Pastoral Care

ITS ROOTS and RENEWAL

Herbert T. Mayer

JOHN KNOX PRESS
ATLANTA

Library of Congress Cataloging in Publication Data

Mayer, Herbert T
  Pastoral care.

  1. Pastoral theology—Case studies. I. Title.
BV4011.M42   253   78-52444
ISBN 0-8042-1130-2

© 1979 John Knox Press

Printed in the United States of America

To Arline

Foreword

A clergyman-friend of mine considers himself an excellent preacher. To tell the truth, what he thinks are first-rate sermons are actually quite dull. But disorganized and incoherent as they are, his sermons nevertheless have significant impact on his parishioners. The reason: he is a master of pastoral care. He communicates in the pulpit in spite of his poor preaching because he is so effective as a pastor in ministering to the needs of his parishioners.

The importance of pastoral care for the life of the church is often underrated. Pulpit committees look for good preachers and teachers and administrators in seeking new pastors. Historians focus on organizational developments and theological movements and major personalities in telling the story of the church. All the while, the faith and life of God's people from generation to generation are nurtured through the unheralded but effective art of pastoral care.

In *Pastoral Care: Its Roots and Renewal,* Herbert T. Mayer puts the spotlight on pastoral care in the church's life and helps us see its significance. Strictly speaking, the book is not a history of pastoral care, though its material spans the church's history from the first to the twentieth century. Mayer presents fifteen cameo portraits of pastors practicing the art, each cameo a window through which we look into a major period of church history. In the variety and diversity of the portraits we see the course and movement of the church's life through the ages.

The author is no stranger to pastoral care. He learned the art in the school of experience as a parish pastor. During his past

twenty years as a professor he has stressed pastoral care in his
church-history courses and has provided a genuine pastoral ministry in his own classroom. He has devoted time and energy to the
cause of social ministry, especially in St. Louis. He is presently
experimenting with new models of pastoral care as he assists
Christian communities in translating theory into practice. His
C.O.M.E. model (Congregations Organizing for Mission Endeavor) is developing small pastoral care units within congregations for the practice of the church's functions of fellowship,
worship, witness, service, and nurture.

What should pastoral care be like in the church today?
Mayer's Cameos provide ample witness against making any one
model of pastoral care normative. Throughout the church's history, time and place have helped shape notions of pastoral care.
Even more formative, as the historical material demonstrates, is
the impact on pastoral care of prevailing views concerning Christ
and the church. In fact is is possible to project from a particular
model of pastoral care the major emphases in the views about
Christ and about the church held by the Christian people among
whom the model of pastoral care is practiced.

Mayer locates the renewal of pastoral care in the recovery of
an understanding of Christ as the suffering servant who gave his
life on behalf of people and in a return of the church to its
vocation of following in Christ's steps. At the same time, the
pastor is the hinge, Mayer tells us, on which the church's mission
swings. A notion of pastoral ministry that flows from an understanding of Christ and of church as suffering servant is essential
for the church to carry out its mission. Only as the pastor follows
in Christ's steps are the people of God properly equipped for
fellowship, worship, witness, service, and nurture.

Size is important too for the renewal of pastoral care, according to Mayer. The bigger the church, the more imposing the
obstacles to effective pastoral care. Mayer argues for the reorgan-
ization of Christian communities into smaller units who select
from among their number the one to exercise pastoral care
among them.

Pastoral Care: Its Roots and Renewal was written for all the people of God, not just for the clergy. So Mayer puts into practice his conviction that proper pastoral care is the concern and the function of the entire Christian community. Mayer has peppered the book with questions for discussion, making the book usable as a basis for study and discussion by small groups within the church. Thus he helps implement his conviction that the renewal of pastoral care must begin with all the people of God, not just with the clergy.

In a seventeenth-century devotional classic, *True Christianity,* which has been an instrument of pastoral care ever since, John Arndt states: "Christ has many disciples, but few followers." Mayer's book will help turn disciples into followers.

John H. Tietjen
President, Christ Seminary—Seminex
St. Augustine's Day, 1977

Pastors		General Western History
Jesus		Persecution
Paul		
	— A.D. 100	
Justin		
Tertullian	— 200	
Cyprian		
	— 300	
Ambrose		Constantine becomes the first
Chrysostom	— 400	Christian emperor
		Fall of Rome
	— 500	
Gregory the Great		Medieval period:
	— 600	Europe becomes Christian
	— 700	
	— 800	
	— 900	
	— 1000	
	— 1100	
	— 1200	
	— 1300	
	— 1400	
Luther	— 1500	Discovery of America
Calvin		Protestant Reform movements
Baxter	— 1600	Puritans and Pilgrims
Edwards		Enlightenment
Asbury	— 1700	Biblical criticism
Loehe	— 1800	American Revolution
Beecher		Civil War
Theim	— 1900	World War I
Daugherty	— 2000	World War II
Marshall		

Contents

Introduction

It has been said that the person who has a *why* to live for can endure almost any *how*. This is a book about the Christian *why*. Because the Christian *why* is always developed, understood, and practiced in a community of people, this is a book about Christians becoming more skilled in caring for each other and in learning to love each other more. Therefore, it is a book about Christian congregations and about Christian people and their pastors. In theological terms, this is a book to enable Christians to understand more fully, to put more fully into practice, and to enjoy more delightedly that which God the Father has done for them in Jesus Christ by the power of his Spirit.

It's no secret that the personal joy and faith of most Christians is at a perilously low ebb today. Patterns of church attendance are changing almost everywhere; but more serious is the fact that so many who go, go out of force of habit, without either expecting anything on Sunday morning or getting anything that increases their faith, hope, or love for the living of their lives. This book will lay before you customs and practices from the church's past that may be used today in programs of reforming and revitalizing congregations.

The book is built around three centers: the person and the work of Jesus Christ (or, more properly, the triune God), the Christian community or congregation, and the called pastoral leader. The interrelationship of these three elements will be studied in the lives of fifteen Christian men, twelve of whom are historical persons who served congregations as pastoral leaders.

The purpose of this book is to help pastors understand and

appreciate the roots of their calling, and to see how styles of pastoral care have changed in response to internal and external pressures. Understanding their permanent roots and constant changes may set pastors free to examine themselves and their work. Some may choose to renew and reform their practice. This is important, because the historical record shows consistently that pastors' style of faith and leadership plays a major role in shaping the life-styles of the people they serve.

The book can also serve as a study tool for lay people. It can help them learn more about pastoral authority and leadership. It can help them think creatively about the relation between faith and life. And finally, it can help them evaluate various patterns of congregational organization for carrying out God's mission. In this book, that mission will be defined as our common Christian privilege, opportunity, and responsibility to proclaim to all people in word and deed that in Jesus Christ God's kingdom is drawing near.

At one point in its development, the book was intended to be a history of pastoral care and was designed to focus narrowly on pastors and their office. But it soon became apparent to me that this perspective was of limited value and could only cause confusion in the minds of most readers. Therefore the perspective of the book was broadened to include the Christian community also. Attention will be given to the ways in which Christians relate to each other in their congregations, to various kinds of congregational structures, and to devices that Christians have found useful in encouraging and supporting each other to be about their Father's business.

Because the book has three centers, three definitions are in order at the beginning. When this book refers to Jesus Christ, it recognizes him as the Son of God who took on human flesh and nature, so that by suffering, dying, and rising he might set all of us free from the tyranny of sin, death, and the devil. The book also affirms that Jesus Christ now sits at the right hand of the Father, that the church on earth is his body, the fullness of him who fills all things. Generally, the word "Christology" will be used as a shorthand term in this book to mean what the Bible and the church fathers teach about the person and work of Jesus Christ.

By the phrase "Christian community" this book means those people who are gathered around preaching and the sacraments in a given place at a given time. The group comes together to worship God, to support each other, and to be about God's mission. The book will spend some time with the important question of how the people come together. Do they come together because they as individuals have decided to do so, or do they come together because God's Spirit has united them? Your answer to this question will affect in a noticeable way how you think about your congregation and the other people who belong to it.

By the term "pastor" this book means that person who leads the congregation in public worship, who does most of the preaching, who usually presides at the celebration of the sacraments, and who is called by such titles as Reverend, Father, Pastor, Preacher, or Brother. The phrase "pastoral care" in this book will be used to describe all the work of the called pastor that helps people to appreciate and to grasp what God the Father has done and is doing for them through the power of his Spirit, both individually and collectively, so that Christians can support each other in mission.

THEMES

Several basic themes or questions will be pursued in this book. Not every theme is covered in each chapter, but the book consistently stresses the following ones.

1. What Christians think about the person and the work of Jesus Christ affects what they think about the church, its nature and its mission. At the same time, what Christians think about the church usually affects what they think about Jesus Christ. The close relationship between Christ and the church and the influence that each has on the other is one of the key concerns of this book. When this principle is rightly understood and implemented, Christians will find new measures of joy and strength and many common churchly problems will not arise.

2. Baptism is the key sacrament of Christian beginning. In that

act, the individual, whether infant or adult, is united with Jesus Christ in a new way that results in the transformation of his or her life.

3. The called pastor is the hinge, the key figure, in the growth of Christian congregations and in the way that Christians understand and pursue mission. A pastor's life-style will be imitated in recognizable ways by many in the congregation. At the same time, it should also be recognized that the people will determine the personality and leadership-style of the pastor. The classic slogan "Like pastor, like people" needs to be modified to read, "Like pastor, like people, like pastor" *(qualis rex, talis grex, talis rex)*.

4. A pastor's successful functioning as hinge depends largely on how the pastor understands pastoral authority. This book will argue that this is the most critical question for pastor and people to answer together. In the past problems often arose as the pastor tried to be both servant and ruler for the people. I will also point to a definite pattern of historical change in the definition of pastoral authority and will show several different kinds of understandings that have been present at various periods in the church's history.

5. Throughout most of the church's history, at least until 1800, Christian pastors and people took seriously St. Paul's exhortation to imitate him as he in turn was imitating Jesus Christ. I will suggest that this "imitation of Christ" principle has been watered down or else badly misunderstood over the past two hundred years. The restoration of its proper understanding will play a crucial role in the reform and renewal of congregations.

6. This book will urge the reader to think hard about whether there is not, in the history of Christian community life, a definite relationship between the size of the community and the vitality of the faith of individual members.

7. There are five activities that have been present in the past in healthy and strong Christian communities. These actions are the worship of the triune God; the practice of warm and intimate fellowship; the practice of self-giving service to all who are in need; the giving of courageous witness that manifests to people that those witnessing are followers of Jesus Christ, and that like

Jesus Christ, they have come not to be served but to serve and to give their lives as a ransom for many; and, finally, the practice of Christian nurture, that is, the practice of mutual education, encouragement, and consolation. Furthermore, in vital communities these five actions are present in balanced and inseparable relationship.

8. Related to the seven foregoing principles is the importance of preaching, the study of the Word, and the celebration of the sacraments.

You are invited and urged to work out your own convictions concerning these eight points from information presented in each chapter and on the basis of your own knowledge of Scripture and of insights you can gain by talking to other Christians.

THE ORGANIZATION OF THE BOOK

This book offers several histories of Christian communities and their pastors. These accounts will help to explain the eight principles and will also show how they have been understood and misunderstood, applied and misapplied, used and abused, in the church's past. Each chapter will place special emphasis on the life and work of one or two communities and their pastors, although other people will be brought in if they can help to make a point clearer. Each pastor and community is selected to illustrate several principles; none is chosen because they adequately understood and practiced all eight. From this it also follows that no single community or pastor is presented as the ideal and perfect model.

The purpose of the book is to enable you to understand these eight principles and to apply them in your Christian community. This will help you to believe more firmly and live out more joyfully your Christian *why*. To accomplish that end, readers are asked to serve as coauthors of the book. In each chapter there are questions that relate to what has been said about the specific pastor and community. These questions are not answered in direct fashion in the chapter; you are encouraged to work out your own answers. The answering process will happen most enjoyably and usefully in group discussion, and so it is recommended that the reading and studying take place, wherever possible, in a congregational discussion group.

There is also an important theological reason for this "question-answer" model, and that is the theological principle that each Christian has been equipped by the Holy Spirit with special gifts that need to be recognized and developed. Each Christian has special wisdom or a different background of experience, and these gifts and insights must all be put into the community hopper if the community is to function at the maximum level of health and effectiveness (1 Cor. 12). This book attempts to draw out these individual gifts with respect to the pastor's understanding of community life and the pastoral work.

The material in each chapter is subtitled "Cameo" and "Commentary." The "Cameo" section describes the pastor at work, while the "Commentary" section calls attention to theological principles and other factors that affected his pastoral work. In ten chapters (Ambrose, John Chrysostom, Luther, Calvin, Jonathan Edwards, Wilhelm Loehe, Henry Ward Beecher, Harley Theim, Daniel Daugherty, and Jack Marshall), the Cameo and Commentary are presented in distinct sections, while in the rest they are combined into a single unit. Some Cameos are taken in large measure from the essays, journals, and letters of the pastors. Some Cameos are in the form of biographies. Four of the Cameos —the ones on Ambrose, Luther, Edwards, and Beecher—are fictionalized history; but they are nevertheless true to the thought and spirit of these pastors. Three of the pastors—Theim, Daugherty, and Marshall—are fictitious people, and for that reason are true to the experiences of hundreds of present-day pastors.

The book is intended to be completely practical. I hope its study will lead to the reform and the renewal of the congregation. Specifically, I hope for three things: (1) that you may grow in understanding the pastor's person and work and thus be better prepared to practice pastoral care; (2) that you may better understand and practice the potentials for growth that are present, although often dormant, in the Christian communities; and (3) that you may become more sensitive to the problems and pitfalls that can destroy pastoral effectiveness.

HOW TO BENEFIT
FROM THE HISTORICAL APPROACH

A word needs to be said about the historical nature of this book. The historical approach grows out of my own life as a teacher of church history in the Lutheran church for more than twenty years. In the course of those years, I have become convinced that the study of history is a valuable but little understood way of comprehending and dealing with contemporary problems. The following guidelines for the profitable study of history are offered to help you gain maximum benefit from the material in this book.

In the first place, keep in mind that the historical way of thinking is different from other ways, although it is not necessarily better, clearer, or more profitable. People think in many ways. Some think emotionally, some scientifically, some artistically, some logically or mathematically, some intuitively, and so forth. Each of these ways has certain strengths and certain weaknesses. It is helpful to understand how one thinks and to learn other ways of analyzing life and trying to solve its problems. The historical way of thinking is one such way. It can produce such benefits as more balance, greater understanding and patience, more confidence for the future, and more sympathy for other people today.

In the second place, remember that historical thinking always begins with a pretty fair knowledge of the basic facts concerning the period or the person. Of course, that can be a time-consuming process. This book will try to sort out and present the more important facts in each chapter but obviously cannot present them all. Some readers may even believe that the chapter omits important facts.

In the third place, having mastered the facts, try to think yourself into the period and even into the person's situation. Understand that these are real people, dealing with problems that are identical with your problems. Learn to ask yourself, "What would I have done in that situation? How would I have dealt with that problem?"

In the fourth place, submit yourself to the scrutiny and judgment of these friends from the past, instead of immediately weighing them in the balance and finding them wanting in one or more respects. Of course, it is much easier and more comfortable to do the latter, but then little learning can take place in your mind. Measure your present understandings and practices against theirs in order to learn from them. Let their ideas judge the adequacy and rightness of yours, rather than the reverse. This practice, by the way, is also an excellent one to apply to your friends and neighbors today.

In the fifth place, try to apply the new understandings and insights to your situation today. Remember that you will scarcely ever be able to apply an insight from the past directly and fully to the present. Seldom, if ever, are past and present situations identical. But you can learn from the past how a given idea or principle developed, how it functioned in the past, what good it accomplished, what harm resulted from it, what happened to it eventually, and so forth. These understandings can be helpful as you think about ideas and practices of today that are similar to past developments.

In sum, then, this is a book about our Christian hope for today and tomorrow. The book shows how hope, grounded in Jesus Christ, has knit Christians together in various communities with widely different patterns of leadership. Hope stimulates us to work together to advance God's kingdom in the world today until hope is fully realized at the end of time.

1.
Paul of Tarsus

CAMEO AND COMMENTARY

The letters of the apostle Paul present seven different pictures of early Christian community life. While each community has its peculiar characteristics, there is at the same time a basic and underlying similarity among them. In these seven communities, all of the eight themes that were listed in the introduction can be identified and their effectiveness can be studied.

In these communities, the general focus always is on building community in the Spirit for the sake of the world that does not yet know Christ. Some of the communities were already beginning to turn in on themselves, to quarrel among themselves, and to seek to enjoy Christianity as a private gift. Paul is concerned that this not happen. He continually calls them to live in Christ with each other for the sake of the world.

The letters are written from the pastor's point of view, but Christian community is the true center of all of these letters. Paul does not think of the pastoral office as important in itself or as something that can be studied in itself. The pastoral office for Paul has meaning only as it participates in the Christian community and is useful for aiding community building for the sake of God's mission.

In these seven communities, the focus of the people's lives is on the triune God. They refuse to permit the spotlight to shine on themselves. They insist that the spotlight shine on the God who created them and was still nourishing them; the God who in

Jesus Christ defeated the powers of sin, death, and the devil which had always terrified them; and the God who now in the power of the Holy Spirit was making faith, hope, and love more powerful and more active in their lives.

Their concentration on the triune God produced the two distinctive elements of Christian community living. In the first place, they responded to the goodness and love of God by worshiping him. Their worship life was important to their living together and was the source of much of their strength. In the second place, their focus on the triune God led them to focus their energies where the triune God had focused its: on the needs of their neighbors throughout the world. Thus, service was the second heartbeat of this community. As a matter of fact, for them, worship and service to their neighbors were opposite sides of the same coin. Neither could have any meaning for them without the other. Neither could effect changes in their lives unless the other was also present.

The members understood that their life together in Christ began in their baptism, and they constantly reflected on the importance of this sacrament for their lives. The baptismal ritual was an important part of their lives together and they spent considerable time preparing for the baptismal services. Probably Peter's first letter is a baptismal sermon prepared for a community that he was associated with to make the next baptismal service as rich and meaningful as possible. The point that Paul made to the Corinthians undergirds all of his thinking and all communal living:

> Christ is like a single body, which has many parts; it is still one body, even though it is made up of different parts. In the same way, all of us, whether Jews or Gentiles, whether slaves or free, have been baptized into the one body by the same Spirit, and we have all been given the one Spirit to drink. [1 Cor. 12:12–13]

These Christians believed that through baptism they had been united with Jesus Christ in a new and strange way so that they lived in him and he lived in them. This thought of henceforth living in Christ is a constant emphasis in the literature of the New Testament. The following examples will serve to illustrate this.

> But God has brought you into union with Christ Jesus, and God has made Christ to be our wisdom. By him we are put right with God; we become God's holy people and are set free. [1 Cor. 1:30]

> We are ruled by the love of Christ, now that we recognize that one man died for everyone, which means that they all share in his death. He died for all, so that those who live should no longer live for themselves, but only for him who died and was raised to life for their sake. [2 Cor. 5:14–15; see also 10:1, 5, 7; 13:3–5]

> For surely you know that when we were baptized into union with Christ Jesus, we were baptized into union with his death. By our baptism, then, we were buried with him and shared his death, in order that, just as Christ was raised from death by the glorious power of the Father, so also we might live a new life. . . . Since we have died with Christ, we believe that we will also live with him. . . . In the same way you are to think of yourselves as dead, so far as sin is concerned, but living in fellowship with God through Christ Jesus. [Rom. 6:3–4, 8, 11]

These Christian communities said exactly the same thing about being alive in the Spirit that they said about being alive in Jesus Christ. They did not make a sharp distinction between the presence of Jesus Christ and that of Christ's Spirit. They knew that the Spirit came from Christ and enabled them to live like Christ. In that sense these Christians were charismatic and Pentecostal. St. Paul talks about life in the Spirit in the following passages:

> But you do not live as your human nature tells you to; instead, you live as the Spirit tells you to—if, in fact, God's Spirit lives in you. Whoever does not have the Spirit of Christ does not belong to him. But if Christ lives in you, the Spirit is life for you because you have been put right with God, even though your bodies are going to die because of sin. If

the Spirit of God, who raised Jesus from death, lives in you, then he who raised Christ from death will also give life to your mortal bodies by the presence of his Spirit in you. [Rom. 8:9–11; see also 1 Cor. 2:10–16]

As the Scripture says about Moses: "His veil was removed when he turned to the Lord." Now, "the Lord" in this passage is the Spirit; and where the Spirit of the Lord is present, there is freedom. All of us, then, reflect the glory of the Lord with uncovered faces; and that same glory, coming from the Lord, who is the Spirit, transforms us into his likeness in an ever greater degree of glory. [2 Cor. 3:16–18]

These Christians believed that the Lord Jesus and the Spirit were present among them as they shared with each other the good news in active, personal ways. They talked with each other about the good things that God had done for them in Jesus Christ. They prophesied or spoke in tongues about this great good news. They wrote to each other about it. They listened to preaching about the good news. They experienced the good news in baptizing and in communing with each other. They knew that the gospel must be gossiped in order to operate with maximum effectiveness in the lives of God's people. They did not hide behind theological formulations and expressions as a substitute for speaking the gospel to each other. In their small communities, they were able to speak the gospel in very personal and intimate ways so that the help and comfort of the gospel was experienced as personally helpful.

As they experienced the sweetness and power of the gospel, they helped each other to realize that the values and the blessings that the gospel was bringing to them were the only ones that really mattered and that truly gave value to life. They affirmed and they helped each other to grow in the affirmation that the spiritual values were the surpassing values. In present-day lingo, they had their heads screwed on straight. They did not permit values of this world to usurp the primary place of the gospel. St. Paul expressed this point of view thus:

But all those things that I might count as profit I now reckon as loss for Christ's sake. Not only those things; I reckon everything as complete loss for the sake of what is so much more valuable, the knowledge of Christ Jesus my Lord. For his sake I have thrown everything away; I consider it all as mere garbage, so that I might gain Christ and be completely united with him. . . . All I want is to know Christ and to experience the power of his resurrection, to share in his sufferings and become like him in his death, in the hope that I myself will be raised from death to life. [Phil. 3:7–11]

This resolve to put Christ first is the source of Christian asceticism. Eventually, asceticism came to be identified with specific practices such as fasting, celibacy, and forms of self-mortification. It is not known whether the earliest Christians engaged in these practices, although there is strong evidence that fasting became a recognized ascetic practice at a very early date. On one thing, however, these Christians were clear: to know Christ and the power of his resurrection was the central experience and value in their lives.

As these Christians experienced Christ and the power of his resurrection, they found themselves naturally joining together with other Christians for worship and service. The exercise and enjoyment of Christian fellowship is a major theme in Paul's letters. The New Testament descriptions of Christian fellowship usually apply to groups that are very limited in number, compared with the average size of congregations today. The Christians were, of course, few in number, and they had no large places to assemble until the third and fourth centuries. Archaeological remains show that there were few places in which more than twenty-five Christians could come together to worship. I plan to argue that the strength of the Christian community is directly related to the small size of the groups. Christian vitality, that is, bears a direct relationship to the size of the basic Christian group.

The following are among the many New Testament passages that stress the mutual love and care of Christians for each other.

We always thank God for you all and always mention you in our prayers. For we remember before our God and Father how you put your faith into practice, how your love made you work so hard, and how your hope in our Lord Jesus Christ is firm. Our brothers, we know that God loves you and has chosen you to be his own. For we brought the Good News to you, not with words only, but also with power and the Holy Spirit, and with complete conviction of its truth. You know how we lived when we were with you; it was for your own good. You imitated us and the Lord; and even though you suffered much, you received the message with the joy that comes from the Holy Spirit. So you became an example to all believers in Macedonia and Achaia [Greece]. [1 Thess. 1:2-7]

I thank my God for you every time I think of you; and every time I pray for you all, I pray with joy because of the way in which you have helped me in the work of the gospel from the very first day until now. And so I am sure that God, who began this good work in you, will carry it on until it is finished on the Day of Christ Jesus. You are always in my heart! And so it is only right for me to feel as I do about you. For you have all shared with me in this privilege that God has given me, both now that I am in prison and also while I was free to defend the gospel and establish it firmly. God is my witness that I tell the truth when I say that my deep feeling for you all comes from the heart of Christ Jesus himself. I pray that your love will keep on growing more and more, together with true knowledge and perfect judgment, so that you will be able to choose what is best. Then you will be free from all impurity and blame on the Day of Christ. Your lives will be filled with the truly good qualities which only Jesus Christ can produce, for the glory and praise of God. [Phil. 1:3-11]

Let us give thanks to the God and Father of our Lord Jesus Christ, the merciful Father, the God from whom all help comes! He helps us in all our troubles, so that we are able to help others who have all kinds of troubles, using the same help that we ourselves have received from God. [2 Cor. 1:3-4]

It was he who "gave gifts to mankind"; he appointed some to be apostles, others to be prophets, others to be evangelists, others to be pastors and teachers. He did this to prepare all God's people for the work of Christian service, in order to build up the body of Christ. And so we shall all come together to that oneness in our faith and in our knowledge of the Son of God; we shall become mature people, reaching to the very height of Christ's full stature. Then we shall no longer be children, carried by the waves and blown about by every shifting wind of the teaching of deceitful men, who lead others into error by the tricks they invent. Instead, by speaking the truth in a spirit of love, we must grow up in every way to Christ, who is the head. Under his control all the different parts of the body fit together, and the whole body is held together by every joint with which it is provided. So when each separate part works as it should, the whole body grows and builds itself up through love. [Eph. 4:11–16]

Paul repeatedly expressed his own deep conviction that his effectiveness as a pastoral leader was totally tied to his relationship with the Christian communities. He knew that he drew his strength from them, and that without their fellowship and their support, his ministry would at once come to an end. The pastoral office and the Christian community were part of the same piece of cloth; they could not be separated or in any way be placed in opposition to each other. One passage is sufficient to illustrate this fundamental understanding of Paul's relationship to the Christian community.

Make room for us in your hearts. . . . Even after we arrived in Macedonia, we did not have any rest. There were troubles everywhere, quarrels with others, fears in our hearts. But God, who encourages the downhearted, encouraged us with the coming of Titus. It was not only his coming that cheered us, but also his report of how you encouraged him. He told us how much you want to see me, how sorry you are, how ready you are to defend me; and so I am even happier now. . . . Not only were we encouraged; how happy Titus made us with his happiness over the way in which all of you helped to cheer him up! I did boast of you to him, and you have not disappointed me. We have always spoken the truth to you, and in the same way the boast we made to Titus has proved true. And so his love for you grows stronger, as he remembers how all of you were ready to obey his instructions, how you welcomed him with fear and trembling. How happy I am that I can depend on you completely! [2 Cor. 7:2, 5–8, 13–16; see also Rom. 1:11; 2 Cor. 2:3–4]

The members of these small Christian communities learned to share with each other and to care for each other. The word that they used to describe their fellowship is *koinonia*. The word means to make things common *(koinos)*. In the Christian vocabulary it came to mean that action whereby Christians took things that were their private possessions and made them the common property of the group. This included private material possessions, but it also came to include their spiritual possessions and their spiritual treasures. It also included their problems and their spiritual weaknesses. These, too, they learned to make the common possession of all members of the *koinonia* so that the burdens could be distributed and thus borne as all took a part of the burden upon themselves. They learned to laugh together and to weep together. They sought for the highest measure of mutual agreement on whatever issues came before them. They practiced mutual admonition and discipline. They also shared the forgiveness of God with each other.

These strong *koinonias* kept the focus of their concern and energy always on the world outside of their community. With Paul's help, they tried to avoid the temptation to become self-centered. They did not always succeed in this effort, but their general record is good. They seemed to sense instinctively that the selfish enjoyment of *koinonia* is a contradiction in terms. They seemed to know that if *koinonia* became a selfish thing, it would not long survive among them. At the same time, there was a strong dynamic within the *koinonia* that kept turning their energies and their attentions outward to the world. Christian *koinonia,* by definition, was an outward-turning, world-embracing power.

The Christian *koinonias* developed around five tasks or functions. They did this in the name of Jesus Christ and by the power of his Spirit. The first function was the one just described, namely, sharing with the other members of the *koinonia* those material and spiritual gifts and problems that God had given each member. The second function was that of worshiping the triune God. The third function was that of serving one another and the world in physical and spiritual matters. The fourth function was that of nurturing and building one another up. The fifth function was that of seeking to share with unbelievers the great gifts and experiences that they shared with each other in Jesus Christ. There is no suggestion in the New Testament that one of these functions is more important than another. Rather, the picture that the New Testament presents is that all five must go on constantly and will go on side by side in a well-ordered Christian *koinonia.*

As part of its concern for others, the members of these early Christian communities devoted considerable time and energy to the pursuit of charity and justice. From the first, they exhibited a strong compassion for the poor. Frequently the bread and wine that were brought to the eucharist by the faithful were shared with the poor following the eucharistic celebration. In other ways, too, they shared their wealth with the poor, with strangers, with those who were in prison or sick, and with those who were persecuted and harassed by a government that was often very cruel. In a word, they imitated the pattern that Jesus set before his followers in the twenty-fifth chapter of Matthew's Gospel.

They were trying to proclaim in word and deed the good news that in Jesus Christ the kingdom of God was drawing near. They did not separate between word and deed in their mission to the unbelievers. They knew that actions speak as loud as words, and they combined them. They were unaware of that much later distinction that theologians made between the primary mission of the church ("to save souls") and the secondary mission of the church ("to minister to bodily needs").

The fellowship of Christian communities in the early centuries was strong and beautiful. Of course, other Christian communities have experienced this same strength and joy in other centuries, but it's good to ask what the secret of this kind of Christian *koinonia* is. Several reasons for the development of unique *koinonia* can be identified. In the first place, many of the members of the *koinonia* faced the possibility of persecution, and some of them actually were put to death for their faith. The constant threat of persecution must have provided a strong bond among these Christians. In the second place, it is probably correct to say that most Christians came from the same social classes. St. Paul does say that there were some who were wealthy and wellborn in the congregation at Corinth, but he adds that such people made up only a small percentage of the congregation.

Perhaps it is easier for Christian *koinonia* to develop among people of approximately the same social standings, but this principle surely can be debated. In the third place, almost everyone in this early Christian world was lonely and frightened. The mystery religions, which had many followers in that day, made no effort to offer an experience of fellowship to their followers. They simply existed as individuals, relating directly to their gods in individual ways. Therefore, the appeal of the Christian *koinonia* must have been strong. But to argue that way is really to put the cart before the horse.

There was another reason for the development of Christian *koinonia*, and this seems to have been the most important one. Christian *koinonias* were developed fundamentally by the full activity of the good news about Jesus Christ working in their midst by the power of God's Spirit. This was always a twofold and inseparable action. The first action was that of the Spirit calling them to faith, strengthening them in the faith, teaching them to enjoy the faith and to share the faith with each other. The second aspect of this action was the Spirit sending them out into the world to imitate their Lord, who came not to be served but to serve and to give his life to set many people free. In that age, this service to the people of the world was frequently a call to suffering, persecution, and martyrdom. These Christians knew something that many subsequent generations of Christians have forgotten: these two actions are inseparable. They could not claim to be God's children without laying down their lives for the sake of the world. It was this constant reality that drove them into each other's arms. Most people, then and now, find it impossible to consider performing heroic deeds of self-sacrifice unless they have the support and the encouragement of a group of people that they love and value highly. These first Christians were not seeking martyrdom in order to be martyrs. They were seeking to live out the gospel, to be guided by the Spirit that was in them. Living out the gospel meant sacrifice and possible death, and that in turn necessitated Christian *koinonia*. And then, in the Christian *koinonias* they found the gospel and the power of the Spirit that they needed to face sacrifice and the possibility of death. This was the real dynamic and the real bond that fostered Christian community.

At this point, reflect on what you have read by asking yourself the following questions.

What do I understand the significance of the phrase "in Christ" or "in the Spirit" to be? Do I think of myself as living in Christ or in the Spirit? What have been my experiences of Christian koinonia or community? Have I participated in a small group and found greater meaning there? Are there factors at work in my life, in the lives of my friends, or in the needs of the world that might call again for the development of small Christian koinonias, on the model of the early centuries?

Paul's letters make it clear that he understood the special role that the pastor plays in the Christian community. He realized that the members of the community would in large measure imitate and reflect his own style of life and his own values. He saw as his first responsibility to the people that of providing them an example of Jesus Christ that they could imitate. This theme appears in every one of his letters. The following examples will illustrate how Paul understood this imitation principle and how important it was to him and to the people that God called him to serve.

> I write this to you, not because I want to make you feel ashamed, but to instruct you as my own dear children. For even if you have ten thousand guardians in your Christian life, you have only one father. For in your life in union with Christ Jesus I have become your father by bringing the Good News to you. I beg you, then, to follow my example. For this purpose I am sending to you Timothy, who is my own dear and faithful son in the Christian life. He will remind you of the principles which I follow in the new life in union with Christ Jesus and which I teach in all the churches everywhere. [1 Cor. 4:14–17]

> I praise you because you always remember me and follow the teachings that I have handed on to you. [1 Cor. 11:2]

Paul also reminded his readers that Jesus Christ, in turn, gives them an example, a likeness of the Father himself to follow.

They do not believe, because their minds have been kept in the dark by the evil god of this world. He keeps them from seeing the light shining on them, the light that comes from the Good News about the glory of Christ, who is the exact likeness of God. For it is not ourselves that we preach; we preach Jesus Christ as Lord, and ourselves as your servants for Jesus' sake. The God who said, "Out of darkness the light shall shine!" is the same God who made his light shine in our hearts, to bring us the knowledge of God's glory shining in the face of Christ. [2 Cor. 4:4–6]

Since you are God's dear children, you must try to be like him. Your life must be controlled by love, just as Christ loved us and gave his life for us as a sweet-smelling offering and sacrifice that pleases God. [Eph. 5:1–2]

Christ is the visible likeness of the invisible God. He is the first-born Son, superior to all created things. . . . For it was by God's own decision that the Son has in himself the full nature of God. Through the Son, then, God decided to bring the whole universe back to himself. [Col. 1:15, 19–20]

All I want is to know Christ and to experience the power of his resurrection, to share in his sufferings and become like him in his death, in the hope that I myself will be raised from death to life. . . . All of us who are spiritually mature should have this same attitude. But if some of you have a different attitude, God will make this clear to you. However that may be, let us go forward according to the same rules we have followed until now. Keep on imitating me, my brothers. Pay attention to those who follow the right example that we have set for you. [Phil. 3:10–11, 15–17]

You imitated us and the Lord; and even though you suffered much, you received the message with the joy that comes from the Holy Spirit. So you became an example to all believers in Macedonia and Achaia [Greece]. [1 Thess. 1:6–7; see also 2:10, 14; 4:2; 2 Thess. 3:7, 9]

Paul believed that an important part of his calling was to imitate Christ in such a way that he could call on Christians to imitate himself.

Is this principle at work in your congregation? How would you define the authority of a pastor? How do your parish leaders define it?

Paul realized that there were other duties that were resting upon him as pastor of Christian groups. So he preached to them, he admonished them, he forgave them when they repented, on occasion he performed baptisms, perhaps he celebrated the holy communion when he was among them.

But the primary characteristic of Paul's pastoral activity was his complete identification of himself with the dreams, the hopes, the fears, the needs of the people. In almost every letter, he stated that he wanted to be their servant, their slave, just as he was the slave of Jesus Christ. At the same time, Paul realized that there were times when the Christian slave-pastor must speak as a guide or ruler. He did not hesitate to do this, especially to the congregation at Corinth in his two letters to them. However, he made it clear that he was ruling and guiding them as their servant or slave. Later generations of pastors frequently functioned as guides and rulers without making clear that their primary calling was to be servant and slave to the community.

Related to this tension between Paul as slave and ruler of the people of God was the question of the authority by which he served. Paul's understanding of pastoral authority was a remarkable blend of personal and official authority. When one studies the work of Jesus Christ, one notes that his authority is based entirely upon himself as a person. When he spoke, he spoke with his own authority. However, the moment a Christian community came into existence, the leader spoke not only from his own authority but also by virtue of the authority that the group had voluntarily given to him. In the case of St. Paul, the authority that he exercised was mostly based on the kind of person he was. His authority among the people was derived from the fact that he lived in Christ and in the Spirit, and his words and deeds made this clear to the people. He did not seek to exercise authority over them nor did he use his pastoral calling to satisfy his own needs or advance his own career. The people sensed this, for it was in marked contrast to those who sought to move in and take over the control of his congregations, and they gladly followed Paul's leadership. His authority was largely personal.

But Paul also recognized that he had a measure of authority

by virtue of the fact that a community existed. A community had to have a leader, and Paul was willing to fill this leadership role as needed, but he always remembered that he was servant of Christ and of his community. Paul's pastoral leadership was based on personal-charismatic authority and on institutional authority. His unique pastoral genius resulted in part from his ability to preserve both bases in a relationship of constructive tension. Many other pastors have based their authority entirely on such institutional factors as ordination or the call of a congregation.

Another aspect of pastoral leadership is illustrated in some of the letters of St. Paul—the fact that in the history of the church, most pastors have emerged from the group to become the natural leaders of the group. Paul himself was an exception to this rule. He came from the outside as a stranger to most of his congregations. He quickly commended himself to them as a friend by his sincerity, his godliness, and his evident devotion to their interests rather than to his own. He was a unique person and became the natural leader of these groups in short order. But Paul did not expect this practice of strangers coming in to be the norm among Christian congregations. Therefore he instructed Titus to ordain elders, that is, members of the group who had emerged as natural leaders, in all the congregations. Historically, this principle of natural leadership has been more frequent and common in the church than the modern practice of the stranger-pastor coming into the group. Of course, thousands of these "stranger-pastors" have commended themselves to Christian groups in the way that Paul did. The practice of Christian congregations calling strangers should not be abolished, but the value of the other practice also needs to be affirmed.

2.

Justin Martyr and Tertullian

CAMEOS AND COMMENTARY

The principles of Christian community life as outlined by St. Paul continued to function in the Christian church for almost three hundred years. These principles are illustrated in the two communities described in this chapter. The first community existed either in Syria or Rome around the middle of the second century; the other community flourished in North Africa toward the end of the same century. A description of the first is found in a writing of Justin Martyr which is known as his *Apology,* or defense of Christianity against pagan opposition. A description of the second is found in Tertullian's *Apology,* which served the same purpose fifty years later.

Justin devoted the first sixty chapters of his *Apology* to theological matters and then in chapter sixty-one and following provided a fascinating picture of Christian community life. In this chapter he described how members of the community began to live their public Christian life. He placed the emphasis in this chapter on baptism, and described it as a sacrament in which people are reborn, in which they receive remission of their past sins, and in which they dedicate themselves to God in a public ritual.

> How we dedicated ourselves to God when we were made new through Christ I will explain, since it might seem to be unfair if I left this out from my exposition. Those who are

persuaded and believe that the things we teach and say are true, and promise that they can live accordingly, are instructed to pray and beseech God with fasting for the remission of their past sins, while we pray and fast along with them. Then they are brought by us where there is water, and are reborn by the same manner of rebirth by which we ourselves were reborn; for they are then washed in the water in the name of God the Father and Master of all, and of our Saviour Jesus Christ, and of the Holy Spirit. For Christ said, "Unless you are born again you will not enter into the Kingdom of heaven." [From *Early Christian Fathers*, vol. 1, trans. and ed. Cyril C. Richardson (Philadelphia: The Westminster Press, 1953), p. 282]

This picture of community baptism suggests quite clearly that the community itself was rather small. The evidence that survives from the early church suggests that the typical Christian community probably was limited to twenty-five to thirty-five or forty-five members. Most of the groups could only meet in members' homes, and no room in the typical house could hold more than a handful of believers. Some larger groups could meet outdoors, perhaps, but the average group was small by our present-day standards.

Justin was talking about the baptism of adults, for that was the general and common practice in the early church. There is some evidence of the limited practice of infant baptism, perhaps beginning after the time of Justin. But down through the fourth and fifth centuries, the baptism of adults was the normal practice, and the baptism of infants was more uncommon and limited. As the adults prepared themselves for baptism, three things were asked of them: (1) do you believe that our Christian teachings are true? (2) will you commit yourself to live according to what you have learned? (3) will you open yourselves to the grace and cleansing of God, Father, Son, and Spirit?

The importance of baptism in these early Christian communities is indicated by the way in which the other members of the congregation participated in the rite. They prayed and fasted along with the candidates for baptism. They joined the candidates in the ceremony at the water. These baptismal ceremonies were held only a few times each year, the great one usually being in connection with the celebration of Easter. The candidates were carefully prepared for baptism. It was explained to them that baptism meant a life-changing commitment to live according to the teachings of Jesus Christ. For many, baptism probably meant that they would be disowned and ostracized by their pagan families and friends.

How do you understand the meaning and importance of your baptism? If you were baptized as an infant, do you understand baptism in any sense as your public commitment to live according to the teachings of Jesus Christ?

Following their baptism, the new-born Christians were led into the company of the worshiping congregation, there for the first time to participate in holy communion. They prepared for this celebration by giving themselves to fervent and earnest prayer. Then the new Christians were for the first time in their lives allowed to join in the eucharistic celebration. Three requirements had been established for joining in the communion service. People must believe the truth of the Christian teachings, they must have been baptized, and they must be living as Jesus Christ lived.

In the eucharistic celebration, they came to the central mystery of their Christian faith, the dramatic reenactment of the proclamation that the almighty God came into the world in the person of Jesus Christ to overcome sin, death, and the devil and thus to set people free from that bondage, to serve other people and to glorify the triune God. The early Christians believed that the body and blood of Jesus Christ were truly present in the bread and wine. Most of them believed that as they received the body and blood in the bread and wine their own physical natures were gradually transformed and in some mysterious way began to share in God's own nature. This experience can be called a process of sacramental deification.

We, however, after thus washing the one who has been convinced and signified his assent, lead him to those who are called brethren, where they are assembled. They then earnestly offer common prayers for themselves and the one who has been illuminated and all others everywhere, that we may be made worthy, having learned the truth, to be found in deed good citizens and keepers of what is commanded, so that we may be saved with eternal salvation. On finishing the prayers we greet each other with a kiss. Then bread and a cup of water and mixed wine are brought to the president of the brethren and he, taking them, sends up praise and glory to the Father of the universe through the name of the Son and of the Holy Spirit, and offers thanksgiving at some length that we have been deemed worthy to receive these things from him. When he has finished the prayers and the thanksgiving, the whole congregation present assents, saying, "Amen." "Amen" in the Hebrew language means, "So be it." When the president has given thanks and the whole congregation has assented, those whom we call deacons give to each of those present a portion of the consecrated bread and wine and water, and they take it to the absent.

This food we call Eucharist, of which no one is allowed to partake except one who believes that the things we teach are true, and has received the washing for forgiveness of sins and for rebirth, and who lives as Christ handed down to us. For we do not receive these things as common bread or common drink; but as Jesus Christ our Saviour being incarnate by God's word took flesh and blood for our salvation, so also we have been taught that the food consecrated by the word of prayer which comes from him, from which our flesh and blood are nourished by transformation, is the flesh and blood of that incarnate Jesus. For the apostles in the memoirs composed by them, which are called Gospels, thus handed down what was commanded them: that Jesus, taking bread and having given thanks, said, "Do this for my memorial, this is my body"; and likewise taking the cup and giving thanks he said, "This is my blood"; and gave it to them alone. [From *Early Christian Fathers,* vol. 1, pp. 285–286]

The role of the pastor in the eucharistic celebration is noteworthy. The pastor is called "president of the brethren," apparently elected to head the group. In all likelihood, the pastor had been a member of the group prior to the election, and was elected because of the group's trust and respect and because they had found the pastor to be a kind and loving person. It can be suggested already at this point that in the history of the Christian church the great majority of pastors have been chosen out of the group to which they belong. Because they were already natural leaders of the group, their pastoral leadership functioned in a different way from that exercised by the pastoral leader who is imported from outside the group. (This important point will be discussed in more detail in other chapters of the book.)

A similar description of the process of pastoral selection is found in Tertullian's *Apology.* He writes:

> Certain approved elders preside [at the eucharistic celebration and worship service], men who have obtained this honor not by money, but by evidence of good character. [Tertullian, *Apologetical Works* and Mincius Felix, *Octavius,* in *The Fathers of the Church: A New Translation,* ed. Roy J. Deferrari et al. (New York: Fathers of the Church, Inc., 1950), p. 98]

These Christians who have been brought together by God's Spirit acting through God's Word and the sacraments of baptism and holy communion, develop a unique kind of relationship and fellowship. This fellowship sets them apart from all associations of unbelievers and becomes the trademark of the early Christian movement. Both Justin and Tertullian describe this life in considerable detail in their *Apologies.* Justin writes:

> After these [services] we constantly remind each other of these things. Those who have more come to the aid of those who lack, and we are constantly together. Over all that we receive we bless the Maker of all things through his Son Jesus Christ and through the Holy Spirit. And on the day called Sunday there is a meeting in one place of those who live in cities or the country, and the memoirs of the apostles or the writings of the prophets are read as long as time permits. When the reader has finished, the president in a discourse urges and invites [us] to the imitation of these noble things. Then we all stand up together and offer prayers. And, as said before, when we have finished the prayer, bread is brought, and wine and water, and the president similarly sends up prayers and thanksgivings to the best of his ability, and the congregation assents, saying the Amen; the distribution, and reception of the consecrated [elements] by each one, takes place and they are sent to the absent by the deacons. Those

who prosper, and who so wish, contribute, each one as much as he chooses to. What is collected is deposited with the president, and he takes care of orphans and widows, and those who are in want on account of sickness or any other cause, and those who are in bonds, and the strangers who are sojourners among [us], and, briefly, he is the protector of all those in need. We all hold this common gathering on Sunday, since it is the first day, on which God transforming darkness and matter made the universe, and Jesus Christ our Saviour rose from the dead on the same day. For they crucified him on the day before Saturday, and on the day after Saturday, he appeared to his apostles and disciples and taught them these things which I have passed on to you also for your serious consideration. [From *Early Christian Fathers,* vol. 1, pp. 287–288]

Their Christian fellowship showed itself in a number of actions. They "constantly remind each other of these things." They "come to the aid of those who lack." They "are constantly together." When communion is celebrated, the deacons take the consecrated elements to those who must be absent so that the bonds of fellowship are preserved. Their fellowship led them to contribute to the relief of the needy, as the Spirit moved them. In their name, the president served as "the protector of all those in need." There is ample evidence in other early Christian literature that the phrase "all those in need" included Christian and non-Christian alike.

Tertullian's description of the Christian fellowship is equally interesting.

(1) Now I myself will explain the practices of the Christian Church, that is, after having refuted the charges that they are evil, I myself will also point out that they are good. We form one body because of our religious convictions, and because of the divine origin of our way of life, and the bond of common hope. (2) We come together for a meeting and a congregation, in order to besiege God with prayers, like an army in battle formation. Such violence is pleasing to God. We pray, also, for the emperors, for their ministers and those in power, that their reign may continue, that the state may be at peace, and that the end of the world may be postponed. (3) We assemble for the consideration of the Holy Scrip-

tures, [to see] if the circumstances of the present time demand that we look ahead or reflect. Certainly, we nourish
our faith with holy conversation, we uplift our hope, we
strengthen our trust, intensifying our discipline at the same
time by the inculcation of moral precepts. (4) At the same
occasion, there are words of encouragement, of correction,
and holy censure. Then, too, judgment is passed which is
very impressive [on an unrepentant public sinner], as it is
before men who are certain of the presence of God, and it
is a deeply affecting foretaste of the future judgment, if anyone has so sinned that he is dismissed from sharing in common prayer, assembly, and all holy intercourse. (5) Certain
approved elders preside, men who have obtained this honor
not by money, but by the evidence of good character. For,
nothing that pertains to God is to be had for money.

Even if there is some kind of treasury, it is not ac-
cumulated from a high initiation fee as if the religion were
something bought and paid for. Each man deposits a small
amount on a certain day of the month or whenever he
wishes, and only on condition that he is willing and able to
do so. No one is forced; each makes his contribution voluntarily. (6) These are, so to speak, the deposits of piety. The
money therefrom is spent not for banquets or drinking parties or good-for-nothing eating houses, but for the support
and burial of the poor, for children who are without their
parents and means of subsistence, for aged men who are
confined to the house; likewise, for shipwrecked sailors, and
for any in the mines, on islands or in prisons. Provided only
it be for the sake of fellowship with God, they become entitled to loving and protective care for their confession. (7)
The practice of such a special love brands us in the eyes of
some. 'See,' they say, 'how they love one another'; (for *they*
hate one another), 'and how ready they are to die for each
other.' (They themselves would be more ready to kill each
other.) . . .

(11) So, we who are united in mind and soul have no
hesitation about sharing what we have. Everything is in common among us—except our wives. . . .

(16) Our repast, by its very name, indicates its purpose.
It is called by a name which to the Greeks means 'love.' [the
Greek word is *agape*] Whatever it costs, it is gain to incur
expense in the name of piety, since by this refreshment we
comfort the needy. . . . (17) . . . No one sits down to table
without first partaking of a prayer to God. They eat as much

as those who are hungry take; they drink as much as temperate people need. (18) They satisfy themselves as men who remember that they must worship God even throughout the night; they converse as men who know that the Lord is listening. After this, the hands are washed and lamps are lit, and each one, according to his ability to do so, reads the Holy Scriptures or is invited into the center to sing a hymn to God. This is the test of how much he has drunk. Similarly, prayer puts an end to the meal. (19) From here they depart, not to unite in bands for murder, or to run around in gangs, or for stealthy attacks of lewdness, but to observe the same regard for modesty and chastity as people do who have partaken not only of a repast but of a rule of life. [From *The Fathers of the Church: A New Translation,* pp. 98–101]

Because their fellowship was the heartbeat of early Christianity, it deserves to be analyzed in more detail. *Koinonia* is a Greek verbal noun to describe the process of making things that are your private property into the common property of a group. Both Justin and Tertullian suggest that *koinonia* in the early church often included material possessions such as money, but it also includes the total action of making common such things as the individual's faith and hope and love or fears and troubles. Christians loved each other and they bore one another's burdens (Gal. 6:2).

The basic action in Christian *koinonia* takes place as members share with each other the gospel promises that they have in Jesus Christ. This practice of intimate and personal sharing and encouragement provides the spiritual energy that establishes *koinonia.* Since most of these early Christians did not own Bibles they had no choice but to "gossip the gospel" to each other. Through this act of gossiping, the Holy Spirit created especially strong ties of friendship.

Historians of the early church have been intrigued and puzzled by the way in which Christians loved one another. Some have argued that this strong love developed because together they faced the daily threat of persecution and death. Others have suggested that this *koinonia* developed because most Christians were members of the same social class. While I don't deny the importance of these two factors, neither one is adequate to explain Christian *koinonia*. The deeper explanation lies in the action of God's Spirit through the gossiping of the gospel, while at the same time Christians supported and encouraged each other in living lives that imitated the self-giving life of their Lord and Master. The action of living the Christian life in that full sense depended on the mutual love and support of the *koinonia*.

As Tertullian points out in number 4 above, another strength of the Christian *koinonia* was the ability of the members to exercise effective control and discipline over each other's conduct. Any Christian who persisted in public sinning was dropped, at least temporarily, from the *koinonia*. Because the *koinonia* had become very important to its members, this banishment created an acute sense of loss in those who were ostracized, and they were ready and usually eager to endure any amount of discipline in order to regain a place in the *koinonia*. Today, when persons are disciplined by a large congregation, it usually means very little to them. For one thing, they are often free to go down the street and join another Christian congregation. Discipline was stronger and more salutary in these small Christian *koinonias*.

Another significant picture is found in Justin's description of the Christian fellowship. He reports that "on the day called Sunday there is a meeting in one place of those who live in cities or the country." Justin seems to be saying here that in addition to the daily meetings in house churches, Christians made a point, whenever possible, of coming together on Sunday morning for larger gatherings and eucharistic celebrations. The experience of the small *koinonia* seems to have impelled them to seek out the larger *koinonia* also. This may be what the writer of the epistle to the Hebrews had in mind in chapter 10:

> Let us be concerned for one another, to help one another to show love and to do good. Let us not give up the habit of meeting together, as some are doing. Instead, let us encourage one another all the more, since you see that the Day of the Lord is coming nearer. [Heb. 10:24–25]

The writer may have heard that members of the small house churches (in Rome?) had begun to skip the Sunday morning *koinonia.* He cautions against this with great firmness. Such was not the problem for Justin's contemporaries.

Reflect on the kinds of fellowship or **koinonia** *that have been important in your lives. Are there things that you can do in your congregation to make possible once again this kind of fellowship experience?*

In the communities Justin and Tertullian describe, the five actions of worship, fellowship, witness, service, and nurture are present. Both writers describe them as natural and important. They do not suggest that one is more important or more necessary than the others. Rather, one gets the impression that the balanced interrelationship among the five is the mark of these communities.

The importance and interrelationship of these five actions can best be illustrated by analyzing how one of them works: the call to witness. The Greek words are *martys,* the one who gives a witness, and *martyria,* the act of giving witness. In these early congregations, *martyria* was frequently defined as the act of imitating the life of Jesus Christ. Justin devotes considerable space to this Christian idea. He writes:

> We have been taught and firmly believe that he accepts only those who imitate the good things which are his—temperance and righteousness and love of mankind, and whatever else truly belongs to the God who is called by no given name. [From *Early Christian Fathers,* vol. 1, p. 247]

In many other places in his *Apology,* Justin describes the teaching of Jesus on specific actions. These statements create the strong impression that Justin believes that Jesus is present in the *koinonia* and that his example controls their own actions. A few examples will suffice.

> About continence he [Jesus] said this: "Whoever looks on a woman to lust after her has already committed adultery in his heart before God." [From *Early Christian Fathers,* vol. 1, p. 250]

This is what he taught on affection for all men: "If you love those who love you, what new thing do you do? For even the harlots do this. But I say to you, Pray for your enemies and love those who hate you and bless those who curse you and pray for those who treat you despitefully."

That we should share with those in need and do nothing for [our] glory, he said these things: "Give to everyone who asks and turn not away him who wishes to borrow." [From *Early Christian Fathers*, vol. 1, p. 251]

The Christian determination to imitate Christ led to the creation of a life-style that was radically different in that world. Justin described the new life-style in his *Apology*, while Tertullian described the sort of life that the pagans lived. Both sections from the two *Apologies*, placed side by side, illustrate why the pagans sought to destroy this new life-style that was calling into judgment and condemning all of their pleasures.

Here is Justin's description of what it meant to imitate Christ:

For they [Justin means demons] struggle to have you as their slaves and servants, and now by manifestations in dreams, now by magic tricks, they get hold of all who do not struggle to their utmost for their own salvation—as we do who, after being persuaded by the Word, renounced them and now follow the only unbegotten God through his Son. Those [Christians] who once rejoiced in fornication now delight in continence alone; those who made use of magic arts have dedicated themselves to the good and unbegotten God; we who once took most pleasure in the means of increasing our wealth and property now bring what we have into a common fund and share with everyone in need; we who hated and killed one another and would not associate with men of different tribes because of [their different] customs, now after the manifestation of Christ live together and pray for our enemies and try to persuade those who unjustly hate us, so that they, living according to the fair commands of Christ, may share with us the good hope of receiving the same things [that we will] from God, the master of all. [From *Early Christian Fathers*, vol. 1, pp. 249–250]

In marked contrast to the conduct of the Christians stands Tertullian's description of the pagan life-style. Of course, not every pagan lived this way, but surviving evidence does indicate

that at least the leaders of society did. The Christian life-style
exposed and condemned the self-serving and sensuous nature of
the pagans. It is no wonder that the pagans responded by repeatedly putting the Christians to death so that they, the pagans,
might continue in their sinful ways. Tertullian writes:

> What has become of those laws which restrained extrava-
> gance and bribery? which forbade the spending of more than
> a hundred asses [a rather small amount] on a supper, or the
> serving of more than one hen—and that an unfatted one?
> which removed a patrician from the Senate because he had
> ten pounds of silver, on the serious pretext of too lofty
> ambition? which destroyed theaters just as soon as they were
> erected, as tending to corrupt morals? which did not permit
> the marks of dignity and noble lineage to be usurped rashly
> or with impunity? (3) I observe that suppers now have to be
> called 'centenarian' because of the 100,000 sesterces [a sub-
> stantial sum] expended on them. Silver from the mines is
> even being converted into dishes—not for the use of Sena-
> tors, which would be a mere trifle—but rather for freedmen
> [a despised class of new rich] or those whip-crackers whose
> backs are even yet breaking the whips. I see, too, that a single
> theater is not sufficient, or one without an awning. . . . I see,
> too, that there is no difference left between honorable ma-
> trons and prostitutes, as far as their dress is concerned.
> (4) As a matter of fact, as regards women, those customs
> of our ancestors which protected their modesty and sobriety
> have fallen into disregard. Why, no woman was acquainted
> with any gold except that on the one finger which her spouse
> had pledged to himself with the engagement ring. . . .
> (6) What has become of that conjugal happiness so fostered
> by high moral living that for nearly six hundred years after
> Rome was founded no home sued for a divorce? Look at
> women now. Every limb is weighed down with gold; because
> of wine [drunk by the women to excess], no kiss is freely
> given. Yes, and now it is a divorce which is prayed for, as
> though that were the natural issue of marriage! [From *The
> Fathers of the Church: A New Translation,* pp. 22–24]

In marked contrast, the Christians pledged themselves to imitate Jesus Christ, and in that imitation they rejected all these
pagan vices. According to Tertullian, the Christians refused to go
to shows and to gladiatorial combats and to participate in any of

the other pagan customs. They did this in order to witness to the new life that they had found in Jesus Christ. Their witness brought down pagan anger upon them and it was for that reason that the witness *(martys)* was often put to death by the pagans (martyred).

As I suggested earlier, the burden and the joy of giving this kind of witness required the mutual support and encouragement of the *koinonia.* Within the *koinonia,* the Christians found strength in worshiping the triune God, they found strength from each other as they gossiped the gospel to each other, and they nurtured and built each other up.

The idea of imitating Christ, as presented by Justin, can be misunderstood and abused. Thus some Christians view Christ as a pattern that provides the answers to all of their decisions. In effect, they make Christ a new law, although our Lord did not want to serve this function among his followers. (The idea of imitating Christ will be studied in more detail in the chapter on John Chrysostom.)

One final idea from Justin's *Apology* requires notice, and that is his description of the Christian's search for the kingdom. He writes:

> When you hear that we look for a kingdom, you rashly suppose that we mean something merely human. But we speak of a Kingdom with God, as is clear from our confessing Christ when you bring us to trial, though we know that death is the penalty for this confession. For if we looked for a human kingdom we would deny it in order to save our lives, and would try to remain in hiding in order to obtain the things we look for. But since we do not place our hopes on the present [order], we are not troubled by being put to death, since we will have to die somehow in any case. [From *Early Christian Fathers,* vol. 1, p. 247]

On first reading, it seems that Justin is making a clear distinction between the earthly kingdom and the heavenly kingdom, as if he were saying that the Christian's chief concern and love is the heavenly kingdom. But that is not the point of this paragraph, as the rest of Justin's *Apology* makes clear. The Christians do indeed seek a kingdom, God's kingdom, but they seek for that kingdom both on this earth and hereafter. In their search for the kingdom, Christians seek to establish God's righteousness in every way that they can. In their search for God's kingdom, they seek justice and they pursue charity. They do good to all people. In this paragraph, Justin is not reflecting the idea that the church has a primary mission (to save souls) and a secondary mission (to do good). Rather, he is assuming that Christians have a single mission: the pursuit of the kingdom which God was bringing near in the life and death and resurrection of his Son. Like his contemporaries and those who followed him through many centuries, Justin took it for granted that the maintenance of justice and charity was the church's business. They did not look to the state for help in this matter. This was all part of their baptismal vocation.

How do you react to Justin's description of the imitation of Christ? Do you agree with the point made in this chapter about imitation in terms of the balanced growth in the five functions of worship, fellowship, witness, service, and nurture? How can you help this growth to occur among your members?

3.
Ambrose of Milan

CAMEO

The report of Auxentius's death was good news for Ambrose. He had not liked the bishop personally and he was intensely angered by the bishop's refusal to use his influence and the wealth of the congregation to deal with the growing social problems in Milan. Furthermore, Auxentius was an Arian, a man who did not believe that Jesus Christ was true God. With the report of his death, Ambrose began thinking of names of possible successors. Simplicianus was the ideal candidate, but he was too old. Of the other priests, in Ambrose's judgment, none stood out.

The election of Auxentius's successor would be public, and a great crowd jammed the church for that event. Various names were put forward and the emotions of the excitable Milanese began to rise. In the growing clamor, Ambrose was startled to hear a youthful voice cry out, "Ambrose for bishop; Ambrose for bishop!" Those standing nearby took up the chant and it quickly filled the building. Ambrose struggled against the mob that was pushing him toward the front. He called for help to the imperial guard that always accompanied him when he was in public, but they couldn't hear him. In a short period of time he found himself standing on the podium with Simplicianus, who was presiding at the meeting. Ambrose protested vigorously, but Simplicianus only grinned, shrugged his arms and shoulders in the famous Italian gesture, and then presented Ambrose to the crowd as the new bishop. A pandemonium of rejoicing broke loose.

There was no sleep for Ambrose for the next week while he struggled with the appointment. He had no desire to be bishop. There were many reasons that he presented to himself. For example, he was not even a priest and had not yet been baptized. Furthermore, he believed that his work as governor of Milan was very important for the welfare of the people. He desperately wanted out, but Simplicianus was able to answer every one of his objections. He pointed out that the church was the only stabilizing force left in northern Italy and that only Ambrose was strong enough to give direction to the church, especially with regard to the deteriorating social conditions. He also argued that Ambrose was the only man who could gain the respect and cooperation of the leaders of the city and the state. As Simplicianus pointed out, Ambrose was related to the powerful Symmachus family, and the people of the church already loved and trusted him as governor. They would transfer that affection to him as bishop.

Added to Simplicianus's arguments was a growing inner feeling that Ambrose had never experienced before and could not explain. He finally accepted the office. The next day he was baptized, on the second day he was ordained to be a reader, the following day as a priest, and on the fourth day was inducted into the office of bishop. Simplicianus agreed to serve as Ambrose's theological tutor. He shared with the new bishop his own enthusiasm for the writings of Origen, the great third-century Christian scholar from Alexandria.

In Origen's writings, Ambrose found a description of the church's mission that he adopted completely. Origen argued that since God was one, God's only goal in this world was to lead everything back to himself so that the perfect unity that existed before Adam sinned would again be established. Thus, according to Origen, God wanted people to again become one with other people and he wanted human beings to become one with nature, God's creation. To restore this unity, Origen wrote, God created the church and the state, each one with separate but related resources and responsibilities. The state was responsible for law and order, for strong social structures, for peace, and so forth.

The church administered forgiveness and reconciliation which reunited people to each other and to God, and also served as the symbol of the unity God was restoring.

In the atmosphere of hopelessness and cynical despair that saturated Milan, Origen's vision and confidence were refreshing breezes. Ambrose set himself the goal of deliberately bringing together *Romanitas,* the spirit and power of old Rome represented in Milan in the powerful pagan noble families, and *Christianitas,* the spirit and power of the new Jerusalem, present, he believed, among the thousands of Christians in Milan.

After getting over the first shock, Ambrose began to enjoy his new career. He thought of himself as a father who suddenly found himself with a large family of children. He discovered that preaching was a joy and the people often told him that his sermons were inspiring and helpful. The preparation of adults for baptism brought him special pleasure as a growing number of young people from the great pagan families began to come for instruction. He was especially delighted when his nephew, Marcus Quintus Symmachus, decided to be baptized. Ambrose was able to awaken among his members a new sense of responsibility for social problems, and especially for the poor and the needy. In his sermons he made constant mention of the cause of charity and justice in Milan, and offerings for those causes increased greatly. He maintained close contact with the Emperor Theodosius and attended most of the imperial council meetings. He was impressed by the sincerity of the emperor's Christianity, and both men developed a feeling of mutual respect and trust.

Ambrose convinced Marcus to become a cathedral priest, and the two developed an effective working relationship. Marcus caught Ambrose's dream of unity and took on the special responsibility of devising ways to implement this.

However, as the years went by, a fundamental difference of opinion between the two men began to emerge. The difference centered on the question of the people's role in the church's mission. Ambrose believed that the priests had the chief responsibility for that mission while Marcus stoutly defended the concept that the whole people of God had responsibility. The disagreement came to a head over a manual of priestly training and duties that Ambrose was writing. In it, Ambrose stressed four points. His first point was to call the people to recognize and honor their priests as their fathers in God, whose example they were to imitate. His second point was that the church had the chief responsibility to defend and enlarge justice in the world and that the state, therefore, was subservient to the church. His third point was to present a list of virtues that were to characterize priestly lives; and the fourth point was to stress that priests, by virtue of their ordination, were better Christians than the people. Ambrose found Marcus in increasingly violent disagreement with all but the second point. Their discussions, which had always been lively and agitated and which both men enjoyed thoroughly, began to become bitter at times. Ambrose held onto the ancient principle of the Roman nobility which held that the common people, the plebs, needed to be led by the aristocracy. Marcus, on the other hand, held to the position that the Gracchi brothers and others had espoused from time to time in Roman history, namely that the common people should share equally in the rulership of Rome and in the benefits of Roman citizenship. Ambrose liked to point out to Marcus that because he was a Symmachus, educated in the aristocratic tradition, he should maintain that aristocratic view. Marcus had read widely in the story of the Social Wars and he admired the populist leaders of that period and espoused their views concerning the role of the people in the total churchly program.

Ambrose spent hours with Marcus, explaining to him from the Scriptures and Roman political history the importance of the father-figure role in Roman life. He cited story after story from the Old Testament to show to Marcus that God had always provided for his people strong leadership. He alluded regularly to his long experience as governor of Milan to further support his case.

On the second point, concerning the mission of the church, the two men were in full agreement and the Christians in Milan sensed this and were inspired by their unanimity to follow their example.

Marcus completely rejected Ambrose's list of Christian virtues. The younger man argued that there was no real difference between the Christian that Ambrose described and a good pagan in Milan. Marcus claimed that Ambrose had really lost the understanding of the essential Christian virtues of love and humility. Instead, Ambrose placed all the emphasis on justice, and according to Marcus this was not the central Christian virtue. Marcus argued that the uniqueness of Christianity was being blurred in Ambrose's list and that it was becoming increasingly comfortable for pagans to become Christians. This argument was often complicated and profound, and many of those who overheard Ambrose and Marcus thought it impossible to follow their argumentation. They could only sense that Marcus believed that something very crucial was at stake.

Ambrose found Marcus in bitterest opposition on his fourth point that priests by virtue of their call to the office were better Christians than lay people. On this point, Ambrose found greatest difficulty in refuting Marcus's arguments, but Ambrose could not yield on this point because of his long aristocratic background. In a nutshell, Marcus argued that Ambrose's principle would destroy the people's sense of mission and thus also the church's power to change the world for the better. He argued that the laity would be anxious to accept Ambrose's principle, because on the basis of that principle they could settle back in their pews and cheer on the priests who were supposed to do the real Christian things like serving, witnessing, and providing nurture. Ambrose appealed regularly to his experience as governor of Milan. His answer finally was reduced to the claim that one can't expect heroic deeds from most people. As he put it to Marcus after one particularly heated encounter, "Let's concentrate on helping the priests to live the best kind of lives and hope that their example will filter through to at least a few people."

While Ambrose and Marcus maintained their friendly relationship at least as far as public appearances were concerned, Ambrose's savvy told him that a bomb was ticking in Milan between himself and Marcus and that when it went off either he or

Marcus would be destroyed. The match was set to the fuse in a way that neither man expected.

It started when an emergency request was brought to Ambrose from three Christian soldiers who had been serving with some of the barbarian Gothic armies that were ravaging northern Italy. The request involved a large group of Parthian soldiers who had been captured by the Goths and were about to be sold into slavery and thus separated forever from their families. The three Christian soldiers had been unable to stand the thought of the Parthian fate and so they deserted the Gothic camp to seek for help among the Christians. When they reached Milan, they were brought to Ambrose who was closeted with Marcus at that moment.

The soldiers described the plight of the Parthians and expressed their hope and confidence that the Christians would not turn their back on fellow human beings facing that disaster. Ambrose did not hesitate; of course, Christians would do all in their power to help these men even though they were not Christians. As Ambrose pointed out, they were still created in the image of God and people in God's image should not be sold into the kind of slavery the Goths had in mind—cruel, killing work, forever separated from their families and their country.

"But we do have a problem," Ambrose added. "There's hardly a penny left in the church treasury. It's our custom to give our gifts to the poor almost as quickly as we receive them. Furthermore we've had some unexpected expenses in recent months and they have eaten up most of our cash reserves. Marcus, you're the financial genius and the fund raiser. Any ideas?"

"How much would it take? Did the Goths establish any price list?"

"There are about six thousand Parthians and the Goths hope to realize an average of $200 per man at the wholesale price."

"One million two hundred thousand dollars!" Marcus whistled. "Can they be bargained for a lump price of one million dollars for all of them?"

"Perhaps. It's possible. We don't know for sure. This is the last major campaign the Goths can wage before winter and so they'll want top prices. But perhaps if the bishop would go to them personally to bargain. . . ."

"No," said Marcus, "Let's work with their first price. It can be done and it will be done by our people. We have somewhere around a hundred and fifty thousand Christians in Milan. Some of them are well-fixed, but most of them are poor. The wealthy will give something, but we've been hitting them pretty hard of late. Our real hope is in the poor."

The four men stared at Marcus, puzzled. Marcus was dreaming again; this was like the old days; he would come up with something exciting.

"We'll need about $6 per person, in addition to what we can expect from the wealthy. Why not propose a six- to eight-day fast, with the food money to go to a 'spring the Parthians' fund?"

Ambrose knew that would not work. His poor people were getting ready for winter. Every dime counted for them. Marcus's plan was unrealistic and idealistic.

"Marcus, I have a different idea that will work quicker and teach our people a lesson that will always inspire them. Your challenge will be too heavy a burden for the faith of most of them. Instead, let's do something that I saw done once when I was a lad. The Christians melted down their eucharistic vessels and sold the metal and the jewels and gave the money to a father who had gone into debt to ransom his daughter from slave traders. We'll make the announcement during the eucharistic celebration this coming Sunday."

Then he turned to the soldiers and assured them that they would have the money within a week. He asked Marcus to lead them to the church hospitality rooms, and as far as Ambrose was concerned, the matter was closed.

As usual on Sunday morning, the divine liturgy carried Ambrose outside of himself. Surrounded by clouds of incense, his eyes feasting on the vestments and the altar, his ears filled with the music of the choir, and his spirit already joined to the bread and wine that would soon be the body and blood of Jesus, Ambrose experienced God's power in a way that always refreshed and strengthened him. In his experience nothing could be compared with the eucharistic liturgy. Here was eternity; here was pure love and grace, as real as the sights, sounds, and smells. No one could destroy this strength; the Arians had tried and failed. This experience of Jesus, seated at the right hand of God, would outlast any barbarian army. Here was justice, strength, power, and unity for the world. In his sermon, Ambrose urged and exhorted the people to bring justice to all people, regardless of the personal costs.

Then in the eucharistic liturgy, after the words of consecration, Ambrose took their largest chalice, a jeweled thing of golden beauty, and holding it high above his head, turned to the congregation.

"Look at this," he cried, "my friends, for you will not see it or drink from it again. Our Master has need of it, and who are we to hold it back? There are slaves that need to be ransomed and our eucharistic vessels are God's chosen means to do that. The church has gold, not to store up, but to lay out and to spend on those who need. Is it not much better to preserve living vessels than gold ones? The sacraments do not need golden vessels in order to be sacraments. In themselves they are golden vessels, for they redeem men from death. That, indeed, is the true treasure of the Lord which works that which God wishes to work. Then, indeed, do we recognize and affirm the vessel that holds the Lord's blood when we use this chalice either to redeem ourselves from sin or to redeem fellow human beings from death. How much more beautiful even than these vessels of ours will be the sight of six thousand Parthians delivered from slavery and returning to their families! What Christian would want only to hear about justice when there is a golden opportunity to perform it? Come, and drink, and then let us be about our Master's business!"

The impact of Ambrose's action was enormous, as Ambrose knew it would be. The people clapped and cheered as they thronged to the altar. Ambrose had never experienced a more meaningful and more spiritual eucharist.

He was still walking halfway between heaven and earth as he returned to the vesting room to find Marcus already dressed in his street clothes. Ambrose emotionally embraced his nephew and said, "Wasn't God's Spirit alive and active this morning?" His nephew tolerated Ambrose's embrace for a brief time and then broke loose with some remark about a luncheon engagement and left.

The next morning Ambrose sought out Marcus in his office when the younger man failed to appear for their usual morning conference. Marcus was packing his belongings from his drawers and his beloved paintings had already been taken down from the walls. Ambrose gasped and sputtered.

"Marcus, what are you doing? What's going on? What do you have in mind?"

Marcus looked into his uncle's face and replied, "Uncle, I cannot work with you any longer. Yesterday was the end for me. I never felt more ashamed of the Christian church in my life, or of you, its chief bishop." Marcus swallowed and continued. "You patronized the people of God with your dramatic show! You denied them an opportunity to serve and to grow. You did not trust them. You had to be the super-Christian. Under that kind of leadership, Uncle, the church is dead. Your dream of unity is baloney. All you want is a unity of the clergy, with the lay people standing idly by in the wings!"

Ambrose's mouth dropped open; he clenched and un-clenched his fists several times, and then managed to squeak, "What in the world do you mean, what did I do, I raised money to ransom the Parthians in the name of God's people, didn't I? Marcus, are you crazy?"

Pausing for a moment, Marcus replied, "Uncle, I love you. You know that but I can no longer agree with you. For the sake of our love, it's better that we part company. I plan to find a position in the municipal administration. I'll continue to seek Origen's goal of the unity of all things, but the church has abandoned that vision, Uncle, and you are responsible for that." Marcus went on, now speaking more slowly. "The church itself is no longer united. It is divided into fathers and children. The fathers don't trust the children; they keep them in their childish condition. The children respect and worship the fathers, but only because the fathers are doing Christian things for them in their place, Christian things that the people should be doing. Uncle, our Lord would not recognize your church as his."

Marcus turned toward the door to hide his tears and walked out into the warm Milanese air.

COMMENTARY

To come to this study of Ambrose, the reader has jumped mentally from A.D. 200 to A.D. 400 and finds himself or herself in a completely different church. It is impossible to recognize Justin's church in the writings and pastoral style of Ambrose. About the only thing that survives is a recognizable commonality in the understanding of mission. Both churches believe they are called by God to proclaim his kingdom, to announce through word and deed that in Jesus Christ a richer, fuller eternal life is coming to be present among people. Both churches share a common determination to imitate Jesus Christ for the sake of the world, to proclaim forgiveness in his name and to pursue charity and justice for all people.

There are two additional steps that the reader needs to take to understand what happened to Christ's vision of the kingdom between Justin and Ambrose. As one German historian has quipped, "Christ came proclaiming his kingdom and what developed was the church!"

The first step occurred as the church became increasingly conscious of itself as an entity separate and distinct from the world and increasingly aware of the need to build walls between itself and the world and between itself and false Christians. This first step is perfectly represented in the writings and pastoral leadership of Cyprian, bishop of Carthage in North Africa from A.D. 248 to 258, when he was martyred by the Roman government.

Like many early Christians, Cyprian was an adult convert. He developed a great admiration for Tertullian and studied the latter's writings throughout his life. His aim was to preserve Tertullian's ideas about the church; had he realized the changes he introduced, he would have been disappointed. Already as a pagan, Cyprian had gained the respect and trust of the people of Carthage. Thus it is not surprising that in A.D. 248 he was chosen as their bishop, even though he had been a priest for less than two years. He was chosen though he had no seminary diploma. Had he known the troubles that lay in store for him, he probably would have declined the office. These troubles and problems brought forth the new ideas about the church that are connected with the name of Cyprian and also sparked new styles of Christian living and new views of the church's mission. During Cyprian's reign as bishop, Roman emperors launched several severe persecutions against the church. Thousands of members renounced the faith and Cyprian twice went into hiding to escape the soldiers. When peace was restored, the so-called traitors applied for readmission to the church. Some of the faithful wanted to let them back in with no questions asked. Cyprian believed that the health and strength of the Christian body could best be preserved by thoroughly testing the sincerity of these people and by subjecting them to a rather long period of church discipline. In this struggle, Cyprian found it desirable to exalt the authority and the power of the bishop's office to a higher level than any of his predecessors had done.

Cyprian also faced the problems of false teachers who created an opposition Christian church in North Africa. The opposition church established its own ministry, and these ministers baptized, celebrated the eucharist, ordained other ministers, and performed other priestly acts. Cyprian believed that the unity of the true church had to be preserved and that to preserve this unity it was necessary to refuse to accept or honor any of the priestly actions of these ministers. Thus if people had been baptized in the other church and then decided to join Cyprian's church, he insisted that they be rebaptized. Not every member of his own church agreed with him, but Cyprian was trying to preserve a fundamental belief that he had about the church.

He believed with all his heart that there could be only one church because Jesus Christ, its head, was only one. But this raised the question: "Which is that one church, that true church?" Cyprian answered: "The older church is the true church; the true church is that church which is more publicly and directly linked with Jesus Christ." According to Cyprian, this public link with Christ existed in the office of the bishop, with special importance being given to the bishop of Rome, since he was St. Peter's successor in a special sense. Cyprian was convinced that the only workable defense against opposition churches and heresy was to be found in the college of bishops. He described it as the glue that holds the church together. In effect, he built the college of bishops into a wall around the church to protect Christians against false teachers.

Cyprian's concern for the spiritual health of his people is praiseworthy, but his solution to the problem contributed to a fundamental change in the way people understood the church. In effect, Cyprian, without ever meaning to, began to define the church as somehow being equal to the college of bishops; other persons are in a separate class. If the church can rightly be likened to a boat, then in the thought of Cyprian, the clergy make up the ark, and lay members are passengers aboard the ark. Cyprian coined the saying "He who will not have the church as his mother, cannot have God as his Father." Cyprian was telling people that their salvation depended on their relationship to an orthodox bishop or other orthodox clergy. The body of Christ has begun to become a two-party, two-level structure. It has changed from the egalitarian, democratic pattern of the time of Justin and Tertullian.

That the nature and purpose of the church was changing can be seen in the many letters and essays of Cyprian that survive to this day. These changes can be noted with reference to the five basic Christian actions of worship, fellowship, service, witness, and nurture. Under Cyprian's leadership, worship probably became richer and more liturgical and in general continued to perform its important Christian function. Not much is known about the practice of fellowship among the people of God in Cyprian's day because Christians no longer wrote about this; instead they wrote more and more about the importance and the work of bishops and other clergy. It seems likely that persecution and heresy must have forced the members of Cyprian's church to hold tightly to each other and thus the bonds of fellowship were preserved, at least to some extent. But at the same time the increasing size of congregations probably decreased the effectiveness of the intimate and personal fellowship-bonds of Justin and Tertullian.

In the area of Christian service, two important developments took place that changed the nature of the way in which Christians understood their mission. In the first place, Cyprian's letters indicate that North African Christians became quite indifferent about their mission call. This seems to be new; previous generations of Christians had maintained uniformly good records of service to all people in need, regardless of creed or race. In contrast, Cyprian expressed his horror about the low level of performance by his people. I believe that the difference in performance is related to the growing size of congregations. In the smaller congregation, people were closer to each other and they knew each other's strengths and weaknesses. Therefore they were able to encourage and support one another as they tried to carry out their baptismal call to imitate Christ for the life of the world. In the larger congregation, this essential kind of Christian nurture did not happen, at least not effectively. In other words, changes in the pattern and style of Christian fellowship affected Christian nurture which affected Christian service.

A second development in the field of Christian service took place with respect to Cyprian's cure for his people's indifference. He taught them that their good deeds done for the poor and needy would gain them great rewards in the heavenly world. While the Bible sets forth this principle in passages like Matthew 25, Cyprian stressed the motivation of reward so strongly that he actually obscured the motivation of the love of Christ present and active within each Christian. The motivation of personal advantage became stronger than the motivation of the needs of the neighbor, who is also Christ's brother or sister. Christian service, originally designed to help others, increasingly became a matter of self-service. Although Cyprian's idea worked very well, at the same time a basic change was taking place in the Christians' understanding of their mission.

Little direct evidence survives concerning the fourth function of witness, but it can be surmised that not much of this was going on either. If the Christians' charitable ministry had deteriorated, it is likely that their witnessing work had also declined. In general, what seems to be happening at Cyprian's time is that Christians were turning in more and more upon themselves and more and more making the church serve their needs. As a result, the earlier attitude of openness to the world's needs was slowly displaced by a new desire to preserve the church as an institution for the sake of their personal salvation. The church was becoming an end in itself, designed to benefit the members, rather than being, as Christ intended it to be, a means, a tool, to the end of establishing God's kingdom or reign among people.

The two-level pattern of clergy-people relationship also radically changed the practice of nurture. In earlier centuries, Christians had been nurtured by leaders of small groups, and they had nurtured each other as they spoke the gospel to one another and encouraged all members to be faithful to Jesus Christ. But now nurture became the sole responsibility of the bishop, and the people participated only as listeners.

In one of his letters, Cyprian presents a classically beautiful picture of the bishop working as shepherd of his flock. The bishop expends his energy without reservation to care for every need of his sheep. He finds their scratches and wounds and pours in oil and wine, he combs their fleece, he beds them down at night, he knows each one by name, he loves each one. It's a moving pastoral picture. The problem is that the bishop has taken over sole responsibility for nurturing Christians. As a consequence, the people become quite content to turn all their baptized responsibility over to this great father-figure. Mutual care and nurture by Christians for Christians began to disappear, with serious consequences for the understanding and practice of God's mission. The spotlight slowly swung from the people of God gathered together in community, and came to rest on the bishop-pastor.

In summary, perhaps it can be said about Cyprian that he loved the church not wisely but too well. He was a fatherly figure and showed a deep fatherly concern for the Christians entrusted to his charge. But in his fatherly concern, he may have been overprotective. Needless to say, many people liked the solicitous concern of Cyprian and failed to see that such concern can sometimes do more harm than good.

Can you daydream for a moment about what you would have done in Cyprian's place? Can you see, within the space of this chapter, how some of Cyprian's seeds began to grow into Ambrose's trees?

Another major change in the shape of Christian congregations and in the commitment to mission on the part of individual Christians took place when Constantine the emperor became a Christian. This happened in the early part of the fourth century. Constantine decided that the Christian church was the social or political group that could do the best job of holding together his tottering empire. Therefore he endorsed Christianity publicly and apparently himself became a Christian. The result was predictable. Hundreds and thousands of pagans suddenly decided that they, too, were Christians and flocked into the church in great numbers. The leaders of the church were totally unprepared for this mass invasion. They did not have the educational resources to train these new members, nor did the new members themselves want to undergo a lengthy period of discipleship training. The leaders of the church were forced to a crucial decision on the question: shall we insist on the old standards of discipleship, or shall we take these people in on the basis of much lower standards and then try to train them? The answer was that the lower standards should be set up. The result was that the higher standards were never taught to or caught by most of the newer members. Thus the general level of Christian commitment and the general pattern of the imitation of Christ sank quite low. As a matter of fact, by Ambrose's time in Milan it was really quite difficult to tell a good pagan from a good Christian simply on the basis of conduct. This is why Marcus was distressed by Ambrose's list of Christian virtues. Marcus believed that the life of the Christian, centered in the imitation of Jesus Christ, should be radically different from that of the typical pagan. It can be argued that between A.D. 325 and A.D. 400 the Christian church underwent the most radical change in its entire history. It can also be suggested that you and I would feel much more at home in the late-fourth-century church than we would have felt in the pre-Constantinian church.

Ambrose wrote a very important and influential book on the work of priests. Throughout this book he assumed the ideas that Marcus disagreed with. Ambrose wrote as the great father of the priests; they were his children. One can well imagine where the laity of the church would fit in this structure, if even the priests are considered children of the bishop. While there are many fine thoughts in Ambrose's manual, there is the underlying assumption that priests are to live at a different level of commitment from the laity. One example from the manual will illustrate this point. Ambrose wrote that in Colossians 3:5 the apostle Paul calls on all Christians to put to death what is earthly in them. Then he observed, "This, indeed, is meant for all the faithful. But thee, especially, my son . . ." In what follows Ambrose lays a special obligation upon the clergy. In quite a number of places in this manual, Ambrose distinguishes between the ordinary duties that Christ has imposed upon all Christians, and the perfect duties that Christ has imposed only on the clergy. Thus he helped widen the gulf between priests and people.

Some of Ambrose's teachings about the duties of the priest are worth noting. The priest is to reject the pleasures and the advantages of this life, in exchange for the blessings of the life to come. The priest has the perfect duty of setting an example of mercy before the people, for in this the priest is imitating the perfect Father. Ambrose has in mind particularly "mercy as shown chiefly towards the poor," that they might be treated as sharers in common with the priests of all that God has provided in nature. Priests are also to clothe the naked, for in so doing they are clothing Christ. The priest is to take the lead in the pursuit of justice and to protect the weak against the strong. The priest is to be in all things "a pattern in all good works, in teaching, in trueness of character, in seriousness." Ambrose encouraged the priests to follow St. Paul who offered himself as a pattern to be copied. The priest is to be humble, of an honorable spirit, chaste, and a person of wise counsel.

Ambrose was a wise man, and realized full well that the demands he was placing upon his priests could not be met by them in isolation. Therefore he placed considerable emphasis upon fellowship among the priests who were assigned to his cathedral. What happened here was that the *koinonia,* the fellowship, that held the early Christians together, now existed chiefly, and sometimes solely, among the priests. For example he wrote in his book of advice for priests that "in accordance with the will of God and the union of nature, we ought to be of mutual help one to the other, and to vie with each other in doing duties" for each other "so that the charm of human fellowship may ever grow sweeter among us." In an earlier period, this objective would have held for all Christians. The importance of the small group is recognized, but the small group from now on is usually a priestly group.

Does Ambrose's distinction between ordinary and perfect virtues continue to describe the calling of priests and laity in our day? Can you prepare a list or description of Christian virtues that will sharply distinguish the Christian from the non-Christian? Would you have agreed with Marcus in his angry charge that Ambrose was patronizing the people of God?

The story of the melting down of the communion vessels actually happened in Ambrose's life. The story of the ransoming of Parthian captives from barbarians is also true. It illustrates the early Christians' concern to do good for all people, regardless of race or creed. It also illustrates their willingness to sacrifice their own possessions so that charity might be carried out.

The writings and sermons of Ambrose present clearly what he thought about Jesus Christ and what he thought about the Christian church. In a nutshell, he loved both of them dearly and with all his heart. He really made no distinction between them. His love for the church was as profound and deep as his love for Jesus

Christ. Perhaps it would be fair to say that in Ambrose Jesus Christ and the church are opposite sides of the same coin. This is something that can be observed in the writings of many of the important leaders in the church. This idea probably will sound strange to many American Protestants and some may even judge it to be idolatrous. But there is good Biblical basis for this attitude in Ephesians and Colossians where the church is identified as the body of Christ.

It is worth noting that what Ambrose thought and believed about Jesus Christ shaped and influenced what he thought and believed about the church. But in his writings this principle can also be inverted to read that what he thought and believed about the church shaped and controlled what he thought and believed about Jesus Christ. This is a principle of fundamental importance for all those who are engaged in carrying out the mission of Jesus Christ or who are engaged in any way in developing parish programs. The point of these remarks is to encourage Christians to unite Jesus Christ and his church in such an intimate way that what they say or do with respect to the one affects what they say or do with respect to the other.

The good and the bad effects of this interrelationship can be illustrated from Ambrose. Ambrose speaks of Christ's saving work in several ways and uses several models to explain what Christ meant to him. For Ambrose Christ was the revealer of the saving knowledge about the triune God. Christ was also the one who made atonement for the sins of humanity. Christ was the bridegroom of the church and there was a real love affair going on between Christ and his church. Christ provided Christians with examples to imitate. Christ was also the bringer of heavenly medicines that he had prepared "from the juices of those celestial fruits that do not wither." This medicine made whole all those who came to Christ.

Note the first and the last models in the preceding paragraph. Both models stress the spiritual qualities, gifts, and graces that Christ gives to the church, rather than his active life, his suffering, and his death. These two models of the work of Jesus Christ support and complement Ambrose's strong emphasis on the centrality of the sacraments in the life of the church. In the sacraments, Christ gives his heavenly medicine to people.

In yet another way, Ambrose's thought about Christ meshed completely with his thought about the church. He spoke about both Christ and the sacraments as channels by which God's grace came into human life. In a sense, both are sacraments and thus the church is the custodian and the dispenser of both. It is clear, then, that Ambrose's thought has a double axis, consisting in almost equal parts of his love for Jesus Christ and his love for the church.

There is a third way that Ambrose's ideas about Jesus and the church reinforce each other, but this is perhaps a less desirable way. With respect to both Christ and the church, Ambrose emphasized the heavenly existence and the heavenly qualities much more strongly than the earthly existence and the earthly qualities. He stressed Christ's divine nature, and he stressed the divine aspects of the church's life, such as the eucharistic liturgy. Christ is no longer the good shepherd, the human brother of all Christians. Rather, he is basically a heavenly being, far removed from this earth and from the lives of people; he is to be feared when he is worshiped. So far away has Christ gone in the thought of Ambrose that the priests must serve as the mediators between the heavenly Christ and sinful, earthbound mortals.

He held the same view of the sacraments. They came down from heaven, he wrote. The bread and wine in the eucharist lose their earthly qualities and are transformed into heavenly realities. Again, to a noticeable degree in the writings of Ambrose, the priest who administers the sacraments becomes a half-heavenly being, or at least a human being who possesses half-heavenly powers. In large measure, the humanity of Christ and the humanity of the sacraments disappear. And it is not surprising, therefore, that the humanity, the earthly qualities, of the church also disappear.

Most of the people in Milan enjoyed this emphasis upon the heavenly qualities of Christ and the heavenly qualities of the church. But this emphasis did tend to obscure their earthly responsibilities and the church's obligation to make them mindful of their earthly mission. In this way, an improper emphasis on the church and an improper understanding of the person and the work of Jesus Christ again supported each other with somewhat harmful results.

Like the pastors who preceded him, Ambrose was always conscious of his call to be both servant to the people of God and their guide or shepherd. This double function created a real tension in Ambrose, as it does in most Christian ministers. It's difficult to keep a proper balance between the two. In Ambrose's case, it is clear that he resolved the tension in favor of the shepherd-guide function. He was much more the leader and the ruler of the people than he was their servant. However, had anyone asked him whether he was among the people to serve, he would have responded with a strong affirmative reply. It seems that he had made a conscious decision to the effect that the best way to serve the people was by being their shepherd and their guide. Given his background as governor of Milan, the shepherding function came out behaving very much like a ruling function. Marcus was distressed by this approach to the pastoral office because he believed it patronized the people of God.

There are reasons why the shepherding-ruling function often becomes more important than the serving function. In the early church, this related to the size of the congregation. The larger the congregation, the more natural it was for the pastor to be ruler rather than servant. But this also relates to human nature, the human nature of Christian people and the human nature of the pastor. Many Christian people prefer to let George do it and they're content when the pastor as ruler does many Christian things in their name. This often gives them a sense of comfort and security at the same time. It is understandable that the pastor often yields to the temptation to rule rather than to serve. For one thing, as a ruler the pastor can get things done much more quickly than as a servant. For another thing, it is human nature to like to rule and to be honored as ruler among your fellow human beings.

By Ambrose's time there was yet another reason for the ruler function almost replacing the servant function. That reason lies in a new understanding of the pastoral office and of pastoral duties. As was indicated a few pages earlier, the people's view toward the eucharist changed. They began to regard it with greater awe and fear, and thus it was only natural that the eucharistic priest came to be regarded with greater awe and fear. The office was exalted in the minds of the people and therefore they preferred to regard the priest as ruler rather than as servant.

It is a rule in Christian community-building that the more the pastor functions as powerful ruler, the more do imbalances occur among the five actions of worship, fellowship, witness, service, and nurture. This rule can be illustrated in the church at Milan. In the congregation there, the worship activity went on gloriously and powerfully. The fellowship activity among the people seems to have been very limited. Among the priests, as has already been reported, it was strong and active. Not much is known about the witnessing lives of the Milanese Christians, but probably not much was going on. One reason for this may have been that most of the people were Christians. On top of that, most of the Christians were poor, and so would have little opportunity to witness to the pagans, who were mostly rich. Quite evidently a great deal of Christian service went on, but, as the Cameo suggests, the Christian service was performed largely through gifts of money rather than through personal service. Christian service became impersonal and was administered by the priests of the church. It's somewhat difficult to determine what kind of mutual nurture and upbuilding was taking place, but there is no strong evidence that the people continued to feed and to nurture each other. However, they did receive much nurture from Ambrose through his sermons and pastoral care and counseling.

In Milan the five functions were not present in equal and balanced relationship. But it strikes me that there are few, if any, cases in church history where the balanced relationship existed in the presence of a strong pastoral ruler. I believe that the balanced development of the five functions is more effective in equipping Christians for mission than strong pastoral rulership.

Though some critical things have been said about Ambrose's approach to church and ministry, one strong positive affirmation must be made. Under his rulership and based solidly on his Biblical studies, the church flourished and became strong. In a society where every other institution was crumbling, the church became the only stable element. As a matter of fact, from the time of Ambrose almost down to our modern times, the church was the major civilizing influence in the Western world. Its strength in large measure is based on Ambrose's teaching and practice. Whether Ambrose's teaching and practice were always the best or whether his ideas contributed to the strongest kind of Christian life is, of course, another question.

Do you think of yourself as loving the church the way Ambrose did? If so, how do you define "church" in that sentence? Think for a few minutes about how your beliefs about Jesus Christ affect your beliefs about what the church is and what its mission is. What factors in your congregation help to shape your definition of pastoral authority?

4.

John Chrysostom

CAMEO

John Chrysostom was born in Antioch, Syria probably in A.D. 345. This made him a contemporary of Ambrose of Milan, but he lived in a quite different world. In the East prosperity was high and the people enjoyed life. Society was stable and the government was strong. Under these circumstances it is not surprising that the people devoted a great deal of time and energy to pleasure. Many of the citizens of the East were Christian, although there is no way of determining exact percentages.

John's parents were Christians, his father being an officer in the Roman army and his mother well known in Antioch for her piety and charity. Like many Christian parents in that period, his parents did not have the baby baptized as an infant. As a matter of fact, John did not present himself as a candidate for baptism until he was in his mid-twenties.

Although John's mother was an outstanding pious Christian, John seems to have led the life of ordinary young people in Antioch, enjoying the disreputable theater and the excitement of the games in the circus. Antioch was an important city, well planned and beautifully laid out with many modern conveniences. Its inhabitants were widely known for their passion for pleasures and their excitability. John seems to have shared in many of these characteristics.

Following a thorough course of baptismal instruction by the priest, John presented himself as a candidate for baptism. In keeping with the custom of the church, he first turned to the west and said, "I renounce thee, Satan, and all thy cult, and pomps, and works." Then, having turned to the east, he also said, "I enter into thy service, O Christ." With the last statement, he meant only that he planned to live the finest kind of Christian life; he did not mean that he planned to enter the priesthood.

Nevertheless he took his baptismal vows so seriously that three years after he was baptized he left Antioch to become a monk in the steep hills around the city. Here for six years or more he lived in absolute solitude, going without sleep for long periods of time. The extreme discipline of these years developed his spiritual sensitivities to the highest degree, while at the same time it ruined his health for the rest of his life. He spent much time studying Scripture and this knowledge made him a powerful preacher after he returned to Antioch.

In the winter of 380–381, he gave in to the pleading of Meletius, the orthodox bishop of Antioch, and left his life of monkish solitude to be appointed as a reader in the church. A short time later he was ordained a deacon, and on February 26, 386, he was ordained a priest. It was at this time that he wrote a manual on the priesthood in the form of a dialogue with his friend Basil. Like Ambrose's manual in the west, Chrysostom's manual deeply influenced the developing character of the Christian priesthood for many centuries.

As priest in Antioch, John had clear understandings of the goals and objectives of the priestly office. He said that the chief goal was to bring the people of God in safety to their heavenly home. A second major goal was to help the people to keep themselves uncontaminated by the sins of the world. For John this meant especially to avoid the baths, the theater, and the circus. A third goal was the mission objective of winning souls for Christ. John was always moved by a deep passion for people, and he tried to inculcate this same compassion in the minds and hearts of his people.

The fourth major goal was to develop in the people a compassion for the poor and the needy, who could be seen all over Antioch. Again and again in his sermons he returned to this topic.

He urged the Christians to share their goods with the needy so that poverty might be eliminated. In vivid words, he explained to his people how the poor of the city maimed themselves and blinded their children to move people to give them a few pennies so that they might buy food. He described other poor people who drove spikes into their heads or sat in ice-cold water in order to earn a few pennies. In his judgment, the care of the poor was at the center of the program of the parish. When members argued that the church had enough wealth to take care of the poor, John always rejected this argument and insisted that each Christian had the duty to help the poor directly and individually.

These were demanding objectives for the people but God had given the priest a variety of means to achieve them. One of the most effective priestly tools was the spoken word, the sermon. In his treatise "On the Priesthood" he wrote:

> Save for good example, there is but one means and method of cure: the spoken word. This is the sole instrument, the only diet, the finest climate. It takes the place of medication, of cautery, and the knife. If it is necessary to burn or cut, this is the instrument which must be used; and if it fails, all else is useless. By this means we raise up the prostrate soul, and cool the fevered; we cut away its excesses and supply its defects; and we do everything else which is required for the health of the soul. [*The Priesthood: A Translation of the PERI HIEROSYNES of St. John Chrysostom* by W. A. Jurgens (New York: Macmillan, 1955), p. 70]

The spoken word possessed great restorative and creative powers. Through it, the Holy Spirit worked to create new hearts and new wills, yes, new people. Through admonition and encouragement, the word caused Christians to mature and to become real men and women as they experienced full despair when the preacher in God's name accused them of their sins, and full joy when God through the priest forgave them and restored them. The ancient Greeks had called this process of maturation *paideia* (from which comes our word "pedagogy"), and they described this as the sum total of experiences that changed a child into an adult. In his sermons and writings, John defined *paideia* as the sum total of experiences that helped Christians to grow to the measure of the stature of the fullness of Christ. *Paideia* included mutual conversation and consolation, preaching, the sacraments, discipline, pain and suffering, joy and rejoicing, and so forth.

John Chrysostom loved to preach. Once after he had been ill for a while, he returned to the pulpit while still too weak with the remark that preaching made him well.

> As soon as I open my mouth, all weariness is gone; as soon as I begin to teach, all fatigue is over. . . . Indeed, I have been chained to my bed until now; but God did not wish to let me die of hunger. For just as you are hungry to hear, so am I hungry to preach. [Chrysostomus Baur, *John Chrysostom and His Time* (Westminster, Md.: Newman Press, 1959), vol. 1, p. 209]

A second primary means that the priest had for achieving the high goals that Jesus Christ had established was that of the priest's own example. It was important that the priests themselves refuse to go to the circus and the theater, and for John this was a great sacrifice because he enjoyed both thoroughly. But in this matter he set a rigorous standard for the people. In his treatise he wrote that the soul of the priest should be as a light which shines in the whole world.

However, the priestly call to imitate Christ did not mean that priests should hide from the people the fact that they were human too. In his treatise he wrote:

> When we blame someone for anything, we ourselves deserve the same. For it is just for this reason that God has called men, not angels, to the priesthood and to be teachers of the gospel; so that we might show more tenderness and pity to sinners as a result of our own experience.

The third basic tool for Christian growth was the sacraments. John emphasized baptism and its daily meaning in the lives of his people. He constantly reminded them of how they had turned first to the west and renounced Satan and his service when they were baptized, and then to the east and publicly declared their intention of enrolling in Christ's service. He reminded them that in baptism they had put on Christ and that Christ was now the controlling power in their lives. The celebration of the eucharist was always an opportunity for the people to give thanks to God for his grace and for the gift of his son. In the eucharist the people received the body and blood of Jesus Christ and through that gift were made more like Christ, a little more divine.

His high view of the sacraments led to an equally high view of the priesthood. In his treatise he wrote:

> Inasmuch as no man can enter into the Kingdom of Heaven unless he be born again of water and spirit, and since unless he eats the flesh of the Lord and drinks his blood he is excluded from eternal life—since, I say, all these things are administered only by these holy hands, the hands of the priests, how could any man without those priests either escape the fire of hell or obtain the crown which is intended for him? The spiritual labor and rebirth accomplished through Baptism is entrusted to priests. By their means we put on Christ [in the sacrament of the altar], and are buried with the Son of God [in baptism], and become members with that Blessed Head. [*The Priesthood*, p. 33]

Even though John's congregation numbered some one hundred thousand members, he maintained a regular schedule of visits. He encouraged the priests to visit both men and women, since the practice seems to have been to ignore women. He even argues that the priest ought to spend more time with women "because of their propensity to sin" (my apologies to modern women).

Finally, John says a great deal about the priest's responsibility to pray for the welfare and the growth of the people. He speaks of the priest as "ambassador to God on behalf of the whole city . . . indeed the whole world—beseeching him to have mercy upon all sinners, be they living or be they dead!"

What kind of person does it take to carry out this forbidding list of priestly duties? In his writings, John offers a full description of the requisite priestly qualities. In his own life he reflected these qualities to a high degree.

A basic priestly quality is that the pastor must love the people. Some of John's own deep love for the people of Antioch shines through in the following words.

> I know no other life but you and the care of souls. . . . That
> is our only care by day and by night, that all of you may
> become holy and perfect. . . . When I see your unsatisfied
> hunger after spiritual teaching, I cannot let a day go by
> without nourishing you with the treasures of the Holy Scrip-
> tures. . . . It is my joy to see you making progress in spiritual
> things. [*John Chrysostom and His Time,* vol. 1, p. 208]

On another occasion when the city had suffered from one of
its frequent earthquakes, John hurried from his sickbed to the
pulpit and said, "My congregation is my crown of glory, and
every single listener means more to me than all the rest of the
city." (*John Chrysostom and His Time,* vol. 1, p. 209)

Furthermore, the priest or pastor must know the people inti-
mately. In this respect, John was a master. The people knew that
he knew them and they listened when he spoke. One paragraph
from a sermon will illustrate this quality.

> But you stand always in the front rank of battle, and are
> always receiving new wounds. . . . Now your wife irritates
> you, then your son worries you; your slaves excite you to
> anger, an enemy sets a snare for you, a friend speaks badly
> of you, a neighbor abuses you, a colleague deceives you; it
> sometimes happens that a judge threatens you; poverty op-
> presses you, the loss of those related to you afflicts you, so
> that fortune makes you arrogant and misfortune makes you
> downcast. All around us are numerous opportunities for
> inducing in us anger, worry, discouragement, affliction, van-
> ity and despair. . . . Therefore we need the divine medicine,
> by which we may heal the wounds we have received. [*John
> Chrysostom and His Time,* vol. 1, p. 323]

It was furthermore essential that the priest be a person of the
Spirit. This meant that the priest should be richly endowed by
God's Spirit with special gifts and that, in the second place, the
priest should discharge the ministry in a spiritual manner.

Part of John's own spiritual living was the rigorous practice of
self-denial. He was an ascetic, long after he had left his monkish
cave. In both Antioch and Constantinople, he stopped the custom of elaborate and costly episcopal banquets, and as a matter
of principle almost always declined invitations. He preferred to

eat a simple meal by himself. His clothing likewise was simple, except for liturgical vestments. Because the liturgy was God's service and a symbol to the people of the glories of heaven, only the finest liturgical garments were suitable. John remained unmarried as a matter of personal choice and part of his ascetic practice. At this time, the church's laws on marriage for priests had not yet been rigidly formulated. John's practice of asceticism was a major source of his priestly effectiveness. In the first place, his disciplined personal life gave the people a brilliant example of his attitude toward the world. He not only preached about rejecting the world, but he lived that kind of life. Like St. Paul, he counted all that the world had to offer as dung because he had come to know Jesus Christ. In the second place, his ascetic life opened him to the presence and the power of God to a unique degree. Almost everyone who met him sensed that God was uniquely present in him. The presence of God and of God's Spirit enabled him to function somehow as a conduit of heavenly powers to weak and earthbound people. He lived close to God already in this world, and the people admired him for this, were encouraged by his example, and many of them strove to imitate him.

In his writings, John also emphasized that the priest must be patient. John knew human weakness first hand because he had discovered it within himself. He discovered it also in his people because he was always among them, visiting and talking with them. He realized that his preaching against the games and the circuses made little real impact on the people. But instead of scolding them for not following his words, John continued his patient program of preaching and educating. In one sermon he said:

> I wish that my admonitions might produce more fruit. But when my listeners continue in their old errors after hearing my sermons, nevertheless we will not stop speaking to them. The brook continues to flow, even when no one comes to fetch water, and the fountain bubbles, even though no one draws from it. . . . We, to whom the service of the Word is entrusted, have received from the dear God the command

never to abandon our duty, and never to be silent, whether anyone listens to us or not. . . . There are those [priests] who . . . make merry over us and say: "Stop the good advice, skip the admonitions; they will not listen to you, let them go!" What are you saying? Have we promised to convert all men in one day? If only ten, or only five, or indeed only one, repents, is not that consolation enough? [*John Chrysostom and His Time,* vol. 1, p. 253]

In order to discharge great responsibilities, God gives great authority to the priest. John believed that the office of the ministry was created by God and that the Holy Spirit made ministers in the act of ordination. He wrote:

For the priestly office is indeed discharged on earth, but it ranks among heavenly ordinances; and very naturally so; for neither man, nor angel, nor arch-angel, nor any other created power, but the Paraclete himself instituted this vocation, and persuaded men while still abiding in the flesh to represent the ministry of angels.

In these words, John does not say that ordination gave priests a new and unchanging character for the rest of their lives. John always wanted to emphasize that the priestly office was one of service and that priests ought never to claim special honor for themselves because they are ordained.

The authority of the priest, according to John, was greater than that of parents, for the latter have authority and power only to beget children for this life, while the priest begets them for eternal life. The power of the priest was also greater than that of the king, who rules people only in this life.

The essential power of the priest was to bind or to forgive sins.

Temporal rulers have indeed the power of binding; but they can bind only the body. Priests, however, can bind with a bond which pertains to the soul itself, and transcends the very heavens. Whatever priests do here on earth, God will confirm in heaven, just as the master ratifies the decisions of his servants. [*The Priesthood,* p.33]

But John always reminded priests that this authority has to be exercised in a spirit of gentleness and pity, never in anger or in a spirit of revenge. He described the priest as "father" or "physician."

Like Ambrose in the west, John had a very high view of the church and he loved it as much as he loved Jesus Christ. John took seriously St. Paul's description (in Ephesians and Colossians) of the church as the body of Christ and the fullness of Christ. He wrote that when Christians are united and bound to one another in peace, then the head finds its completion and a complete body arises. To this body belong "all believers in the whole world, who are, were and shall be."

> It is one spirit that makes us into one single body and causes us to be born again. We were not baptized that we might become different bodies, but rather that by baptism we might preserve, with mutual attention, the unity of this one body.

> The body of the church can be nourished only if members communicate with one another.

> As the human body is only in its right order, and can serve the spirit as support and instrument only if all the members are in their places and fulfill their natural functions, so also is the case with the spiritual body of Christ, the church. So whoever evokes schisms in the church acts just as though he had torn asunder the members of a body.

In John's thinking, the church is spotless and holy. Its members should love it and revere it. The church can only be one. Friendly intercommunion among all members is essential for the life of the church. Maintenance of the proper hierarchical order and distinction among clergy and between clergy and laity is necessary for the healthy life of the church. John believed that the priests are the glue that holds the congregations together as they minister God's good gifts to the people. Priests are the mainsprings that keep congregations going. They represent God and Christ and make God and Christ again present among the people.

Again like Ambrose, John emphasized the divine nature of the church even as he emphasized the divine nature of Jesus Christ. In the thought of John, the sacrament of the altar was a celebration of heavenly life. He placed great emphasis upon a beautiful and ornate liturgy, and the people loved this. Jesus Christ was not so much the people's brother as he was their Savior and their Judge. Just as in the thought of Ambrose, so also in the thought of John, beliefs about Jesus Christ affected beliefs about the church and *vice versa*.

COMMENTARY

To enter the world of John Chrysostom is to enter a world of spiritual love and devotion that is not often experienced. But John's world is the kind of world that God's Spirit intends people to have. According to John, the priest plays a crucial role in leading people into this world and in preserving this world among people. The priest is the hinge upon whom the spiritual life of the people swings. The priest's example is to be a source of constant inspiration and encouragement to the people. One cannot read John's writings without developing a strong hunger for his kind of living.

It seems that John retained a creative balance between the serving function and the shepherding-guiding function of the priest. In Ambrose's writings, the priest emerged as the ruler and the father of the people. By contrast, in John's writings the priest was there to serve the people and to help them to grow in spiritual strength through example, through preaching, through visits, through forgiving or refusing to forgive sins, and through other priestly means. John was much less a ruling figure, and much more a supportive-serving figure.

John emphasized the importance of intercommunion among all the members of his congregation. This stress is not found in the writings of Ambrose. Obviously John believed that the life of the spirit was made present also through the mutual conversation and encouragement of the brothers and sisters. In other words, John insisted that the actions of fellowship and nurture were the responsibility of the people just as much as of the priest. If the priest was the hinge, then the people were the door. Neither was worth anything without the other. It is remarkable that John stressed this in view of the huge size of his congregation. Perhaps the very size of his congregation led to that emphasis. There is no way of determining how successfully the people implemented their mutual fellowship and nurture.

Like Ambrose, John Chrysostom had a clear view of the goals of the Christian community. He spoke of four: (1) that the people reach their heavenly goal; (2) that they live lives that are distinctly different from the world; (3) that they win others for Christ; (4) that they care for the poor and the needy.

Can you list in your own mind or share with your friends the goals that your parish has established? Who is responsible for evaluating and reporting the progress that you are making in achieving your goals?

Attention needs to be given to John's consuming passion for the poor and the needy. For him, as for many of his predecessors and successors, charity was a major center of Christian community life. God's people were gathered together in order to care for all classes and kinds of needy. At one point John said that the closer he came to God in the practice of spiritual exercises and devotion, the closer he came to the needy.

It is unfortunate that in many areas of Christianity today the practice of charity and justice is placed in secondary importance behind the goal of "winning souls." The history of the church reveals that this division into primary and secondary missions is a recent development. It does not become common until after 1700, when the church received a series of setbacks which greatly reduced its prestige and power. As a result of this loss of influence, the church generally abandoned its traditional responsibility for charity and justice. To justify and to explain this loss of influence, theologians taught that the church had no business in the affairs of this world, but should concentrate on the life after death. Thus there developed the common idea that the church's primary business was to win souls and that, at best, its secondary mission was to be responsible for charity and justice.

John Chrysostom's attitude is in marked contrast to this position. Not only was the congregation as such responsible for charity and justice, but each individual Christian had a direct calling in these respects. John would have agreed with the principle laid down in *The Apostolic Constitutions,* a manual of Christian life that was probably put together during John's lifetime. This manual stipulated that Christians are to care for the needy, and it encouraged poor Christians to fast for a day or two so that they might have something to give to the truly poor!

Like all his contemporaries, John did not have our modern understanding of economic principles and interrelationships. He believed that all poverty and human suffering was the consequence of sin and that moral reform was the only solution. Therefore none of the church fathers took an active part in politics or worked hard to secure legislation that would alleviate social evils. Of course, in the totalitarian society of their day, such action would not have been especially fruitful either. If the fathers were alive today, it seems safe to say that they would be in the forefront of corporate political action and economic reform movements in the name of Jesus and of his church.

How do you and the members of your parish understand your individual or corporate responsibility for charity and justice? Would the pursuit of charity and justice in your community be a good way to witness and to serve your neighbor?

John believed that Christians witnessed by what they were as well as by what they said. He believed that they were to be salt and leaven in the corrupt society of fourth-century Antioch and Constantinople. By their conduct they were both to rebuke non-Christian conduct and to invite these people to join them. They were to be honest in a dishonest world regardless of the cost to themselves, scrupulous among unscrupulous people, chaste in a lecherous society, decorous in a society that was lacking in decorum, self-giving in a world where most people sought their own advantage, meek and humble among people who were cruel and power-oriented. John realized full well that this kind of conduct would anger people and bring wrath and punishment down upon his own people. But his understanding of Christianity gave him no choice. John himself paid with his life because he insisted upon being consistent with his beliefs. John understood pastoral care to include a great variety of tools and activities, all to enable the people to be active in their fourfold mission. Preaching, teaching, the sacraments, visiting, personal example, discipline: all these were essential parts of pastoral care. This broad and inclusive program had only one goal, to help his people to announce to all the people of Antioch that the kingdom of God was drawing near to them in Jesus Christ, and that life—real life—was available to them, already in the here and now. He did not believe that the goal of pastoral care was simply to help the weak individual or to restore the sinner to Christian fellowship. These might be intermediate goals, but the real goal was to help all people to "be about their Master's business." He carried on pastoral care for the sake of God's mission.

How would you define the goals and objectives of pastoral care? Is there a difference, or should there be a difference, between the pastoral care offered by a pastor and that offered by a Christian psychiatrist who is a member of your parish?

In his writings, John placed considerable emphasis on the importance of the priestly example. Like Paul, the priest was to urge the people to imitate him, even as he imitated Christ. The idea of imitating needs careful thought, for in our day the idea has largely disappeared from Christian vocabulary. It needs to be restored, for Christians are baptized into Christ in order that they might grow into Christ's likeness so that their example would help other people to sense the presence of Christ in their lives. In this process of imitating, the priest or pastor gives the chief example of Christlike living.

Many find this a frightening thought, partly because they believe it to be unattainable and partly because it seems to make Christ a new lawgiver. The first fear can be dismissed because in this life Christians do not achieve the perfect imitation of Jesus Christ. The second fear rests on a misunderstanding of the Christian practice of imitation. In his writings, John provided valuable insights into what imitation means. He said that the first characteristic of priests who imitate Jesus Christ is that they are "eminently free and confident." The priest does not see Christ as a new lawgiver, but has found in Christ a new freedom and a new power to meet new situations in a creative and constructive manner. In the second place, priests imitate Christ in Christ's trust and confidence in the Father's will. Like Christ, priests learn to trust the Father's will even when the Father's will is that they pay with their lives for their beliefs. Furthermore, like Christ the priest is filled with compassion for all manner of human need. The priest's example of compassion is to inspire other people to imitation. Like Christ, the priest seeks to serve rather than to be served. Like Christ, the priest understands that people come first and that laws are made for the sake of people and that people are never made for the sake of laws. Like Christ, the priest is forgiving and patient, forgiving another seventy times seven. Like Christ, priests spend a great deal of time in prayer to the Father. Like Christ, they practice self-discipline and asceticism. And finally, like Christ, they find their basic authority in the word of forgiveness that God has given them to speak to the people. This challenging pattern of imitation is the priest's finest gift to people.

But this is indeed a frightening responsibility laid upon the priest. Priests cannot imitate Christ by themselves. They need the support, the comfort, and the encouragement of their people to achieve that goal. The people learn to hold up the priest's hands so that the priest can place those hands in blessing upon the people or in admonition and rebuke when the people fail. Thus the people pastor the pastor so that the pastor can pastor them. This kind of action can go on effectively only in a small group. One thinks of the garden of Gethsemane. Our Lord himself needed the pastoring of Peter, James, and John that he might be faithful to his pastoral calling.

Do you see this pastor-people-pastor relationship going on in your parish? How can people help the pastor to imitate Christ more fully so that that imitation can inspire them to imitate Christ more fully?

John's example has been an inspiration to hundreds and thousands of Christians. His witness to Jesus Christ was consistent, even to his own death. In his work as bishop of Constantinople, he insisted upon calling even the royal family to a higher level of Christian living. The anger of the empress finally resulted in John's banishment. He existed for several years under difficult circumstances, but steadfastly refused to change his position. At last, during the course of a long, difficult winter march, he passed from this world to the other world. But, to paraphrase a Biblical text, "John, being dead, still speaks."

5.
Martin Luther

CAMEO

Martin saw the puzzled look on John Uhrig's face as Philipp Melanchthon spoke with growing vehemence. On the point of the public ministry, he and Philipp were reaching a higher level of disagreement with each passing week, and the present debate was neither pleasant to Martin nor helpful to John as he tried to reach a decision concerning the future shape of ministry for St. Perpetua's parish on the south bank of the Elbe.

Philipp clasped and unclasped his hands as he spoke and that was as close as he ever came to losing his academic composure. "John, I appreciate your disappointment and your dilemma. In a sense, the people of St. Perpetua were betrayed by Father Roscellinus, especially with respect to his conduct with his housekeeper. But that is no reason for rejecting the ancient and honorable institution of the ordained public ministry, established by Jesus Christ forevermore. The stability of the congregation is always dependent on the presence of a properly trained and properly ordained person. This is a lesson clearly taught by Scripture and church history. Somewhere there is a good man waiting to become your new priest. Someday, soon, Archbishop Albrecht will send you that person."

Rather than responding, John indicated by a gesture that he wanted to hear Luther's response. "Philipp, you're talking about a side issue, a minor issue, the public ministry. The basic issue is what is a Christian, and until we get that settled, only confusion will be present in the mind of John and the other members of his parish." Luther paused to take another noisy swallow of his warm Augustinian beer, while Philipp barely moistened his lips from his own tankard. Martin could tell from the look on Philipp's face that the latter was displeased because Luther was drinking from the mug that some students had molded in the likeness of Pope Leo. Martin almost hated himself when he did things deliberately to twist Philipp's tail. But on the other hand, the younger man still failed to understand some of Luther's basic insights and was often far too theoretical and almost pompous in his attempts to explain Luther's understanding of the gospel to others.

"The major issue here, as I said, is 'What is a Christian?' The answer is profoundly simple: A Christian is one who has Christ! How does he have Christ? He has him in the word that promises forgiveness to each repentant sinner! He has him in his baptism and in the celebration of the Lord's Supper! He has him in the words of love and forgiveness that his wife speaks to him! He has him in the sermon you preached last Sunday, Philipp. He has him in the office of the public ministry of which you spoke a few minutes ago. The point is that the Christian has Christ, and with Christ, has received everything. No one can lord it over the Christian. No one can terrify or threaten him—the Christian has Christ! Now, when the ordained priest seeks to do any of these things—to lord it over Christians, to terrify them with the threat of damnation, to threaten them so they'll give more to John Tetzel for the building of St. Peter's, to behave so badly that Christians cannot understand that they have Christ—then the public ministry has become an execrable abomination."

Luther noticed that John was listening intently and subconsciously beginning to nod his head in agreement, while Philipp's hands were clasping and unclasping at an increasing rate.

"From this follows the second fundamental point," Martin went on, "and that is that every Christian is a priest in God's eyes by virtue of baptism. As I wrote in my letter to the Bohemian Christians last year, Philipp, priests are born, not made, while ministers are made, not born. And Father Roscellinus has twisted this around so completely that in his mind, ministers, or as he called them, priests, were more important in God's eyes than priests, that is, the people of God. This is the lesson that the people of St. Perpetua's, yes, the people at the Castle Church right here in Wittenberg, must learn. They are kings, as Christ is king; they are sons of God as he is son; they are priests as he is priest. In him they possess all things that are necessary for this life and for the life that is to come!"

Philipp knew from long experience that an interruption would be of no use when Martin had gotten his mind into top speed. It was like trying to stop a man on one of those new long Norwegian snowshoes that were becoming popular in Thuringia. But John Uhrig had been carried away by Luther's argument and by the intense look in his eyes, and he jumped into the conversation next.

"Yes, yes, Father Martin, that is the point that we people need to learn, that is what draws me to your understanding of the gospel. To teach people that chief lesson of the Christian faith we need to find a new kind of priest, er, uh, minister, and we need to develop a new kind of relationship between minister and people. That is what you are saying, is it not, when you urge me to present myself, poor John Uhrig, untaught, unable to write, unskilled in speaking, to the people of St. Perpetua as a candidate for the office that is vacant now that Father Roscellinus is dead?"

"But don't overlook what is the third and main issue of all," Luther broke in. "Christ has made you a Christian, a priest, a king so that you can offer up royal sacrifices in whatever calling you occupy, sacrifices that will lead others to fall down and worship God along with you." He turned directly to Philipp and continued. "Ah, no, the priesthood has not been abolished. You are quite correct on that point, Philipp. But it is now being restored from a state of hopeless corruption that began when these Romish fakes taught the people that ordination, tonsure, robe, and the dread power to make Christ present in the mass belonged only to them; when they claimed for themselves an indelible character that gave them the right to do anything they wanted to do without ever losing any of their powers. According to my gospel, the priesthood is at the center of parish life, but the priesthood belongs to all believers because Christ gives it to each of them when he baptizes them."

Philipp could not restrain himself any longer. "Martin, Martin, you are creating a devil's harvest. This priesthood of believers idea that you have is surely not what Peter was talking about when he said that Christians were a royal priesthood. He had something quite different in mind, as I have argued in my recent pamphlet on the proper interpretation of Peter's First Letter. Your priesthood idea is really a damnable notion. It smacks of peasant propaganda, of Thomas Münzer, of all that is most to be feared in the German spirit." Philipp paused; his face grew beet red as he remembered that he was in the presence of John Uhrig, peasant, German, and interested in some of the ideas of Münzer.

John grinned at Philipp, enjoying the widely respected academic's discomfiture. "On this matter, Master Philipp, I can only listen to my heart which tells me that Father Martin has understood the mind of the Lord, while you have listened more carefully to Erasmus." The careful distinction in John's use of titles was not lost on Philipp. "But I must start home. It is getting dark, and some of Wittenberg's students enjoy activities after dark other than studying Greek." He grasped Philipp's hand and then turned to Martin to thank him for his hospitality and to assure him that he intended to take the latter's radical ideas back to the people of St. Perpetua. "But you understand," he threw over his shoulder, "that I have no intention of persuading the people to become Protestant or leaving St. Perpetua because it remains a fief of Archbishop Albrecht." John's honesty and steadfastness were two of the characteristics that moved Luther to admire and respect him.

Luther became acquainted with John Uhrig when he purchased a small farm next to John's prosperous farm. Because he knew almost nothing about farming, Luther had become dependent on the advice of Uhrig and the two men became good friends. Uhrig had in general accepted Luther's understanding of the gospel with the comment that that was the gospel in which he had lived as husband and father for many years. However, he had retained his membership in St. Perpetua's parish under the priestly control of Father Roscellinus. During the last eighteen months, the situation in the parish had changed for the worse and John had shared his fears with Luther.

Parish members were being placed under fierce pressure to increase their gifts and their purchases of indulgences so that the work of building St. Peter's might again get under way. Loyal son of the church that he was, John had responded to the best of his ability, but that was no longer sufficient. The priest had not reacted well to the pressure that Archbishop Albrecht of Mainz, the owner of the little parish, was putting on him. To increase the revenues, Roscellinus had begun to act more and more like a little pope, stipulating amounts that were larger than almost any of the members, including the Uhrigs, could afford.

Even worse than that, he had begun to conduct the services in a completely different spirit from the low-level, warm style that John and Gertrude had come to appreciate. Apparently his strategy was to awe the people into greater support for the church by emphasizing his own authority and the people's total dependence on the masses that he celebrated and the absolutions that he pronounced. For the first time in the years that he had been priest, he excommunicated a family because they had failed to meet his giving standards. This had disturbed the Uhrigs, but John had refused to let the family panic and join the Wittenberg church, as the children were urging. "It's easy to run away from the farm when somebody's barn is burning," he said. "Real people don't do that." Luther could only watch his friend's agony increase, but until recently had refused to offer any advice.

The affair came to a head when Father Roscellinus was accused of misbehaving with his housekeeper. He refused to defend himself, appealing instead to the indelible character that had become his in his ordination, and his priestly power and prerogatives. The little congregation was being torn to pieces. Some began to listen to Martin Luther. At the height of the controversy, Father Roscellinus suffered a stroke and died.

After the funeral, the parishioners gathered in the church building to consider their plans. Normally, they would have sent messengers to Archbishop Albrecht and he would eventually have assigned another priest to care for them. However, John suggested that they move slowly and with care, in the realization that they might receive another tyrant who cared only for revenues and pleasure. The more faithful members were ready to consider John's suggestion, provided that they would not be deprived of priestly ministrations during the period of discussion.

That was the last report that Luther had had from John and it had been the subject of the previous evening's discussion. The issue of priestly authority was very much on Luther's mind the next day and he decided to pay John an immediate return visit. He received his usual cordial welcome, especially from Magdalene, the three-year-old who at once preempted the position of honor on Luther's lap. Gertrude looked at the pair and observed that God and Mother Nature had clearly intended Luther to be a father. "What a shame," she added, "that such marvelous natural gifts are wasted on books and theological arguments." Luther was accustomed to her good-natured teasing and responded by handing Magdalene a piece of the hard candy that she knew was always hidden somewhere in his flowing robe.

"You know," he began, chuckling as little Lenchen struck a ticklish spot in his anatomy while foraging for more candy, "one thing has become crystal-clear to me in the last year or two, and that is the importance of forgiveness. I once thought that I could overcome sin and live perfectly in this life. But I have slowly come to the conclusion that is not possible. Why our dear heavenly Father put us together in that way, I do not know. Maybe it was so that we would always have to depend on his grace for everything we need for our bodies and souls. At any rate, forgiveness is the central point; that is what religion is all about.

"Forgiveness belongs to every Christian, to be used freely for himself—or herself—and to be shared freely with others. Forgiveness is like the dust in this house, meaning no offense, Gertrude. But like dust, it is everywhere, under the table, under the bed, between the bedsheets, on the plates, on the candy," he added as Lenchen scored a victory in his right pocket. "That means that no one dare monopolize it, and no one dare say it is available only on this day from this person or only upon the payment of so much money. If that were true, we would all die, for forgiveness would not be there when we need it. Therefore, whatever you do with your parish, you must preserve the common ownership and use of the word of forgiveness.

"However, if you call another priest, he will immediately assert his personal monopoly of forgiveness. You know that, as well as I do. That is the way he is trained to think. He cannot do otherwise.

"Now, the second point to keep in mind," Luther leaned forward as he became more intense, "is that Christ gave the word of forgiveness to you, not to the priests. That is your most precious possession. 'Forgive one another's sins,' he said. 'If he will not hear you, tell it to the church,' not to the pope, not to the bishop, not to the priest. And John, anyone who has Christ's word of forgiveness as a free gift possesses all spiritual rights and powers. You cannot speak the word of forgiveness without public preaching, without baptizing, without celebrating the mass, and so forth and so on.

"This point is so fundamental, so basic, and so often overlooked, that I would again urge you to implement it among your people by calling one of your own people to serve as your priest, perhaps permanently, but at least until your people have come to understand this fundamental truth that while I think the ordained public ministry is of vital importance, I also believe that Philipp exaggerates its importance because he has not yet fully understood what is central in our lives: the word of forgiveness. Sometimes I wish he would commit a dreadful sin so that he would gain a personal appreciation of God's grace. I went through that blessed experience and in that experience I learned all my theology."

Martin noted that John, Gertrude, and Hans, their elder son whom Luther had come to love as his own, were completely caught up in what he was saying. Martin, their younger son, was playing with the cat and Lenchen had fallen asleep, her sticky fingers wrapped around Luther's rosary.

"I've heard you say all this before, in other words," John

responded. "Or at least, I have concluded that this is where your ideas must lead. And I am sympathetic, I think you are right. I believe this is what the Bible teaches. But the people," John shook his head, "they are not ready for such an idea."

Luther interrupted, almost rudely. "But that is not for you to decide in advance, John. The people make that decision. As a Christian, your only calling is to speak God's word as you understand it. You cannot be quiet because those words will upset people, or threaten your life, or cause you to lose money, property, perhaps even your wife and family. God says that clearly in Psalm 46. He will be your refuge. But the word must remain, the sweet word of forgiveness must be your possession so that your loved ones can stay alive." Luther's excitment caused Lenchen to squirm and whimper and so he subsided. "You see," he grinned "how women make theological discussion impossible in one way or another."

Hans, mature and responsible for his age, the delight of his father, spoke up in support of what Martin had said. "It is the right way, father, you must ask the people to call you as their pastor."

At Hans's clear statement of the issue, John became pale. "Hans, you don't know what you're saying. Not me, perhaps some good man in the congregation. You would want me to take the body and blood of Jesus into my own hands without being ordained? I could never do that."

But Hans would not be put off. "But, father, ordination is not the point. The point is that you believe in Jesus and that you want to help others live Christlike lives, as you have helped us. After all, who ordained Peter or Paul? Who ordained Jesus? Who ordained the first bishop of Rome to be bishop? No, no, I think the people have the right and the duty to call you, and I hope they do. You would make a wonderful pastor." Luther felt emotional pain that was almost physical as he saw the look of respect and love pass between father and son. That relationship he could never enjoy.

While John was still stunned by what Martin and Hans had said, Gertrude chimed in. "Hans is right, John. The only priest that I have known for the past twenty years, now that I think about it, is you. The only real mass that I have celebrated is the bread and wine that we share after you bless it. The only real forgiveness that I have accepted is that which has come from you and Hans and Martin and even Lenchen." She reached over and relieved Martin of the squirming child. "You have better credentials even than Albrecht of Hohenzollern, though I have never seen him."

The topic was obviously painful to John. His deep love for his Lord, combined with his strong affection for his family and his fellow townspeople and his respect for priestly authority was placing a heavy burden on him. Luther suggested that they drop the subject. Gertrude invited him to supper that night. Much of the remainder of the evening was taken up by Hans and Martin as they discussed St. James's misunderstanding of Jesus' teaching.

After two weeks of little sleep and much counsel with family and friends, John Uhrig concluded that Luther was correct. After months of patient argument and discussion, most of the members of the parish agreed with him, and he was selected for the office of priest. Martin officiated at his installation. In his sermon, Martin assured the people that they had acted rightly. He pointed out that they had called John to be their priest, and by that action they were pledging themselves to listen to God's word as he spoke it and to follow his example of love and service, and to respect and honor him. At the same time, Luther reminded John that he was pledging himself to preach the word in its truth and purity, to be a godly and Christlike example to them and to love and respect them as God's children. There were no dry eyes in the parish house. A new relationship had come into being, and no one could miss the implications. When John faced the people to speak the benediction, his voice broke and he could not complete it. Nor did the people need to hear the words; they sensed that they had never been so richly blessed.

Luther's schedule and obligations caused him to be absent from Wittenberg quite a bit for the next several months. He saw little of the Uhrigs, but he heard enough from others to be convinced that John was indeed the called and ordained servant of the word in the Elbekirche, and that the people were being richly fed and were developing a new sense of ownership and responsibility for the Christian mission. They were indeed learning to offer up spiritual sacrifices. He was delighted to learn in the summer of 1524 that the church had decided to affiliate publicly with the Protestant movement.

One day when his travels had taken him to Marburg in the territory of Duke Philip of Hesse, Luther was delighted to run into Hans in the duke's courtyard. After they had embraced each other, Martin found out that Hans had been offered a position in Philip's court because of his talent with the violin. Yes, things were going well in the orchestra; yes, he was coming along very well as a soloist; yes, he was pleased with the religious life at the court, with one exception. Luther did not need to ask what that exception was. Almost every Protestant was concerned that Philip had become disenchanted with his shrewish wife and had fallen in love with another, younger woman. As Luther and Hans sat down in the shade of an oak, Martin shared Hans's uneasiness.

Duke Philip had become strongly identified as a leader of the Protestants and now, if his personal dilemma could not be resolved, he might discredit the entire movement.

"Hans, I've been giving the duke's problem a great deal of thought. I have finally reached a decision, which I think is evangelical, although it frightens even me, it is so new. You must keep this absolutely to yourself and not tell anyone." Hans indicated his readiness to keep silence. "This morning I advised the duke to marry his young friend without divorcing his wife!" Luther waited for Hans's shocked reaction, but nothing happened, except for a look of new vision in Hans's eyes.

"You know, Father Martin, that advice is good and it's true to your basic principles. It's shocking, all right, but it's proper. But how many people are ready for it?"

"Now you sound like your father, Hans, and I must say the same thing I said to him. The task of evangelical Christians is to speak the truth of God's word as they understand it. It's not their task to decide whether a given statement will be popular or will advance their own ambitions. I think you understand that, don't you?" Luther noticed a deep shadow in Hans's eyes, and decided he must pursue the subject.

Before he could do so, the shadow had passed and Hans was speaking again. "These past months in my spare time, Father Martin, I've been plowing through the book you wrote in 1520 called *The Freedom of a Christian*. It's difficult, not like some of your sermons that I can easily understand. However, I did learn your two points, namely that the Christian is free from the threat of sin, from the threat of any human ordinance or pressure, completely free in Christ. This also means that Christians need never devote their energy to making up for their past sins. Christians are freed by their Savior in order to make themselves slaves to all people. Do I understand you correctly?"

"I wish I had said it that simply and then shut up," the reformer replied. "You understand me correctly. Duke Philip does indeed have that freedom, although not many people have come to that understanding of what it means to live in Christ." Luther paused for a moment, and then went on. "Hans, something else is bothering you. Are you facing a major decision?"

Hans looked at Luther with the open manly glance that he had inherited from his father. "Yes, there is. And it also relates to Duke Philip. Here in Hesse, Father, I have talked with many peasants and I have been horrified when I understand their conditions and they tell me how they must live. I do not understand how Philip will allow these conditions to continue. I am happy that such a Christian man as Thomas Münzer has their plight at heart and has decided to do something about it in the name of Jesus Christ. But now my problem is this. I cannot just talk and think about the peasants. For Christ's sake, I must do something for them. But if I do, then I am a traitor to my duke. Do I have the freedom to follow Thomas or am I bound to Philip?"

Luther was struck by his young friend's naiveté, but was at a loss to counsel him. Luther personally disliked Münzer for his theology and for the strange way in which the latter was mixing church and state, gospel and life. He also knew that Münzer and his associates had thousands of followers in the so-called Anabaptist movement. If Hans followed Thomas, he would be infected by his theology and would be exposing himself to great danger. However, if Luther counseled against doing that, then Hans would be suspicious that Luther was not being true to his own principles or perhaps was jealous of Münzer. That much Luther understood about the mind of a young man.

But Luther also knew about the condition of the peasants, especially in Thuringia and South Germany, and he knew that Hans's concern was proper. He also believed that it was a proper expression of the gospel to do something about one's suffering neighbor. But how angry John and Gertrude would be if he counseled Hans to side with the peasants! Luther drew a deep sigh, and then said to Hans. "I cannot disagree with your thinking. I believe you should do something for peasants. I would hope that you could find some way of doing it without following Thomas Münzer too closely. He has some strange theological ideas."

Hans smiled and looked relieved. "Will you tell Duke Philip," he began, and then stopped. "No, of course not," he went on. "That is my responsibility. I shall try to talk with him today about the freedom of a Christian." Martin and Hans winked at each other, despite the solemness of the moment and the implications for Hans's future. Philip could hardly claim his own radical freedom and deny it to the young violinist.

The next month was a busy one for Luther. He wrote two pamphlets about the peasants' grievances. The first one was mildly supportive and suggested that the peasants' complaints were legitimate, although he cautioned against violence. Many peasants heard only the first idea: Luther supported them. Others listened to Münzer and his dreams of a Golden Age in Germany in the cause of Christ's kingdom. The result was a sudden increase in the number of peasant attacks, followed by a major resistance effort by the German princes. When Luther learned how his pamphlet was being taken, and when he visited his brother-in-law in Eisleben in mid-April and saw firsthand the brutal atrocities that the peasants had committed, he returned to Wittenberg and penned a harsh pamphlet against what he now called "the murdering, robbing bands among the peasants."

The appearance of the pamphlet almost coincided with several royal victories over the peasants, climaxing in Philip of Hesse's defeat of a large army led by Münzer at Frankenhausen.

Luther was more disturbed than he had ever been, more unsure of himself. His mood was intensified when John Uhrig came to the Black Cloister to report that Hans had been killed by Philip's troops at Frankenhausen. Luther was overwhelmed by sorrow and a sense of guilt. He told his friend the conversation he had had with Hans and the advice he had given him. John crossed over to Martin and embraced the distraught monk, now become one of the most famous men in Germany. John said nothing; his gesture said it all. Martin knew that somehow this great man had found it in his heart truly to forgive him for the suffering he had in part caused. Martin and John wept together over the loss of a son and over the peace that the gospel was providing in a moment of deep crisis.

During the weeks that followed, Luther wrote nothing, said nothing, did nothing. His spirit had been badly bruised. The only person in the cloister family that could get through to him was Katharina von Bora, a nun whose escape from a nunnery Luther had earlier helped to plan. Luther was moved by Katharina's concern because he knew how badly she had been hurt in an earlier romance that he had also helped to arrange. The memory of Hans and of the relationship between Hans and John continued to haunt his every waking moment. Then one evening, as he and Katharina sat by the fire in the hall, alone for the first time in weeks, Martin asked her if she would consider marrying him. "Katharina, before God, I do not yet love you, but I like you. I think we need each other. I believe God will bless our marriage." For several minutes, she hesitated.

Then finally she reached out, took Martin's hand and said, "Nor do I love you—yet. But I respect you, I would be pleased to be your wife."

The wedding took place on June 15, in the presence of five or six friends. Martin and Katharina quickly developed a warm and compassionate relationship. She had a way of looking right through him and sensing what was going on in his heart. She had a way of talking to him, or just looking at him, that helped Luther to unburden himself in a way that he had not been able to do with his male friends. She was often brutally honest in her assessment of her man. She knew that he needed to unburden himself with respect to his role in the Peasants' War, and she needled him gently to do so.

Little by little, he unburdened himself, and Katie, as he preferred to call her, realized, more than any other person in Germany, how the Peasants' Revolt and Hans's death had come close to destroying the man whom so many respected for his "childlike, undaunted faith in God's goodness."

In a nutshell, Luther defended the position he had adopted in the two pamphlets and for which he was being widely criticized by friend and foe. The princes *were* mistreating the peasants; the peasants had legitimate grievances. But, as he had pointed out in the second pamphlet, no matter how serious their grievances, they had no right to take up arms against their superiors. But Katie's questions raised doubts about where this position could finally lead. She was especially concerned about what she called the interior, private nature of this position. "No one," she said to him in one of their rare free evenings, "sees that religion has any relationship to life. It is a private matter, between the person and God. Is that really how you mean to be understood?"

Luther knew that she had reached a vital spot, and he hemmed and hawed as he tried to formulate an answer. "No, no, that's not what I mean. Of course, religion calls us to serve our neighbor. Faith is always a living, active thing. But God never allows us to revolt against authority. Romans 13 is clear here."

Katie was not satisfied. "What about your rebellion against the pope?" she asked. "He was one of God's authorities, was he not?" Again Luther squirmed and Katie did not pursue the point. She was concerned to learn that there were unresolved tension points in her husband's theological system. She was also concerned to note that his positions more and more seemed to favor constituted authorities at the expense of the religio-political help that the masses needed.

She bearded him on that point several months later. "Martin, as you know, the expenses of running the Black Cloister as a hotel for all travelers is more than our income will bear, although we usually manage to survive. But being hostess does allow me to see who comes to visit and I note that John Uhrig has not been here in a long time, and that men of his class and rank are not coming any longer. Is my observation correct?"

Luther admitted that she was right and when she pressed him for a reason, he shrugged his shoulders and said that he did not know. She was not satisfied. "I think you know, and are afraid to admit it! You have begun to become a pawn of the princes! You have begun to put peace and tranquility above preaching what you think the word of God says. You have allowed your interpretation of Romans 13 to color your understanding of many other verses." Katie paused as she saw the naked hurt in Martin's eyes, but then plunged on. "And I think you're doing this somehow to make atonement with God for Hans's death. Am I right?"

Martin was silent for a long time and Katie said nothing more. She reached over and took his cold hand in hers. He squeezed her hand, then slowly began to talk. "No, Katie, I do not think you are right about my selling out, although I have asked myself the same question. I have certain deep problems that I have difficulty handling. A major one centers in Philipp Melanchthon. Katie, he is constantly pushing me toward theological positions that I do not like, and I no longer can find the time to argue with him. He is very much oriented to the princes and to the conservative tradition on almost every issue. I am frightened at the thought of his influence, though I continue to love him as a person.

"You are right about Hans. Katie, I loved him as a son; he was my life and my future, just as he was for John and Gertrude. I cannot ever again be an agent for violence. Therefore in this world we must be content with our lot. Our dear heavenly Father will more than make up for our suffering in the world he has already prepared."

Again Martin paused for a long time. "Yes, Katie, I think you have hit a very sore spot in my heart. I think that I could not believe that God could forgive me for what I did to Hans. And now you, my dear one, have rubbed salt in that wound. It hurts like hell. Will you also now please pour in the sweet oil of the gospel lest I perish?" Martin was crying uncontrollably.

"Oh, Martin, my Martin. I forgive you that sin and all your sins in the name of the Father and of the Son and of the Holy Ghost. And more than that, I offer you another Hans. Martin, we're going to have a baby!"

Martin's sobbings stopped. He held Katie at arms' length. "You bitch!" he exclaimed and then enfolded her in a hug that threatened to crush her spine.

COMMENTARY

The Cameo emphasizes three aspects of Martin Luther's understanding of the gospel that directly affected his approach to pastoral care. These three emphases are the central importance of the word of forgiveness, the resultant importance of the priesthood of believers, and his understanding of the connection between the church and the world, as this understanding was crystallized in his attitude toward the Peasants' War. The Cameo also seeks to present Martin Luther as a normal human being, sharing the emotions, desires, and fears that characterize most people.

The Cameo takes some liberties with fact to establish these emphases. The Uhrigs are fictitious people, although Luther dealt with hundreds of people who spoke and thought as the Uhrigs did. The tension between Luther and Melanchthon is heightened for dramatic effect, although it was a real tension in their lives. Most of Luther's words are taken from actual writings or speeches, although some have beeen reshaped to fit the dramatic needs of the Cameo. In other words, the portrait of Luther is true to life and reliable, even if some parts of the Cameo are not historical.

Luther's characteristic central emphasis was on the person and the work of Jesus Christ, in whom all people have forgiveness and through whom they may approach God the Creator. Though Jesus Christ was the dynamic center of his thinking and living, this Christ-concern often took the form of Luther's emphasis on the word. He was indeed a theologian of the word and in this respect has had few, if any, equals in the history of the church. However, unlike many of his heirs, Luther did not equate "word" with "Scripture." Rather, he understood word in the sense of God's vital power and presence in Jesus Christ. For Luther, "word" was every power or force that came forth from God's Spirit. This included the word that rebuked the hardened sinner, as well as the word that brought sweet comfort to the repentant and terrified sinner. It also covered all of God's actions that had the betterment of human life as their purpose.

But chiefly Luther related word to Christ. He was God's last and great word. He represented God to humans in a unique way and thus was also God's special word to us about what he, God, was like and about what he wanted for people. Jesus Christ was God's creating word, through whom all things were made. Jesus Christ was the word that revealed God's inmost heart, and showed it to be a heart filled with justice and mercy, a heart in which God's last word was always a gracious word, except when people sometimes forced him to speak a final word of judgment against them.

With these fundamental ideas in mind, we can now connect Luther's understanding of word with the Holy Scriptures. Luther was not only a theologian of the word in the sense described in the previous paragraphs, he was also most decidedly and most enthusiastically a man of the book. He loved the Bible and devoted his entire life to its study. In the Bible he found God revealing himself in Jesus Christ. He believed that the Biblical words carry God's power to save because they all point to Jesus Christ. The only task of the interpreter is to point out what the passages proclaim about God's work in Jesus. No passage was properly or fully interpreted until it somehow made Christ more real or more necessary to people. Any interpretation that ended only in debate about the age of the earth or the historicity of miracles or the authorship of any Biblical book had no meaning or value for Luther. The gospel, God's good word of grace and forgiveness, was the only key that could unlock the Spirit-given treasures of Holy Scripture. In a single-minded way in his later life, Luther insisted that every question addressed to the Bible must finally be reduced to the question of the meaning and purpose of the gospel.

Luther devoted all his intellect and energies to helping people discover in the Bible that God was gracious and forgiving. This message was good news for a generation that had been taught that God either did not really care about them or else was a stern God who demanded perfection of people. Luther's words were life-giving water for the parched soil of thousands of German souls. His understanding of the gospel was reflected also by reformers in other lands, but it is generally acknowledged that though he had reforming contemporaries, Luther's insight into the nature of God's word made each reformation possible.

How do you understand the phrase "the word of God"? In what sense is Jesus Christ the word of God? How is God's forgiving word, Jesus Christ, the center of your private life? Your parish life?

Against the Roman Catholic Christians, Luther argued that the word had been obscured by their magical, mystical understanding of the mass and their views concerning the power and the authority of both the pope and ordained priests. His theology of the word, centering in Jesus Christ, led him to new views concerning the ministry and the rights of all believers.

For example, he taught that all Christians were priests by virtue of their baptism. In baptism, they received the highest kind of ordination and the most sweeping Christian rights and powers. No person could lord it over them or threaten them. They possessed Christ, and in him they possessed all things. He scolded Roman priests who believed that their ordination had given them an indelible character, that is, a nature that was different from what they had had before they were ordained and powers and authority that were superhuman. These priestly powers showed themselves most clearly in Roman teachings concerning priesthood and mass. Only priests could take the body and the blood of Jesus into their own hands. Only an ordained priest could celebrate the mass. The other Christians were second-class citizens, with no rights or powers in the congregation. It was not remarkable, given this understanding of priesthood and ordination, that few lay people felt any direct sense of responsibility for the welfare of the church or its mission.

Luther taught that this view of the priesthood took away from people God's greatest gift to them, his personal word of forgiveness. This word was theirs, to be appealed to at any hour of the day or night, and to be orally and freely shared among other Christians. Those who in any way belittled this privilege and right were depriving Christians of their birthright. They were taking away from them God's word; they were denying their baptismal ordination.

By doing these things, Roman priests were also immobilizing the Christian laity. Because they had no rights, they felt no sense of responsibility, even for one another's spiritual and temporal welfare. The Cameo presents the Uhrig family as exceptional. They did care richly for each other; they did share the word of forgiveness with each other; and they did, in a sense, celebrate the holy communion around their supper table.

Luther believed that this kind of relationship, in and under Jesus Christ the word, was not only most natural for Christians, but also the only way in which the gospel could perform its creating and renewing tasks in the lives of people. Impersonal preaching did little good. Magical celebrations of the mass did no good. At one point in his life, Luther went so far as to suggest that sincere Christians should meet together in homes, for preaching, holy communion, prayer, and sacrificial giving for the needy. His theology of the word led him to be a forerunner of the present-day small group movements within the church. But he never aggressively or systematically pressed this idea upon others.

What we have said about Luther gives us an opportunity to raise once again the question of ordination and ministerial authority. Do you agree with Luther's position? How do you define ordination? Would you agree that the achievement of a mutually acceptable definition of ministerial authority is a crucial task for pastor and people to undertake?

Given Luther's emphasis on Jesus Christ, his dynamic understanding of the central role of God's word, and his high views of the rights and privileges that Christians possess because of their baptism, one would expect Lutheran congregations to have been beehives of Christian love and service. But as a general rule that was not the case, although there have been many Lutheran congregations and individuals who have put into practice Luther's thought that they are bona fide priests, called to offer sacrifices of love and kindness to all they meet.

Many explanations of this curious failure have been offered, and I have no new ones to suggest. However, the Cameo focused on one thing that may help us understand Lutheranism's general failure to take seriously its social responsibilities in the name of Jesus Christ. The Cameo suggests, and there is enough evidence to support this suggestion, that the Peasants' War produced a change in Luther's theology in two respects.

The first change showed itself in his strengthened insistence that rebellion against any constituted authority is always wrong. Luther believed that Paul's words in chapter thirteen of Romans supported him in this conclusion. Whether he was right or wrong, the historical fact is that most Lutherans have accepted his exegesis and have conducted themselves accordingly. They have often permitted constituted authorities to perpetrate gross injustice and oppression while they have remained silent. I do not agree with William L. Shirer who argues that Martin Luther created the climate in which Hitler could flourish, but it does appear to be true that many Lutheran pastors and people remained silent in the face of Nazi brutality and pogroms. In fairness, though, it must also be pointed out that other Lutherans like Martin Niemöller and Dietrich Bonhoeffer behaved in heroic fashion.

In the Cameo, Katie suggests another consequence of the Peasants' War. She questioned Luther sharply about what she called the individualization and interiorization of his thought. In other words, as she saw it, Luther was coming to regard religion as a personal and private relationship between the individual and God. This meant, in her judgment, that Christians could ignore public needs as long as their individual hearts were right with God. It also meant that the pious congregational members could ignore other members of the same congregation.

There may be some truth in these suggestions. The purpose of them is not to place Luther and his thought in a negative light, but rather to challenge each reader to examine his or her own thinking on the twin fundamental issues of the private nature of faith and the question of the Christian's responsibility for social justice for those who suffer any form of oppression. The assumption of this Commentary is that there is a direct causal relation between people's theology and their views of what their individual Christian obligations and responsibilities are.

Do you think that the quietism that Katie began to suspect in Luther's theology is peculiarly Lutheran? What seems to produce it in the lives of people of your acquaintance? What do you think your proper Christian responsibilities are toward all your neighbors in this world?

Following the Peasants' War, two things happened (over which Luther had really no control) that changed the shape and style of the German Reformation. The first was the serious shortage of trained clergy throughout those areas of Germany into which Lutheranism was coming. Luther devoted great amounts of his time and energy to dealing with this problem. So bad was the situation that for a time about all he could insist on from the new emergency preachers was that they have a vague idea of the difference between Lutheranism and Roman Catholicism. Frequently these preachers had almost no idea of Luther's teachings. In many cases, they enjoyed the respect that they claimed as members of the clergy while their conduct denied their holy calling. They were, in effect, again insisting that by virtue of their ordination they had an "indelible character" which entitled them to do what they wanted and which they could not lose. To Luther's credit, he did encourage people to dismiss unworthy clergy. As he pointed out in one of his writings, "What we give them today [ordination], we take away from them tomorrow [if they prove to be unworthy]."

To deal with this problem, Luther began to publish copies of his sermons, hoping that this would help to raise the quality of Lutheran preaching. It must have done some good, although one can also imagine Lutheran pastors becoming lazy as far as their own preparation and theological growth were concerned. The second thing that Luther did was to arrange for learned theologians and lay people to visit all the new Protestant congregations to examine their spiritual and temporal welfare. To help the visitors, Luther and his associates produced a series of questions to guide them. Once again, both the visitors and the visited clergy took the easy way out, and pleaded with Luther for more and more detailed regulations and directions. Luther refused this pressure. His pastoral motto was "Be free, but discreet." He resisted any new forms of clerical control and supervision, but was not always successful in these efforts. The clergy preferred to yield their freedom in Christ for the security of specific directions.

In view of the increasing unrest and disturbance in the Protestant lands, Luther also had to turn his attention to this problem. He began to learn how archbishops and bishops had done yeoman work in preserving some degree of peace and stability in their regions. Since he did not favor powerful bishops again, Luther turned instead to the princes and asked them to form committees to supervise church life and to stabilize general life in their principalities. These committees were called consistories, and their history represents the second unfortunate development over which Luther had little control.

Under the leadership of the princes, the gospel tended to become a gospel of the rich and a gospel that favored and supported the status quo, regardless of how corrupt and oppressive it might be. The Cameo suggests that Duke Philip of Hesse is an example of this kind of political abuse of the gospel.

After the peasants had been betrayed by Luther, as they judged his conduct, they turned away from his reformation. They either returned to Roman Catholicism or affiliated with the various Anabaptist leaders in Germany. Because of this, already by the time of Luther's death in 1546, the German Reformation had lost a significant portion of its earlier vitality. It became more conservative and more traditional. By the end of the sixteenth century, Lutheran churches frequently witnessed a resurgence of clerical authority, a reemergence of canon or church law, and a muddying of Luther's clear gospel. However, Luther's dynamic understanding of the word of forgiveness had given the Christian church an insight and an orientation that would continue to be a reforming power in the following centuries.

6.
John Calvin

CAMEO

Gerard Perrin threw open his bedroom windows and looked out over the red tile roofs of Geneva that flowed from the hill down to the Rhone. It was his city, it had been good to him in many ways, and he loved it. The name Perrin was a good name in the city, for it was connected with respect and prosperity. Ami had been a good father in the sense that he had never been quite sure how to bring up Gerard, anymore than he had ever been quite sure how to handle his wife. Each had done what he or she had pleased. Franchequine was a typical member of the Favre family, rich, spoiled, beautiful, and sensual; in a sense, a typical Genevan aristocrat. She had always demanded of her father and then of her husband that she receive today gifts and pleasures that should have been denied her for weeks, months, and even years. Gerard had inherited many of the traits that made Franchequine exciting, attractive, and the cause of endless problems to those who loved her.

Gerard smiled at the thought of his mother, whom he understood much better than his father ever would. The smile broadened as he thought of the escapades of the previous evening. His gang had spent several hours in taverns, flirting with waitresses, making love in their dirty attic rooms. Gerard could not even remember the name of the girl who had pleased him for the moment. Nor did the name matter. She was a servant; he was a Perrin. Then had come the brawl with the nightwatch, a regular

event that never ceased to delight the gang, for they always han-
dled the watch with no problems. If complaints were filed, the
magistrates were sure to dismiss them. And a brawl was always
fun. Of course, the watchmen had developed venomous hatred
for the gang and particularly for Gerard, its leader, but there was
little they could do to limit them or to punish them.

By the time Gerard reached the porch to be served breakfast,
his father had left the house. In this way, Ami avoided a confrontation with his son which would also lead to one with his wife. He
would spend the day seeking ways and means of advancing the
welfare of the city that he also loved, while his son would spend
the day deciding what pleasure he would take from the city.

In the Little Council of Geneva, Ami received the respect that
was denied him by the members of his family. For the past years,
he had taken the lead in introducing the new Protestant beliefs
and practices into Geneva and supported the fiery preaching of
William Farel. He had been the chief author of the 1536 ordinance by which the citizens had rejected the rule of the Roman
Catholic Church and had instead pledged themselves to be
guided and governed by the law and the Word of God. He had
also supported the earlier Council action against blasphemy,
oaths, card-playing and certain forms of conduct in the taverns.
The ordinance requiring compulsory church attendance had
been drafted by him and then also adopted by the Council. As
Gerard learned of his father's achievements in the Council, he
cynically concluded that his father was going to use the might and
force of all Geneva to tame the wife and son that he could not
handle by himself.

Two actions of the Council in early August were bound to
have shattering effects on the life of father and son. The first
action was the long-delayed, often-frustrated declaration of independence from the powerful city of Bern, which had sometimes
used its leadership of the Swiss Protestant movement as a pretext
for gaining control over Geneva. The second action was the
Council's decision to accept the recommendation of William
Farel and invite the French humanist scholar and preacher John
Calvin to become preacher in Geneva. Ami felt certain along with

many others in Geneva that Calvin had the ability to stabilize Protestantism in Geneva and to further the development of true Christian life, in keeping with previous Council laws. Gerard paid no attention to any of these developments; his time and energy were devoted to more satisfying pursuits.

Farel and Calvin immediately went to work on a new set of ordinances for Geneva, in keeping with the instructions of the Council. By January 16, 1537 the first draft was completed. Gerard learned of their contents as his father discussed them enthusiastically with his mother, who listened with a slight cynical smile playing at the corners of her mouth. The first proposal was that all Protestant citizens of Geneva be expected to attend the Lord's Supper once a month, even though, according to Ami, the Frenchman preferred weekly communion. The Council, led by the elder Perrin, had refused that recommendation. They themselves were not ready and they knew the people of Geneva well enough to know that an ordinance requiring weekly communion would excite them unduly. "Nevertheless," Ami pointed out to his wife and son, "this shows how truly religious M. Calvin is and how successful, therefore, the reform of Geneva will be." Gerard was thinking of a different kind of communion he had enjoyed the night before in the tavern.

"More than that," Ami went on, "M. Calvin insists that only true believers can worthily receive the sacrament, and he, therefore, proposes a system of church discipline very much like the one that has worked so well at Bern." Gerard and Franchequine looked at each other and winked. "In his system, there will be elders appointed by the Council for each section of the city who will have the duty of overseeing the life and conduct of each citizen. If they see any fault, they are to call the ministers to admonish the offender and to urge the offender in a loving spirit to reform. Any offender who refuses to reform will be reported to the church; any offender who will not hear the church is to be regarded by us as a heathen and a publican. If the person continues in these stubborn ways, the civil magistrates must be called in. I am really excited about what this system can do for our city." Franchequine and Gerard knew that in his subconscious mind

Ami was hoping for effective discipline of the two people he loved too much.

The second statute adopted by the Council caused no embarrassment whatever to the Perrins, mother and son. This proposal ordered each citizen to give a public confession and account of his or her faith so that, in the words of the ordinance, "it may be understood who of them agree with the gospel, and who love better to be of the kingdom of the pope than of the kingdom of Jesus Christ." The members of the Council were encouraged to set examples to the people and then each person was ordered to confess his or her faith before a committee consisting of at least one minister and one member of the Little Council. No people in Geneva gave a more resounding Protestant confession than Franchequine and Gerard. Ami's eyes filled with tears as he witnessed this act on their part. He embraced each one warmly, and looked forward to a new life and a new spirit in his house.

The third major proposal put forth by Farel and Calvin called for an intensive program of education for the children of Geneva. Parents were to be primarily responsible for the course of instruction, and the children were to be examined at fixed times of the year by the ministers. Ami had hoped to involve his talented son in the preparation of the course of study, but the Council assigned that task to John Calvin. But at least Ami made arrangements for the austere Frenchman and his son to become acquainted. Gerard was impressed by the humanistic learning and wit of Calvin, and pretended to be equally interested in the latter's religious concerns. They made a point of getting together once a week, for Calvin, against his will, enjoyed discussing the Latin classics and speaking good Latin with Gerard. The fact that they shared July 10 as their birthday and that Gerard bore Calvin's father's name served to strengthen the bond between them.

Much more than his father, Gerard from the beginning sensed an inevitable and dreadful clash of wills between his kind of people and those who accepted the principles of the new man. When the clash came, Gerard believed that either he and his mother or his father would be destroyed.

In one of their weekly meetings, Gerard brought up the topic of Calvin's proposed disciplinary system. "How," he asked, "does your system of control really differ from that of Rome, which you claim to despise?" Calvin was intrigued; this was the first time that Gerard had initiated a theological discussion or showed any real interest in Calvin's program. Calvin fixed Gerard with his deep-set eyes and would not let him escape his stare. "A good question, Gerard," he began, "the kind I expect from you." Despite himself, Gerard felt warmed toward the man. "Let me at least list the differences that I see between my system of moral control and that set forth in theory by the church of Rome.

"In the first place, my system is based on the conviction that God's will is the greatest thing humans can experience, while Romans, I believe, would argue that the church and its clergy are the greatest things in our existence. It is, in the second place, God's will that all people should live to his glory. He has described this style of living for us in his law and we are to be excited by his law, not by the fear of punishment or the expectation of rewards in heaven, as the papalists teach. But more than that, we learn to know God, first and foremost, in the love that he showed for us in the gift of his Son, by whose life, death, and resurrection we receive forgiveness of sins, life, and salvation. So the motive for proper living in my system is the experience of God's love, and nothing else. Finally, my system calls for the creative supervision of daily life by the laity, people like yourself, rather than by a dead, spiritless code of church laws drawn up eight hundred or more years ago, or by dissolute, shameless clergy. It is really a quite different system, Gerard, and therefore I believe it will work."

Gerard allowed that Calvin's thinking was new and different and asked for time to reflect on it. Calvin gave Gerard a copy of his new catechism and lent him a copy of the *Institutes of the Christian Religion,* in which the Frenchman had set forth the teachings of Reformed Protestantism in an attempt to persuade Francis, the king of France, to allow Protestantism to exist without persecution in his realms. Gerard found the *Institutes* fascinating, more because of the author's mind and ability than because of its theological content, but he continued to read it. When Ami saw a copy of the *Institutes* lying on his son's bed one morning, he fell to his knees and gave thanks to God for his gift to Geneva of John Calvin.

However, within less than twelve months, the Council had turned against Calvin and Farel, and dismissed them from Geneva, though Ami voted against the action. Even Gerard was angered by the dismissal. He had begun to argue with his free-wheeling friends that Geneva should be broad-minded enough to tolerate a person of Calvin's views, but that citizens should be free to reject them, even as he personally did. The ruckus developed as Bern once again tried to assert its control over Geneva, despite the declaration of independence of 1536. This time, the Bernese camel's nose was inserted into the Genevan tent by an attempt to enforce Bernese religious ceremonies upon the Genevans. Calvin refused to adopt the Bernese ceremonies, the situation became more upset, largely for political reasons, until the Little Council finally bowed to Bernese pressure and pressure from many of its own citizens, and adopted the resolution asking the reformers to leave.

Calvin's behavior in this affair was a new experience to Gerard and it shook him deeply. It was the first time he had known a person who put principle above personal advantage. As a matter of fact, that concept had rarely been heard of by any of the people of Geneva. Gerard knew that Calvin had a good life in Geneva, adequate income and housing, growing respect and honor, even time for the study and writing that Calvin loved so dearly. He had made for himself the good life. Gerard could not understand how celebrating the Lord's Supper according to the rites of Bern could jeopardize Calvin's work at Geneva. The Frenchman talked to Gerard at length about the importance of the church's independence from any kind of earthly pressure in order to be free to be God's creation and agent at its particular place and time in history. Gerard was too Machiavellian in his thinking even to understand Calvin. But he could not dismiss the man from his mind. Gerard even allowed a moment of fleeting respect for his father's courageous stand to enter his mind.

Calvin made a special point of calling on the Perrins before he left. He expressed his appreciation to Ami for his support and revealed no bitterness over the Council's action. He assured Gerard of the pleasure he had always derived from his company and expressed the sincere wish that they would meet again in order to continue them. "Next time," the Frenchman said, "I will move more directly to questions concerning your eternal welfare. I was delinquent in that respect." Gerard was moved by his evident love and sincerity. He felt a tear trying to break through the hard mask of cynicism that he thought he had perfected. As he left, Calvin observed that he had learned an important pastoral lesson from his stay in Geneva. "I tried too much, too soon, too harshly," he commented.

Calvin's departure seemed to bring out the worst in Gerard. Perhaps the young man compared Calvin's own high-principled conduct with his own meaningless life and hated himself the more. Perhaps it was anger at the shortsighted action of the Council. Perhaps it was the fear that he would find that his father was a good and strong man. At any rate, he sought out his own companions and pursued his old rounds of pleasure with a new vehemence. Scarcely a night passed that did not see a brawl between the gang and the nightwatch. Reports kept coming back to Ami, and because he was too weak where his son was concerned to deal with him effectively, he became angrier until one morning he roused him from bed and threw him out of the house, cut him off without a penny. Franchequine threw a tantrum, but Ami refused to budge.

For several months, his mother managed to smuggle money to Gerard but Ami put an end even to that. But so naive was Ami that he was genuinely surprised when a few months later Gerard broke into his house and tried to make off with the money that Ami had always kept in a closet. In a fit of rage, Ami called for the guard and then tried to grapple with his son. Gerard cursed and threw him to the floor, grabbed the money and headed for the door. The watch met him there, headed by one man whom he had frequently humiliated. The captain drew his sword and slashed at Gerard, cutting a huge red slash in his leg between the knee and the thigh. So powerful was the thrust that the vessels, nerves and even bones were cut. The doctor was unable to save the leg, and Gerard had to submit to the agonizing procedure of amputation, held down by three strong attendants with a bullet in his mouth.

Ami did not visit his son or offer him any help. When Gerard recovered enough to return to the streets, he discovered that his old friends did not want to be handicapped by his company, and that few girls cared for it, either. Bitterness turned Gerard against his father and against Genevans in general.

Calvin's departure did not soothe the situation in Geneva. The pot continued to boil. Through a letter from Cardinal Jacopo Sadoleto, the Roman Church made a massive effort to persuade the troubled Genevans to return to the fold. The Bernese continued to press for additional advantages and control. In desperation the Little Council finally yielded to Ami's continued urging and voted to authorize him to invite Calvin to return to Geneva from Strasbourg, where he had spent more than two delightful and productive years. Once again against his will, Calvin finally yielded to Ami's urgings and agreed to return to Geneva with his wife of one month. On September 13, 1541 he reentered the city and this time the Council in effect gave him a blank check to introduce whatever measures were needed to solve Geneva's internal and external problems.

Gerard was stunned, surprised, and delighted when John Calvin sought him out and asked him to help draft the new set of ordinances. To make matters more convenient, Calvin invited Gerard to move in with him, his wife, her daughter, Judith, and his hunchbacked servant, Pierre Daguet. Calvin could offer him only bed and board with occasionally a small amount of money. But Gerard, with no other options open to him, learned a measure of contentment. Gerard threw himself into the drafting work, reasoning that it was not a religious task, but only political in purpose. He had not yet learned that John Calvin could not entertain any thought that was not religious in character and that did not somehow encourage people to know God more completely and to live more fully to His glory. Calvin had high hopes for the young man whom God had brought very low.

The new *Ordonnances* were chiefly the work of Calvin and were quickly done, for they drew heavily on the earlier set. Having been burned by previous governmental interference, Calvin made clear in the new *Ordonnances* that the church in Geneva would be self-governed and independent of the government. The magistrates *as* magistrates were not permitted to interfere in church life with respect to theology, liturgy, or discipline. They became involved as magistrates only when the level of excommunication was reached. And then it was only a matter of determining the form of punishment. More than fifteen hundred years of church-state relationships were thus brought to an end in Geneva. Gerard knew enough church history to catch the great significance of this provision.

A second major provision of the *Ordonnances* was the establishment of four offices, and only four offices, in the church. The first office was that of pastor, and according to Calvin it made no difference whether it was called pastor, bishop, or anything else. The pastor was to preach, admonish, reprove in public and private, administer the sacraments, and make "fraternal corrections." The pastor was to be elected by fellow ministers, then approved by the magistrates with the consent of the people.

As part of the pastoral program, the *Ordonnances* called for communion to be celebrated four times a year, although Calvin continued to express his opinion to Gerard that weekly communion was the better practice by far. The document also called for weekly Bible study for ministers and any others who could attend, and for a session of mutual, helpful criticism every three months. Calvin explained to Gerard that his goal was to create a corps of educated, disciplined, mutually supportive clergy as the core of his entire program. To himself, Gerard compared Calvin's ideal with the present reality of the poorly equipped, poorly qualified ministry in Geneva and the surrounding countryside. But even those relatively weak men were known as the *Vénérable Compaigne* and came to occupy a major position of leadership in Genevan affairs.

The next office was that of the teacher, whose task was to train especially the young in all needed knowledge, with special emphasis on skills that would aid in Bible study and in applying Biblical knowledge to daily life. John surprised Gerard one day by expressing the hope that he, Gerard, would think seriously about seeking this office. Gerard reminded his master that he was not yet a Christian. Calvin's brief response continued to bother Gerard. "Not yet," was the reply, "at least not in public." As Gerard meditated on that answer, he began to realize that Calvin knew his heart better than Gerard himself did.

The third office was that of elder, just as in the earlier set of provisions for organizing religious life in Geneva. Elders were called to "watch over the life of each individual to admonish affectionately those who are seen to err and to lead a disorderly life, and, where there shall be need, to make fraternal corrections." Twelve elders were to be elected to supervise all the citizens of Geneva, for none were counted to be outside the pale of Christian responsibility. These twelve elders plus a number of pastors made up the *Consistoire,* which met once a week under the presidency of one of the secular magistrates to discuss the various cases that were brought before them. The *Consistoire* was responsible for church discipline up to the point of excommunication and was charged to report to the Little Council which was obligated to render judgment according to the merits of the case.

The emphasis upon discipline bothered Gerard, but he had trouble summoning up enough courage to challenge the master on this point. When Gerard finally did so, Calvin smiled and invited him to sit with him and enjoy a glass of wine while discussing the issue. "Grace and discipline, faith and disciplined living, go hand in hand," Calvin began. "It is the very nature of God's will to find expression in his law, and law cannot exist apart from discipline. Without discipline, the church would quickly become a rope of sand, a laughingstock. Furthermore, all of us are so weak, so beset with sin, that we need the help of a strong discipline to find the real joy of living the sacrificial lives that God calls us to live." Calvin paused a moment, and then looked deep into Gerard's eyes, almost hypnotizing him, and went on. "You, Gerard, are a perfect illustration of the importance of discipline. For his own reasons, your father chose not to discipline you, and the result thus far has been an outrageous waste of gifts and talents, leading to a true hatred of yourself. When you compare what you might have been with what you now are, you cannot be proud of what you have done. Discipline, fraternal correction, admonition from concerned elders or brothers would have made all the difference in the world." Without meaning to, Calvin allowed his gaze to drop to Gerard's stump of a leg. He blushed in embarrassment for his action, and Gerard fell to the floor before John Calvin, and in between great gasping sobs, confessed that Calvin was indeed right. He spoke of his own sinful past, of the dread evil master he had cheerfully served and who had brought him to ruin, and of the great fear he now had of God.

Calvin let him talk and then placed his hands on Gerard's head and began to speak to him of God's love in Christ, of the victory that Christ had won for him, Gerard, over sin, death, and the devil, of the fact that God had chosen him from all eternity to share eternal blessedness with the saints in light. As Gerard listened, he experienced a miracle within himself. He felt a hand lift a huge burden from his heart, he felt new life, joy, and peace, such as he had never known. A bright light filled his mind and he saw God enthroned in glory with the four and twenty elders falling down before him. With tears in his eyes, he cried out, "My God, my God, you have not forsaken me. Such a glory! Such a wonder!" Calvin raised him up and embraced him. Because Gerard had been baptized by his parents, it was not necessary to rebaptize him. His first visit to the Lord's Table caused new thrilling sensations of peace and love in Gerard, and surprised almost everyone else in Geneva.

More and more, Gerard found himself to be an extension of the man Calvin, and he enjoyed this relationship. He was delighted to be useful to Calvin and through him to the church and to God. He never failed to be at Calvin's bedside at 5:00 A.M. to begin the day's dictation. He was doubly useful as an amanuensis because of his own learning and acquaintance with books. He gradually replaced Pierre Daguet as Calvin's valet and premier secretary.

He was always astounded and uplifted by Calvin's singleness

of purpose, by his iron will, and by the fact that he never swerved from his announced purpose and refused to employ less than honest means to achieve a goal. He had always admired Calvin's intellect; now he also came to understand his love and compassion for other people. He became a Calvinist through and through. He had but one purpose in life and that was to know God, to experience God's glory and to serve him. In God's law, he found a constant stimulus to greater exertion and more God-pleasing works. Religion became for him, as one Calvin scholar observed, not so much a life-giving principle, but a system of law and government in which he found himself to be the subject of an absolute sovereign whose will is expressed in ordinances.

The work of the *Consistoire* went well and the supervision of the elders contributed to a new moral tone throughout the city. Geneva was becoming the most perfect school of discipleship on earth, as John Knox would describe it after his visit. But there were other problems that plagued Calvin's leadership and Gerard suffered through most of them with him. He was bothered by incapable ministers through the years of 1543 and 1544, by which time the caliber of men improved noticeably. The plague struck Geneva and the ministers refused to pay hospital visits, despite Calvin's order to that effect. He contented himself finally by observing that "God had not yet given them grace to have force and constancy to go to the hospital." The tension between the old Genevan families and the rising influx of French expatriates was almost a daily threat to peace and stability. The old rivalry with Bern would not die.

Perhaps the most threatening problem for Calvin was that posed by Sébastien Castellio, who applied for a ministerial post in Geneva in 1543. Castellio refused to recognize the inspiration of the Song of Solomon, and thus, in Calvin's judgment, threatened to undermine and destroy the entire Genevan enterprise. Calvin argued that the church at Geneva was built on the unquestioned authority of every word of Scripture. If any word could be questioned, the whole book could be questioned and thus destroyed, and this would destroy the Christian faith. Furthermore, Castellio was in effect also challenging Calvin's credentials as a teacher of the church, for Calvin taught that every book and every word was inspired. Gerard could see that Calvin considered the struggle with Castellio to be a life-and-death matter, although he could not agree with either of Calvin's premises. Finally, Calvin persuaded the Little Council to banish Castellio from Geneva, and thus also, in effect, to affirm the inspiration of the entire Scripture and Calvin's position as teacher of the Word.

The greatest challenge to Calvin was presented in 1551 by a wandering former Roman Catholic priest by the name of Jérome Bolsec. He had the temerity to reject Calvin's doctrine of predestination, the view that God had by his own will chosen some for salvation and others for damnation. Again, Calvin mustered the might of the Little Council to refute Bolsec and to have him driven from Geneva. Then at Calvin's request, the Council affirmed that he was an "unassailable interpreter of the will of God." Gerard regretted the last action, for he knew that in the long run it would weaken Calvin's position. The Council's action based Calvin's authority in Geneva on their own political power rather than on his repeatedly demonstrated mastery of Scripture and devotion to God's will. Gerard wondered how often the Council would be forced to repeat that affirmation in the years ahead.

Despite the problems and troubles that Calvin frequently discussed with him and that he saw taking a terrible toll on his sickly friend, life was good for Gerard. Until one night when he fell into the sin from which he thought he had been forever rescued. With a few pennies in his pocket, he had wandered into town and out of curiosity had stopped before a tavern. His old gang happened by at that moment and dragged him in. A few beers later, one of the waitresses began to flirt with Gerard. He was flattered because he had not thought of himself as a man since the amputation. He felt the old passion arise within himself and before he knew what was happening, was making love to the serving girl.

His feelings of remorse the next morning caused him to avoid Calvin and to pretend sickness. After a few days, the master could not be fooled any longer. A few probing questions, and he discovered Gerard's sin. Kindly, but strictly, Calvin led him to see the seriousness of what he had done, but then also led him to Jesus Christ for forgiveness and to the Holy Spirit for new supplies of grace and determination. Gerard felt almost as good as he had on the day of his conversion, and he vowed to Calvin that it would not happen again. Again, Calvin drew comfort for Gerard from his doctrine of predestination. He pointed to the powerful passions that could rage within Gerard as proof of the immense power that sin still wielded in his life. From that observation, Calvin pointed to the good news of the divine purpose to rescue him from his sins by an all-powerful transforming might. "Nothing," he concluded, "but the will of God can give anyone rational ground for hope of salvation." Gerard found himself comforted, although somehow disturbed by Calvin's teaching about God's will to save him.

Gerard wondered whether Calvin's law could produce any final relief from temptation. He received an answer that satisfied him a few weeks later when Pierre Daguet, with a glass of wine too many, confided that he and Calvin's brother's wife were carrying on an affair. Was this happening all over Geneva—without the knowledge of the ever-present elders? Was the bawdy jest literally true that if adultery merited death then all the women of Geneva should be sewn into sacks and thrown into the Rhone?

In the years that followed, Gerard redoubled his own efforts to keep God's law and was rewarded with a growing sense of piety and discipline. As he increased in these graces, he also experienced a growing sense of kinship with Calvin. The two men became closer than brothers, as Calvin phrased it one day. Gerard wanted the Genevan experiment to succeed and shared Calvin's conviction that it was well on its way to success. By 1555, Calvin was the acknowledged leader of Genevan life, though he held no official position. It almost seemed to Gerard that a new spirit was being created in the people, a spirit that made them want to keep God's law.

In 1558 Calvin climaxed his Genevan program with the construction of an *Academie* that was to draw pupils from all over Europe and become a major factor in the spread of Calvinistic Protestantism. This time, Gerard was persuaded to take a post as teacher of classics and Protestant theology. He regretted that his father could not witness this development but Ami had earlier turned against Calvin for petty reasons and had been sentenced to be hanged and quartered. Fortunately, Ami had already fled from Geneva.

One evening, Gerard attempted to condense his understanding of Calvinism into a single paragraph. When he showed the effort to Calvin, the master accepted it as a fair summary. It subsequently became the operational belief of the entire *Academie*. The paragraph read as follows: "People are rescued by the mercy of God in an act of his sovereign will through the work of Jesus Christ. Faith makes God's will and Christ's work a personal possession. The result of faith is the sanctified life, which is a constant struggle. In this struggle, the law excites people to the study of purity and holiness by reminding them of their duty."

Gerard was troubled by increasing signs of weakness in John Calvin, but nothing would slow him down. In caring for his master, he found himself increasingly in contact with Judith, Calvin's deceased wife's daughter. Early one morning the two sat down in Judith's room to discuss John's condition. Wearied by their around-the-clock efforts and frightened by the thought of his death, emotionally exhausted, they were drawn to each other for comfort, and contact led to intercourse. The act could not long be kept from Calvin, and although he refused to rebuke either of these people whom he loved dearly, he did leave Geneva for three days to consider in solitary the future of the Genevan experiment and his entire system. He made only one slight modification in the system by allowing a larger place for the power of sin that remained in people even after their conversion. Then he resumed his leadership of Geneva, while Gerard moved out of his house, since Judith had nowhere to go.

Gerard saw Calvin only once more and that was the day before he died. He came into the master's bedroom along with the members of the *Vénérable Compaigne,* though he kept to the shadows so that Calvin could not recognize him. His heart broke as Calvin reviewed the troubles he had encountered in Geneva and the sacrifices he had made. He wept as John exhorted the ministers to follow the good of his example and his teaching and to continue faithfully the pursuit of what they thought to be for the glory of God.

Calvin died May 27, 1564 and was buried in an unmarked grave in Geneva. Gerard concurred completely with the resolution passed by the Little Council, which affirmed simply that "God gave him a character of great majesty."

COMMENTARY

The Cameo tried to depict the many-sided character of John Calvin and the religious movement that he launched at Geneva. The Commentary will underscore limited parts of three aspects of the total program: the pastoral goals that Calvin pursued, the pastoral means that he used, and the theological foundation of his pastoral care. The Commentary will also offer some evaluatory comments on the program and its theology. Those who have read Williston Walker's biography of John Calvin and E. William Monter's study of Calvin's Geneva will recognize my dependence on especially these two books. Several essays presented at the Colloquium on Calvin and Calvin Studies at Grand Rapids, Michigan in April 1976 also proved especially helpful.

The goals that John Calvin set out to attain at Geneva were not so novel; rather it was the combination of goals, means, and theology that gave the experiment its far-reaching consequences. It is probably also correct to add that the experiment could have been conducted on such a massive scale only in sixteenth-century Switzerland or Germany. Societies have frequently tried to control the morals and private lives of their citizens by law. Sumptuary laws were passed in great number by the Roman Senate. The Romans also spent a great deal of time and money trying to enforce those laws and punish offenders—all with little evident success.

At Geneva, Calvin determined to enable each citizen to live according to the law of God to the glory of God in a framework of regular worship and regular participation in the sacrament of the altar, under the constant "affectionate" guidance of the elders. To achieve his goals, Calvin believed that it was absolutely necessary to establish the full independence of the church from every form of governmental control. In this he succeeded.

What kind of life did Calvin define as suitably Christian? Fortunately, the records of the *Consistoire* survive, making it possible to provide a detailed description of Calvin's perfect Christian. This ideal person is best described negatively as one who avoided scandals and lying, domestic quarrels, quarrels with others, fornication, resistance to the theological authority of the elders, quarrels with relatives, drunkenness, superstition, blasphemy and swearing, theft, ignorance (which frequently showed itself in the practice of old Roman Catholic customs and rites), clandestine marriages, business fraud, gambling, profane dancing and singing, usury, overeating, and idleness. The records of the *Consistoire*, as analyzed by Dr. Monter, reveal that these sins were exposed among the Genevans in descending number of frequency, beginning with scandals and lying and ending with overeating and idleness. With respect to many of these acts, it is difficult to draw the line between behavior that is socially acceptable and that which is religiously sinful. It is interesting to note that in the rural areas around Geneva, the pattern of sins and the frequency of occurrence was quite different.

Did Calvin's program succeed? The testimony of John Knox and of other contemporaries indicates that it did. The records of the Little Council and of the *Consistoire* in general support the same conclusion. However, the Cameo presents another piece of evidence by focusing on the sexual sins that were committed even by members of Calvin's own household, as late as two years before his death. It is furthermore important to note the steady increase in the number of excommunications from church life in Geneva. Beginning with perhaps four people in 1551, the register swelled to include 535 in 1569. The rural excommunications tripled from forty-two in 1557 to 130 in 1569. While the vast majority of these excommunications were for a period of two or three months, they nevertheless suggest that Calvin's Genevan approach to Christian living called for increasing control. However, it may be argued to the contrary that as Calvin's system succeeded, the *Consistoire* was able to give more time to more petty sins; hence the growing number of excommunications.

Is it possible for a present-day Christian community to reintroduce Calvin's concept of sanctification through discipline? Can the control of external sinful acts be equated with the development of positive Christian character? Is it possible to create a modified form of Calvin's goals for a congregation? Was the Genevan definition of sin inclusive enough? What list might you draw up today?

If some validity is granted to Calvin's understanding of the Christian life, then the means that were adopted in Geneva to achieve these goals are important to modern-day Christians. A considerable number of means were employed. Perhaps the chief means was the personality and leadership of Calvin himself. Of course, he would have denied this and would have pointed to the system of elders, to the work of teachers and preachers in expounding the infallible Word of God, and to the emphasis on church attendance and participation in the Lord's Supper. At the same time, the mood of the times contributed significantly to the success of Calvin's work. People were listening for a new religious trumpet; they had given up hope of hearing such a sound from the church of Rome. They needed once again to link religion and life, to add the sacred dimension to the daily secular routine. The response in Germany to Luther's Visitation Articles and to the call of the Anabaptists indicates that the time was ripe for Calvin's kind of religious revival. Throughout western Europe, people were on an emotional jag, caused by the new discoveries, new inventions, new freedom to move about. Genevans were notoriously self-confident, but fifty percent of their self-confidence was still derived from their faith in God.

Calvin's personality and theology were inseparable. He was a man of strong intellect and will and so he tended to emphasize these same qualities in God and to dwell on those Scripture passages that stressed them. He was a tightly disciplined person himself, and he viewed God in that light. Of course, one can debate at length whether his personality shaped his belief in God or whether his beliefs about God formed his personality. Perhaps the two interrelated in a supportive and creative way, as would later be true of Jonathan Edwards, a true heir of John Calvin. Through sheer force of his will and intellect, he became the commanding figure in Genevan life after 1555 and he was also the spiritual sparkplug that set the basic tone for the community. A less stable person, like William Farel, would undoubtedly have achieved some of Calvin's goals but would also have frustrated many of his plans by keeping the city in constant turmoil and unrest.

Calvin himself believed that the system of elders was the most important cog at Geneva. The elder plan was one of his most radical and important innovations. For one thing, it gave to the laity a position and office of central importance to serve as an effective counterbalance to the ever-present tendency of clericalization. This system received probably its finest development in the Scottish Presbyterian church under the leadership of John Knox. This system also provided for supervision of life by fellow human beings who were experiencing the same problems and temptations as the persons they were admonishing. It was usually a humane system for "fraternal correction." It was an important step back toward the early church's pattern of constant mutual admonition and exhortation. It was also a happy halfway house between the medieval Roman penitential system and the shapelessness that characterizes most of present-day Protestantism. It stopped short of Luther's insistence that all people should provide "conversation and consolation" for all others, but was considerably more effective than Luther's model.

What role do elders play in your parish? What additional roles could they play? Do you see any reason for reintroducing Calvin's insistence on their key role as "fraternal correctors"? How would your people, elders and non-elders, react?

Calvin scholars have argued whether his system of discipline for daily living bore any direct relationship to his preaching about justification by grace through faith. Many of them have decided that it did not, but somehow stood as an unrelated development.

The Cameo suggests that there is a connection, but at best it seems rather dubious. Much more evident is the connection between discipline and Calvin's understanding of the will and the law of God. God's will was that people should live to his glory; none were exempt from that demand. To enable all people to reach that goal, God gave his law to perform three vital functions. The law functioned as a mirror to enable sinners to see themselves as they truly were, as in the case of Gerard's conversion in the Cameo. Second, the law served to create fear and terror in the mind of the sinner. Third, the law was designed by God to excite people to the study of holiness and duty, and thus to inspire them to more sanctified living.

Concerning this third point, endless debate has taken place between Calvinists and Lutherans. Calvin saw the law as a positive force for righteous living, while Luther seems to have seen it, sometimes primarily and sometimes only, as a harsh, judgmental power in the lives of Christians and non-Christians. It is clear that in Geneva the law did indeed excite people to the study of holiness and duty, and thus played a significant role in affecting and effecting behavior. But the question remains: does the law have this power in itself, or was it only a fortunate combination of social, political, and theological circumstances that apparently made it effective in Geneva? The excommunication records of the *Consistoire* suggest that there is no simple answer to this question.

But it was also in his doctrine about the law that Calvin linked justification by grace through faith with daily living. The law was a manifestation of God's will, the same will that led him to save people through the work of Jesus Christ. Upon that almighty will to save rested all hope of salvation. From that will, Calvin drew all comfort for disturbed sinners like Gerard. Furthermore, the law had to do its work of frightening and condemning before sinners would be open to the good news of their deliverance through the work of Jesus Christ.

Almost against his will, his teaching about the will of God under the label of predestination became central to his system while at Geneva. It happened in connection with his debate with the Jesuit Bolsec, which is reported briefly in the Cameo. For Calvin the original issue in the Bolsec matter was not his peculiar understanding of predestination, but rather his authority as an "unassailable interpreter of God's Word." This battle was fought on the ground of predestination, and in his effort to defend his authority as an expositor, Calvin gave to predestination a new importance that alienated to some degree even some of his supporters from other Swiss cities. It must be said to Calvin's credit that he never used the doctrine except to provide comfort for troubled souls like Gerard.

But perhaps the most distinguishing feature of Calvin's theological system was his insistence upon the absolute authority and reliability of every word of the inspired Scriptures. As he pointed out in his own letters and writings, this doctrine set him apart from Rome, for they substituted other authorities than that of Scripture. In this insistence, Calvin seems to have given a new emphasis to Christian theology which has raised considerable turmoil in the nineteenth and twentieth centuries. The problems associated with this view are hinted at in the Cameo in the case of Sébastien Castellio. It was apparently an all-or-nothing requirement at Geneva, and in many of the denominations that have followed Calvin on this point.

What place does God's law have in your system of pastoral care? Would you agree with Irenaeus of Lyons (ca. A.D. 180) who said that for Jews the law was a ceiling to control and limit conduct while for Christians it was the floor? How do you connect justification and sanctification?

7.
Richard Baxter

CAMEO AND COMMENTARY

The practice of Protestant pastoral care in England and North America from 1650 to 1850 was largely shaped by the example and the works of Richard Baxter. He was born in England in 1615 and died in 1691. Thus his life spans the turbulent seventeenth century of England's history. During his lifetime a king was beheaded, Oliver Cromwell established the Commonwealth, and the parliament overthrew the Commonwealth and reestablished the kingship by calling Charles II to the throne. In many of these events Baxter played an important role, and throughout all of them he tried to carry on a pastoral ministry, especially among the hard-working people of Kidderminster. Despite a busy parish schedule, Baxter found time to do a great amount of writing. His book *The Reformed Pastor* influenced the development of pastoral styles on both sides of the Atlantic for two centuries.

In his book on pastoral care and in other writings, Baxter tried to establish a balance between pre-Reformation styles of pastoral care and Christian community and post-Reformation patterns. He was well acquainted with the earlier fathers, some of whose writings have already been discussed in this book, and he tried to incorporate their ideas into his thinking on pastoral care. The pre-Reformation church had placed most of its emphasis on the sacrament of the altar and the practice of penance. In contrast, the Reformation church placed most of its emphasis on preaching and on the fellowship of the saints. The pre-Reformation church often thought of itself as the vessel of salvation, the ark that was carrying a freight of souls to the heavenly harbor. The post-Reformation church placed more emphasis upon the mission of the church in this world. These diverse strands and sometimes competing emphases are held together in the thought and the writing of Richard Baxter.

In addition, Baxter adds some elements that are uniquely his own and some ideas that developed in the post-Reformation English churches. Richard Baxter was a practicing theologian; that is, he understood the importance of a carefully developed theology for the successful conduct of parish duties. His own parish theology centered in the idea of the covenant, by which he meant, first, that God enters into a covenant relationship with people and that, second, people respond by pledging to live a godly life. In Baxter's thought, both sides of the covenant were solidly based in Biblical ideas. Thus he insisted that God had entered into the covenant prompted only by his infinite mercy. Nothing in people themselves moved him to do so. God sealed the covenant, renewed, ratified, and offered it in Christ's life, death, and resurrection. In no sense did Baxter think of this as a covenant between two equals. God's act of freely entering into the covenant relation causes two ideas or attitudes to become present in the souls of people. In the first place, people adore and worship God because of his gift of free salvation through the blood of Jesus Christ. In the second place, people accept a new position of responsibility for the world and its peoples. But they recognize that even this kind of stewardship living depends solely on the grace of God for its effective development.

In many parishes both in England and in what would become the United States, church members were asked to sign a covenant in which they recognized their dependence on God's grace and promised to live lives of love and service for their neighbors. It was hoped that this act of signing would inspire each person. Following a century of more or less unsuccessful experimentation in the United States, the signed covenant idea was abandoned.

Covenant theology can lead to an overemphasis upon human

responsibility and human reaction to God's gracious offer. Baxter endeavored to avoid this by centering his covenant theology in Jesus Christ. This Christ-centered character of his thought is brought out in a strikingly beautiful paragraph in his autobiography, where he reflects on the relationship between grace and works in the Christian life.

> Though my works were never such as could be any temptation to me to dream of obliging God by proper merit in commutative justice [that is, that his works could in any sense earn forgiveness], yet one of the most ready, constant, undoubted evidences of my uprightness and interest in his covenant is the consciousness of my living as devoted to him. And I the easilier believe the pardon of my failings through my Redeemer while I know that I serve no other master, and that I know no other end, or trade, or business, but that I am employed in his work, and make it the business of my life, and live to him in the world, notwithstanding my infirmities. And this bent [purpose] and business of my life, with my longing desires after perfection, in the knowledge and belief and love of God, and in a holy and heavenly mind and life, are the two standing, constant, discernible evidences [evident proofs] which most put me out of doubt of my [Christian] sincerity. [*Autobiography of Richard Baxter*, ed. J. M. Lloyd Thomas (London: J. M. Dent, 1925), p. 125]

Baxter's covenant theology was clearly based on the Biblical idea that believers form the body of Christ on earth. Once, in a speech delivered to a group of ministers who were troubled by jealousy and envy among themselves, Baxter explained his beliefs on this point. What he says here about ministers could be directly applied to the attitude of Christians toward each other in the congregation.

> Oh that it ever should be spoken of godly ministers that they are so set upon popular air [favor], and of sitting highest in men's estimation, that they envy the parts [talents] and names of their brethren that are preferred before them, as if all were taken from their praises that is given to another. . . . What? a saint, a preacher for Christ, and yet envy that which hath the image of Christ, and malign His gifts for which He should have the glory, and all because they seem

to hinder our glory? Is not every true Christian a member of the Body [of Christ], and, therefore, partaketh of the blessings of the whole, and of each particular member thereof? And doth not every man owe thanks to God for his brethren's gifts, not only as having himself a part in them, as the foot hath the benefit of the guidance of the eye; but also because his own ends may be attained by his brethren's gifts as well as by his own? For if the glory of God and the Church's felicity be not his end [goal] he is not a Christian. Will any workman malign another because he helpeth him to do his master's work? [*The Reformed Pastor,* ed. Hugh Martin (Richmond: John Knox Press, 1956), pp. 90–91]

Baxter liked to refer to the congregation as a family. Once he wrote, "All Christians are bound to teach and help each other in love but the ministers are set in the church (as parents in families) to do it by office."

Because the church was a family, Baxter also placed special stress upon ministries to families. He wrote:

We must also have a special eye upon families, to see that they be well ordered, and the duties of each relation performed. The life of religion and the welfare and glory of Church and State, dependeth much on family government and duty. If we suffer the neglect of this, we undo all. What are we like to do to ourselves to the reforming of a congregation, if all the work be cast on us alone, and masters [i. e., heads] of families will let fall [neglect] that necessary duty of their own, by which they are bound to help us! If any good be begun by the ministry in any soul in a family, a careless, prayerless, worldly family is like to stifle it, or very much hinder it. I beseech you therefore to do all that you can to promote this business [family religion], as ever you desire the true reformation and welfare of your parishes. [*The Reformed Pastor,* ed. Hugh Martin, p. 58]

As a man of the Reformation, Baxter was convinced that the clergy needed the people as much as the people needed them. In pre-Reformation thought, this mutual-dependence pattern usually did not exist. It is a mark of Baxter's greatness that he can publicly affirm his need for his people.

We must carry ourselves meekly and condescendingly to all; and so teach others as to be as ready to learn of any that can teach us, and so both teach and learn at once; not proudly venting our own conceits, and disdaining all that [in] any way contradict them, as if we had attained to the height of knowledge, and were destined for the chair [of teaching at a university], and other men to sit at our feet. Pride is a vice that ill beseems [fits] them that must lead people in such a humble way to heaven. . . . Methinks we should remember at least the title of a minister [by which Baxter means "servant"], which, though the popish priests disdain, yet so do not we. It is indeed pride that feedeth all the rest of our sins. Hence the envy, the contention, and unpeaceableness of ministers; hence the stops to all reformation; all would lead, and few will follow or concur. [*The Reformed Pastor,* rev. and abridged by William Brown (New York: American Tract Society, 1829), pp. 176–177]

Richard Baxter's great sense of balance is shown also in his attitude toward church discipline. He grants that many abuses had crept into the medieval practice of discipline, but refuses to allow that these abuses justify the scrapping of the practice. And even though he stressed the familial and fellowship character of the church in the post-Reformation model, he insisted that discipline was crucial for family life. In his day it was possible for a person who had been placed under discipline by one congregation to join another. For that reason, in his own community Baxter developed a ministerial association, one of whose objectives was the mutual respect of each other's discipline. In an address to pastors, he said:

My second request to ministers is, that they would at last, without any more delay, unanimously set themselves to the practice of those parts of Christian discipline which are unquestionably necessary, and part of their work. It is a sad case, that good men should settle themselves so long in the constant neglect of so important a duty. The common cry is, "Our people are not ready for it; they will not bear it." But is not the fact rather, that you will not bear the trouble and hatred which it will occasion? If, indeed, you proclaim our churches incapable of the order and government of Christ, what do you but give up the cause to them that withdraw from us, and encourage men to look out for better societies, where that discipline may be had? [Baxter refers to stricter, puritanical gatherings of Christians that had separated from the Anglican church on the ground that the church was too loose.] [*The Reformed Pastor,* rev. and abridged by William Brown, p. 84]

Baxter also appealed to the people to listen to their pastors and to repent when the latter, in meekness and love, convinced them of their sins and admonished them. He pleaded with the people not to resist the word of God which pastors lay on their consciences, and not to force pastors to cut them off with grief from the communion of the church as people who remained fixed in scandalous sins.

Baxter's convictions concerning the unity of the body of Christ were firm and grew as he grew older. This led him to stress not only unity in the local congregation, but also unity in the broader church. He admitted that as he grew older he decreased the requirements for church unity while his own convictions concerning its importance increased. Thus he wrote:

My last request is, that all the faithful ministers of Christ would, without any more delay, unite and associate for the furtherance [advancement] of each other in the work of the Lord, and the maintaining of unity and concord in his churches. [*The Reformed Pastor,* rev. and abridged by William Brown, p. 85]

They [the pastors] must, therefore, keep close to the ancient simplicity of the Christian faith, and the foundation and centre of . . . unity [by which he meant Jesus Christ]. They must abhor the arrogancy of them that frame new engines to rack and tear the Church of God, under pretence of obviating errors, and maintaining the truth. The Scripture sufficiency must be maintained, and nothing beyond it imposed on others. [*The Reformed Pastor,* ed. Hugh Martin, pp. 78–79]

He liked the ancient motto that unity is to be observed in essential matters, freedom in nonessential, and love in both areas. He was realistic about the difficulties in the way of true unity. He wrote:

When we are perfect in love, and perfect in humility, and meekness, and patience, and perfect in self-denial, and all other graces, then, and never till then, shall we be perfect in our union and agreement among ourselves. [Irvonwy Morgan, *The Nonconformity of Richard Baxter* (London: Epworth Press, 1946), p. 100]

Although Baxter never used the fivefold description of healthy parish life that this book stresses, all five actions are clearly evident in the parish at Kidderminster. Baxter constantly stressed the importance of worship and insisted that the people must always present themselves on Sunday morning to engage in this activity. Further, Baxter stressed the importance of Christian nurture, especially in the form of preaching and the sacrament of the altar. As a man of the Reformation, Baxter gave preaching the central role and ascribed to the sacrament of the altar a somewhat secondary role. In the medieval church the sacrament of the altar had the primary role and preaching was decidedly deemphasized. Baxter repeatedly reflected his conviction concerning the central role of preaching, and he himself preached with great effectiveness. He explained that his own pulpit power came from the fact that his people knew that he loved them, that he drew his sermons directly from Scripture, that he gave them something in each sermon that would stretch their minds, and that he had a "familiar voice," a very important asset. While he does not define what he means by a "familiar voice," probably he means a voice that is comfortable to listen to and a voice that the people trust. Like many of the new breed of Protestant preachers, Baxter ended most sermons with an appeal to the people to decide to serve Christ then and now. One example follows:

And now . . . having laid down these undeniable arguments, I do, in the name of God, demand thy resolution: wilt thou yield obedience or not? I am confident thy conscience is convinced of thy duty. Darest thou now go on in thy common, careless course, against the plain evidence of reason and commands of God, and against the light of thy own conscience? . . . Or dost thou not rather resolve to "gird up the loins of thy mind," and set thyself wholly to the work of thy salvation, and break through [all] . . . oppositions, and slight [pay no attention to] the scoffs and persecutions of the world . . . ? I hope these are thy full resolutions. [Richard Baxter, *The Saints' Everlasting Rest*, abridged by Benjamin Fawcett (New York: American Tract Society, 1840) pp. 176–177]

With respect to the sacrament of the altar, Baxter again sought and followed a middle road. He set himself against the Roman Catholics and Anglicans on the one hand, who placed the sacrament of the altar at the center of parish life, and against the new anti-liturgical Christian groups that were beginning to emerge, who minimized this sacrament and thought of it almost as a fellowship meal. With these new groups, Baxter agreed that preaching was the chief work of the pastor and was the center of parish life. But unlike them, he continued to emphasize the importance of the sacrament of the altar for healthy parish life. He also thought that other ceremonies and rituals that were useful should be preserved. In contrast to the sectarians, who threw organs out of their church buildings, he believed that organ music was of supreme importance.

In Baxter's view, Christian nurture was also very heavily dependent upon the work of the Holy Spirit. Here, again, Baxter maintains his balance. Theologians in Roman Catholic and Anglican circles in seventeenth-century England were paying hardly any attention to the work of the Holy Spirit, while the sectarians placed him and his work in the center of their individual and parish lives. Baxter frankly admitted in his writings that in the earlier years of his ministry he had not placed sufficient emphasis upon the work of the Holy Spirit. But then he added that he had done this because he wanted to avoid the extreme emphasis of the sectarians. But as he grew older, he writes, he came to the conviction that the sectarians had a valid point, and he was man enough publicly to admit his own error and to change his mind. But in this matter, also, he avoided an extreme position, and in opposition to the sectarians continued to emphasize that the Spirit ordinarily came through preaching and the sacraments.

Baxter's emphasis upon regular family visitations demonstrates his concern both for nurture and for fellowship. In his

Have we the conduct of those saints that shall live forever with God in glory, and shall we overlook [neglect] them? God forbid! . . . Are the souls of men thought meet by God to see his face, and live for ever in heaven, and are they not worthy of your utmost cost and labor on earth? Do you think so basely of the church of God, as if it deserved not the best of your care and help? . . . They are "a chosen generation, a royal priesthood, a holy nation, a peculiar people, to show forth the praises of Him that hath called them." And will you neglect them? [*The Reformed Pastor,* rev. and abridged by William Brown, p. 196]

To pastors who argued that they did not have the time to minister faithfully to families and individuals in their parishes, Baxter, who made it his habit to meet regularly with the eight hundred families in his parish, addressed the following words:

To this I answer, Is it necessity, or is it not, that hath cast upon you such a charge [of a parish]? If it be not, you excuse one sin by another. How durst [dare] you undertake what you knew yourself unable to perform, were you not forced to it? It would seem you had some other end in undertaking it, and never intended to be faithful to your trust. But if you think that you were necessitated [forced] to undertake it, I would ask you, might you not have procured assistance for so great a charge? Have you done all you could with your friends and neighbors, to get maintenance [support] for another to help you? Have you not as much maintenance yourself, as might serve yourself and another? What though it will not serve to maintain you in fulness? Is it not more reasonable that you should pinch your flesh and family, than undertake a work that you cannot perform, and neglect the souls of so many of your flock? . . . Nay, should you not rather beg your bread, than put so important a matter as man's salvation upon a hazard or disadvantage? . . . [Is it not] inhuman cruelty to let souls go to hell, for fear my wife and children should fare somewhat the harder, or live at lower rates; when, according to God's ordinary way of working by means, I might do much to prevent their misery, if I would but a little displease my flesh, which all who are Christ's have crucified with its lust? [*The Reformed Pastor,* rev. and abridged by William Brown, pp. 141, 143]

These stern remarks to clergy make clear how important the regular program of visitation was for Baxter's ongoing program of fellowship and nurture.

Baxter stressed the activity of Christian service repeatedly. He taught that the goal of pastoral leadership is

> true morality or Christian ethics [which] is the love of God and man stirred up by the Spirit of Christ through faith, and exercised in works of piety, justice, charity and temperance, in order to attain everlasting happiness in the perfect vision and enjoyment of God. [*Autobiography of Richard Baxter,* p. 117]

In similar manner, Baxter exhorted his people to be active in mission and to always be seeking the conversion of people. He wrote:

> The work of conversion is the great thing we must strive at; after this we must labor with all our might. Alas, the misery of the unconverted is so great, that it calleth loudest to us for compassion. . . . It is so sad a case to see men in a state of damnation, wherein if they should die, they are lost for ever, that methinks we should not be able to let them alone, either in public or private, whatever other work we have to do. . . . Methinks I see them entering upon their final woe. Methinks I hear them crying out for help—for speediest help. [*The Reformed Pastor,* rev. and abridged by William Brown, pp. 144–145]

> My soul is much more afflicted with the thoughts of the miserable world and more drawn out in desire for their conversion than heretofore. I used to look little further than England in my prayers, as not considering the state of the rest of the world. . . . But now, as I better understand the case of the world and the method of the Lord's Prayer, there is nothing in the world that lies so heavy upon my heart as the thought of the miserable nations of the earth. . . . No part of my prayers are so deeply serious as those for the conversion of the infidel and ungodly world, that God's name may be sanctified and his kingdom come and his will be done on earth as it is in heaven.[Richard Baxter, *The Life of Faith,* cited in Morgan, *The Nonconformity of Richard Baxter, p. 97*]

How do you view the relative importance of preaching and the sacraments in parish life? What place does the Holy Spirit play in your life? Do you agree with Baxter on the importance of a visitation program?

In his views of parish life and structure, Baxter is firmly convinced that the pastor is the central figure. The pastor is the hinge around whom the entire life of the parish turns. But two other points must be kept in mind as one considers Baxter's teaching about the importance and role of the pastor. The first point is that he wrote these words in seventeenth-century England. At this period the commandment to obey one's elders was of extreme importance in family life, in political life, and in church life. Baxter lived in a structured, authoritarian society, and he was convinced that the church required a form of hierarchical structure just as surely as family and state did. Had he lived in a more democratic society, it is possible that his description of the pastor's role might have been different. At the same time, one must remember that the level of education of most of Baxter's parishioners was low. They were weavers and had seen little or nothing of the inside of even an elementary school. Again one asks whether Baxter would have the same view of the pastor's role in today's society where most people are rather well educated.

The second general point to keep in mind is that Baxter thinks of the pastor as functioning in the congregation of saints and in the family of God's people. The pastor is not lord over the people of God, but rather their minister, their servant. Baxter rejects what he calls the "popish" views of ministerial authority and leadership. Although his descriptions of the pastor often sound highly authoritarian, he intends them to sound very democratic and community-oriented. However, a good many of the pastors who read Baxter's book understood him to be describing a hierarchical and authoritarian view of the pastor's office.

Like some others who have already been described in this book, Baxter sees pride as the pastor's worst enemy. The chief problem with pride is that it convinces pastors that somehow they have earned or deserved the office. It encourages them to forget that they are God's choice and that it is God's grace alone that enables them to pastor the people of God. Baxter returned again and again to the work of the Holy Spirit in creating and supporting pastors. He writes:

> It is God by His spirit that makes us overseers of His Church, and, therefore, it concerneth us to take heed to it. The Holy Ghost makes men bishops or pastors of the Church in three several respects: By qualifying them for the office; by directing the ordainers to discern their qualifications, and know the fittest men; and by directing them, the people and themselves, for the affixing [of] them to a particular charge. All these things were then [in the time of the New Testament] done in an extraordinary way, by inspiration. . . . The same are done now by the ordinary way of the Spirit's assistance. . . . God also giveth men the qualifications which He requireth; so that all the Church hath to do, whether pastors or people, ordainers or electors, is but to discern and determine which are the men that God hath thus qualified and to accept of them that are so provided, and upon [their] consent, to instal them solemnly in this office. [*The Reformed Pastor,* ed. Hugh Martin, pp. 82–83]

> Ordination . . . is God's orderly and ordinary means of regular admittance: and [it is] to be sought and used where it may be had (as the solemnising of a marriage). And it is a sin to neglect it wilfully and so it is usually necessary. . . . But it is not of absolute necessity. [Richard Baxter, *Five Disputations,* p. 149]

Because the Anglican church was being agitated by questions concerning the necessity and the nature of ordination, Baxter continued to speak to that topic.

> If the way of regular ordination cannot be followed, God may otherwise (by the church's necessity and the evident aptitude of the person) notify his will to the church, what person they shall receive (as if a layman were cast on the Indian shore and converted thousands who could have no ordination), and upon the people's reception or consent that man will be a true pastor. . . . It is better that man should be disorderly saved than orderly damned; and that the church be disorderly preserved than orderly destroyed. [Baxter, *Five Disputations*, p. 165]

Baxter sets forth his high view of pastoral work and responsibility in the following paragraph.

> Christ makes them the chief instruments for the propagating of his truth and kingdom in the world, for the gathering of the churches and preserving and defending contradicted truth. They are the lights of the world and the salt of the earth. All Christians are bound to teach and help each other in charity but ministers are set in the church (as parents in families) to do it by office. And therefore [they] must be qualified above others for it and be wholly dedicated to it and attend continually upon it. . . . Never yet was the Gospel well propagated nor continued in any country in the world but by means of the ministers of Christ. . . . And how great an honor it is to be blessed instruments of building up the house of God and propagating the Gospel and the kingdom of Christ, and the Christian faith and godliness in the world. [Richard Baxter, *The Saints' Everlasting Rest,* ed. John Wilkinson (London: Epworth, 1962), p. 139]

While it is clear that Baxter rejects the medieval view of the pastor's role and authority, it is also apparent that he has not completely divorced himself from a high view of pastoral authority. If one compares Baxter's views in the preceding paragraph with the descriptions of the pastor that are found in the New Testament and in the writings of Justin and Tertullian, one notices a difference. In the thought of Baxter, the pastor is far more authoritative and important than in the literature of the first and second centuries in the church's history. Baxter is a paternalistic pastor; he calls himself that in the paragraph cited above. Usually the presence of a paternalistic figure in a group tends to retard the maturation of individuals in the group. The kind and loving father usually does more for the individuals than is good for them. Thus it is likely that Baxter's kind of pastors would actually retard the development of *koinonia,* though they are far superior to the medieval pastor and to many other pastors who have a heightened view of their own authority.

Baxter's views of pastoral authority were kept in balance by his own deep love for his people. He loved them in deed and in word. Once when a member rebuked Baxter for not showing him the proper degree of "respect and gratitude," especially in view of the fact that the member claimed that he had twice engineered for Baxter a call to Kidderminster, Baxter fired off the following letter.

> I purposely kept myself unplaced all the wars [the years of civil war in England when he served as a chaplain] for [the] love of my people that I might be free to return to you. And did my love to them draw me to take ninety pounds per annum (for that is my share) when I was offered five hundred pounds [to go to another parish]; and am I beholden to you as my patron? It beseems me not to say the open truth, that, sure, my people were beholden to me! Have *you* ever lost three hundred pounds per annum for the church, or love of your friends; and were [then] "hit in the tooth with it," when you had done, as if you were beholden to *them*? Do you think I cannot, in worldly respects, be quickly better provided for than here, if I would leave my friends that are so dear to me? And for whose sake do I thus deny myself? Truly, much more for the sake of many a humble godly man in Kidderminster that has scarce bread in his mouth than [I do] for yours. [Cited in Frederick J. Powicke, *A Life of the Reverend Richard Baxter* (London: Jonathan Cape, 1924), pp. 84–85]

And in another moving paragraph Baxter wrote:

> The whole of our ministry must be carried on in tender love to our people. We must let them see that nothing pleaseth us but what profiteth them; and that what doth them good, doth us good; and that nothing troubleth us more than their hurt. We must feel toward our people, as a father toward his children; yea, the tenderest love of a mother must not surpass ours. We must even travail in birth till Christ be formed in them. They should see that we care for no outward thing, neither wealth, nor liberty, nor honor, nor life, in comparison of [with] their salvation. Thus should we, as John saith, be ready to "lay down our lives for the brethren," and with Paul, not count our lives dear to us, so we may but "finish our course with joy, and the ministry which we have received of the Lord Jesus." When the people see that you unfeignedly love them, they will hear any thing and bear any thing from you. . . . Let them see that you spend, and are spent for their sakes; and that all that you do is for them, and not for any private

ends of your own. [*The Reformed Pastor,* rev. and abridged by William Brown, pp. 178–179]

Like other pastors whose views have been discussed in this book, Baxter took seriously his responsibility to set an example for his people. He wrote:

> Let me entreat you, brothers, to do well as well as say well: be zealous of good works. . . . Maintain your innocency and walk without offence. Let your lives condemn sin, and persuade men to duty. Would you have your people more careful of their souls, than you will be of yours? If you would have them redeem their time, do not you mis-spend yours. If you would not have them vain in their conference [conversation], see that you speak yourselves the things which may edify, and tend to minister grace to the hearers. Order your own families well if you would have them do so by theirs. Be not proud and lordly if you would have them to be lowly. There is no virtue wherein your example will do more, at least to abate men's prejudice, than humility, and meekness, and self-denial. Forgive injuries, and be not overcome of evil, but overcome evil with good; do as our Lord, who when He was reviled, reviled not again. [*The Reformed Pastor,* ed. Hugh Martin, pp. 35–36]

Do you agree with Baxter that the pastor is the hinge (Latin: cardinal) in the parish? Do you share Baxter's view of total pastoral dedication to the needs of his people?

It is important to note that Baxter does not call upon his people to imitate him as he imitates Jesus Christ. Rather, he calls upon the pastors to set before their people an example of Christian virtues so that the people may have examples before their eyes. Baxter approaches the idea of example in a moral vein, somewhat as Ambrose had done. The idea of example does not have the full impact and dynamic that it does in St. Paul and Justin Martyr, to cite only two examples.

Richard Baxter had learned the importance of solitude for contemplation and self-discipline in daily living. He was in the best sense of the word an ascetic. His asceticism was not just limited to peculiar personal habits, but it was a whole attitude toward life. He reflected the ideas that St. Paul put forward in the third chapter of Philippians, where he told his readers that he rejected everything but Jesus Christ. Likewise for Baxter, asceticism was a discipline that opened him to the outpouring of the grace and power of God's Spirit. He wrote:

> [The ministerial] work must be carried on in a sense of our insufficiency and in a pious, believing dependence on Christ. We must go to Him for light and life and strength, who sends us on the work. And when we feel our own faith weak and our hearts grown dull and unsuitable to so great a work as we have to do, we must have recourse to the Lord that sendeth us and say, "Lord, wilt thou send me with such an unbelieving heart to persuade others to believe? Must I daily plead with sinners about everlasting life and everlasting death, and have no more belief or feeling of these weighty things myself? Oh, send me not naked and unprovided to the work; but, as Thou commandest me to do it, furnish me with a spirit suitable thereto." Prayer must carry on our work as well as preaching: he preacheth not heartily to his people, that will not pray for them. If we prevail not with God to give them faith and repentance, we are unlikely to prevail with them to believe and repent. When our own hearts are so far out of order, and theirs so far out of order, if we prevail not with God to mend and help them, we are like to make but unsuccessful work. [*The Reformed Pastor,* ed. Hugh Martin, pp. 77–78]

In prayer Baxter found the confidence that he believed to be an essential ingredient of the pastor's work. He wrote:

> If you would prosper in the ministerial work, be sure to keep up earnest desires and expectations of success. If your hearts be not set on the end of your labors, and you long not to see the conversion and edification of your hearers, and do not study and preach in hope, you are not likely to see much success. As it is the sign of a false, self-seeking heart, that can be content to be still doing, and yet see no fruit of his labor, so I have observed that God seldom blesseth any man's work so much as his whose heart is set upon the success of it. [*The Reformed Pastor,* rev. and abridged by William Brown, pp. 182–183]

Do you agree with Baxter that pastors are specially qualified by the Spirit for their work? Do you think that pastors possess spiritual gifts in stronger measure than lay people? How do you understand the place of ordination in the life of God's people? Do you like Baxter's kind of paternalistic pastor?

Baxter's own deep commitment to the ministry and its joys provides a fitting conclusion to the discussion of this chapter.

Such thoughts as these [namely, to leave the ministry because of abuse and opposition] my flesh has too often suggested; so that I confess, had I but liberty to put aside this calling, which you so reproach, my flesh would take it for the happiest hour that ever I saw. But do I approve of this or grudge at my employment and the disposal of my God? No, I bless the Lord daily that he called me to this blessed work! It is only my flesh that regrets this. God has paid me for all these sufferings a thousandfold. O the sweetness of sacred studies and contemplations! These are the recreations of my spirit though a weariness to the flesh. O the consolations that I have in the very opening his Gospel mysteries, and in revealing the hopes of the saints and the unseen glory of the life to come. O how the Lord does sweetly revive my own faith and love and desire and joy and resolution and all graces, while he sets me on these thoughts in my studies, and those persuasions in my preaching which tend to revive the graces of my hearers! O the sweet comfort that I have in the abundant success of my labors, in the conversion and confirmation of souls, and in the mortification and vivification of my godly friends. . . . Truly God's work is most precious wages! Yes, even my sufferings for him are the inlets of my joy! And my constant experience assures me that the dearer it costs me to serve him the more abundant will be the incomes of my peace; and that no man shall ever be a loser by him. I would not therefore change my life for any of the greatest dignities on earth. . . . I am willing to wait on God in this work and think my lines and lot well fallen. I am contented to consume my body, to sacrifice my reputation to his service, and to spend all that I have and to be spent myself, for the souls of men—though the more I love, the less I may be beloved. [Cited in Powicke, *A Life of the Reverend Richard Baxter,* pp. 287–288]

8.
Jonathan Edwards

CAMEO

Sarah Edwards tried to keep her mind occupied with routine household chores, but her thoughts were with her husband in the meeting in the church across the green. The church council was in session to decide whether her husband's ministry at Northampton could continue. Sarah's agony for Jonathan was intense because she knew the depth of his pride and, she added hesitantly even to herself, his stubbornness. Her anger at the leaders of the disloyal opposition was equally intense, although she knew that this anger was prompted in part by her dislike of common people like Seth Pomeroy and Timothy Root. Sarah found some relief in muttering to Venus, the new maid, even though she knew that the girl had no understanding of what she was saying. But at least she grunted sympathetically at the right times. "How much good Jonathan has done for them," Sarah fumed and Venus grunted. "Two big revivals have been sent from God to Northampton through Jonathan's ministry and both of them spread to all of New England. Jonathan has trained their children in the ways of the Lord for twenty-two years, and has watched over their morals like a hawk." Again Venus made the appropriate sound. "He has turned down appointments to better churches. He has worked thirteen hours a day on sermons and lectures. Now all this is threatened by men who aren't worthy to clean his boots." No grunt from Venus on that one; she did clean them.

"Do you know why, Venus? Do you know why?" Venus, not listening really, grunted sympathetically. Sarah ignored that sound and went on. "All because he wants to spark a third revival that will surely bring the kingdom of God to the Connecticut Valley. Oh, Venus, what will happen to my man?" This time Venus's sound was genuinely sympathetic; she could understand the sounds of love's suffering.

Sarah's one-way conversation was interrupted by Jonathan's appearance, along with John Cotton and Dr. Isaac Mather, Jonathan's strongest supporters in the council. Sarah could see the strain of the meeting in Jonathan's eyes and in the subdued appearance of the other two. Jonathan put his arms around Sarah, something he rarely did in public, and thus silently confirmed her fears. She waited for him to speak, but Dr. Mather was the first to break the silence.

"It's a shame, Mrs. Edwards, it's a shame. Mr. Cotton and I did our best to put it off, but we could not." Then he broke off awkwardly, as he sought for the right words. "In effect, Mrs. Edwards, the majority are asking Mr. Edwards to resign. It breaks our hearts and it fills us with anger when we think of men like Pomeroy and Root and their followers forcing this action upon your man."

Jonathan, optimist at least on the outside, took up the story. "It's not really final, Sarah. Dr. Mather is too weak in faith; God will still act to sustain and defend us. Thanks to Dr. Mather and Mr. Cotton, I am being given the opportunity to give five lectures to the people defending my position with respect to the covenant idea. And I'll persuade them once again, Sarah. They'll see that it is God's will and a good thing for all true Christians. They'll see." Sarah wanted to share her husband's optimism, but she knew the mood of the town much better than he. She suspected that Dr. Mather and Mr. Cotton also did not share Jonathan's conviction. The two men excused themselves and left. Jonathan told Sarah that he wanted to walk in the woods while it was still light and would be back for supper within the hour.

Sarah knew what these walks in the woods did for her man, and that they were usually more important to him than her own company. He would come back changed and refreshed, and then he would share his most intimate experiences with her, and she, too, would be helped. She watched him walk across the yard toward the river to give thanks to God even in this time of adversity and defeat. Sometimes, being a Calvinist woman was an awful trial! Was there no place for genuine anger or despair?

After the children were in bed, Jonathan and Sarah sat before the fire, and he thrilled her with his story of how his spirit had joined itself to God in the woods, filled with the color that only New England trees can produce in the fall. He described to her how he felt strong and powerful as he again renewed his pledge of absolute dependence on the grace and power of the sovereign God to whom he had originally dedicated himself at Yale College. He spoke with confidence and conviction about the outcome of his lecture series before his people.

Unlike Jonathan, Sarah dreaded the outcome of the lectures. She fully expected him to be dismissed, but Sarah knew that the action itself would probably destroy her husband. The people of Northampton were his life. She had always had to share his love with them. To be separated from them would be like cutting the cord of one of her babies while it was still in her womb. He would never let the world know the dimension of his defeat. Perhaps by employing his singular will power, he would disguise it even from himself. But Sarah knew her man well enough to know that he could not survive this blow to his self-esteem. She almost thought of it as his pride. Sometimes she even permitted herself a vision of a broken Jonathan, morosely rocking before the fire, saying nothing, thinking nothing. Gone would be his tender love and care for her and the children. She hoped that the great reservoir of her love for him that he had kept filled would not go dry as long as he lived.

Sarah gave him her encouraging smile and in the flickering firelight he could not see the deep shadow in her eyes. She knew the new mood of the town in a way that Jonathan never could. Locked in his study for thirteen hours each day, he had no understanding of the spirit that was abroad. When Sarah tried to tell him about it, he put her off with remarks about respect and obedience for parents and elders. So Sarah stopped trying to tell him about the hostility she encountered, about remarks that were deliberately made to be overheard. Abigail Miller told Eunice that her father thought that Edwards's preaching sounded just like his old cow after a good mess. It had taken Sarah an hour to soothe the girl. But that was not Jonathan's world; he refused to admit its existence.

His words interrupted her musings. "You'll see, dear, all the people will see God's Word and his will triumph. God's Spirit will once again warm their hearts. They will return to their first love for God and for us. Those who now call me snooty will learn again that I am not. They will come to respect anew my fatherly love and care for them. They will see that we must live in a certain way so that we may always have their respect. Respect and authority go together, and they must give me the authority to guide their growth in Christ's virtues. They must and they will again permit me to judge and rebuke when necessary. They will see the glory of God's kingdom here in Northampton, and they will pass into it. Most will want to sign the public covenant."

Jonathan's complete devotion to God and to his people was strangely moving. Sarah felt her doubts begin to erode. She thought she saw the ghost of an approving smile on John Cotton's portrait on the wall. Perhaps Jonathan was right. Perhaps God's Spirit was stronger than Pomeroy's new vision. Perhaps the kingdom would come. Yes, surely it would. At that moment their old cow mooed, the spell was broken, and the shadow crossed Sarah's eyes again.

For the next weeks Jonathan and Sarah saw little of each other. Jonathan spent all his time in the study. He took many of his meals there, and sometimes Venus would find the tray untouched while her master scribbled furiously. He outlined the lectures to Sarah in the rare moments they spent together. Jonathan's thoughts organized themselves with beautiful clarity. He began his first lecture by reminding the people of the important role that the covenant had played in the first Puritan settlement. It had been God's effective instrument for maintaining that high level of discipline, spirituality, and devotion that had won the admiration of European Christians. It had failed in the third generation because pastors had lost confidence in it and had weakened it into a halfway model. The Half-Way Covenant had allowed the unconverted spouses and children of full covenanters to participate in the ordinances of God's house. This action meant that Puritans no longer had to take upon themselves the full yoke in order to receive the sacraments. The results had been catastrophic. Puritanism had all but vanished from the face of the earth. So far, his argument was clear and sharp.

He experienced greater difficulty in dealing with the ghost of his grandfather, Solomon Stoddard, who had invited even unconverted Christians to receive the sacrament of the altar at Northampton. Instead of disagreeing head-on with his grandfather, Jonathan refused to offer any criticism of his position, and contented himself with explaining and defending his new, yet very old, views.

While Jonathan worked, Sarah was left with too much time to think. At times she almost felt a return of her troubles of eight years before, when she had been concerned that she might be losing her mind. At times then and again now she received visions that enabled her to understand things with a clarity that amazed her. She had always failed, however, to communicate the visions to Jonathan. During that long winter he had spent almost all of his time at her side when he was at home, praying or simply holding her hand.

She was surprised and frightened to find her sympathies increasingly going out to the townspeople in their contention with her husband as the day of the first lecture drew near. At first, she ascribed this to a womanly intuition which told her that the covenant requirement was unfair and unworkable. She believed that most of the people of Northampton loved God and wanted to live according to his will. But she also knew that they knew from their own experience that their obedience would not be perfect. Was it fair to force them to stand up before God and make a public promise that they knew they could not keep? Would that public promise strengthen their resolve? Had that been the secret of the first Puritan success?

During one of their increasingly infrequent walks in the woods, she had tried to share her questions and concerns with Jonathan. She knew that she would be touching close to his heart, but she did not know that she was striking directly into his heart through the one flaw in his magnificent Calvinistic system. Jonathan had suspected the presence of the flaw only once or twice, but he had quickly dismissed its existence. The brusqueness of his rejection of Sarah's questions should have alerted them both to the danger she had almost exposed. Instead, they attributed his explosion to his demanding schedule.

The true nature of the flaw hit Sarah with terrible clarity a few days later when she was playing her green-dress game. With Jonathan safely locked in the study, she had slipped on the new dress he had bought in Boston. She did this frequently, for it gave her considerable pleasure. The satin sheen highlighted the color of her eyes and complemented her dark hair. She looked at her figure with satisfaction. It was still good, despite her eight children. Of course, she had worked hard at keeping it, while most of the women in the town let themselves go. She had worn the same size corset for many years, while they had given up the battle even to get one locked around themselves. Perhaps their own slovenliness was one reason they kept after their husbands about Mrs. Edwards's fancy Boston clothes.

Sarah smiled to herself, did a brief waltz step and ended with a deep curtsy before the looking glass. As she straightened up, she realized in a moment of revealing clarity that she had wanted to bow to herself. That was her tribute to a good woman who was successfully carrying out a demanding mission. There was only one proper word to describe that attitude! Pride! Hers was not the ordinary kind of pride that her husband preached against so powerfully: the pride of position or wealth or family or even of good deeds done to God's glory. She knew how to deal with that kind of pride. That was the core of Puritan behavior.

She had just discovered that her habits of Puritan pride-control had served to obscure her real problem. Her pride did not consist of a series of public and private thoughts and acts for which she could easily obtain pardon. No, her problem was that the real Sarah Edwards, carefully hidden from everyone, was uncontrollably proud. Her pride was a growth lodged in her heart. Over the years in Northampton it had grown. Eventually it would cause her to challenge God himself and to seek to throw him from his throne. Sarah sat down on the bed and buried her face in her hands. She had given in to Satan's temptations to admire herself and to compliment herself on her great motherly successes because deep in her heart she wanted to. She wanted all the kingdoms of the world; she wanted to turn stones into bread to demonstrate her independence; she wanted the people to applaud when she cast herself unharmed down from the temple.

There was no one to whom she could go. Certainly not Jonathan. His system did not allow for Sarah's kind of deep-rooted controlling pride. That was supposed to disappear when you gave yourself to God. Her husband truly believed that God's Spirit had banished it from his life and from hers also. It was because of that spiritual cleansing that he could make a public covenant with God and ask the people of Northampton to do likewise. Her husband, she realized, did not understand the problems and the agonies that went with being human. He did not and could not understand his wife's nature. Sarah wondered whether he even understood himself.

She began to understand why so many people had come to hate Jonathan. For twenty-two years they had listened to his glowing descriptions of the Christian who had been indwelt by God in Christ. They wanted that experience. They had listened with stricken hearts while he painted God's anger against their sins in vivid colors. They had admitted that he was right. They were sinners and a great gulf separated them from God's holiness. But he had not helped most of them to cross that gulf. Instead, he had burdened them with demands for public pledges of perfect obedience that was totally beyond their power. Now Sarah understood why Jonathan was truly a failure at Northampton. He did not understand human nature, even though he loved people so much. He had not probed the nature of sin deeply enough. He had contented himself with rebuking sins of thought, word, and deed. He knew nothing about SIN as a controlling and uncontrollable lust lodged even within the wife of his bosom. This crack threatened to destroy the foundation on which he had built his system and his life.

Jonathan's tragedy consisted in the fact that the fatal flaw was located in the central point of his system. The strength and appeal of his system had been his understanding of sin. He helped people to understand much about the problems and the terrible limitations that went with being human. He helped them to see something of the powers of evil and destruction that resided in each of them. As Sarah reflected on Jonathan's preaching, she realized that both of the Awakenings in the Valley had been launched by a series of powerful sermons on sin. That was indeed his strength. Now she knew that that strength contained the fatal flaw. Jonathan's entire system was built on an inadequate understanding of sin's power. Jonathan had nothing to give her in her desperate need. Nor would he ever change or redesign his great system. The kingdom would not be built at Northampton as long as Jonathan was the preacher. Sarah sighed, brushed away a tear, slipped out of the green dress, knowing she would never wear it again, and went to the kitchen to help Venus with the baking chores. The old cow lowed as Timothy led her into the shed.

On the day of the first lecture, Jonathan crossed the commons to the church, climbed quickly to the desk, arranged the manuscript, nodded pleasantly to Colonel Dwight and Colonel Stoddard's widow sitting in their boxes, raised his eyes to the audience, smiled his thin, pinched smile which made people feel uncomfortable, and then returned his eyes to his manuscript and began reading. It took several minutes for the bomb to go off in the back of his mind and Sarah waited in anguish for the realization to hit her man. Jonathan read for a while and then, contrary to his manner, raised his eyes to sweep the audience. The church indeed was filled, but with few exceptions the people were not from Northampton. Confusion and anger washed over Jonathan. So that was how they would protect themselves against the Word of God. He lost his place, momentarily thought he would faint, but then regained sufficient composure to finish his reading.

The rest was a blur in Sarah's mind. She restrained tears only with the greatest effort. When the meeting was over, she fled back to the house accompanied by her children. She had no idea when Jonathan finally crawled into bed, although it must have been hours later. She suspected he had walked in the moonlight to one of his places overlooking the river and there had experienced the grace and sufficiency of God in Christ. She knew that *she* had not, as she tried hard not to toss and turn. Jonathan should sleep, he was tired.

For hours her spirit ranged frantically, looking for help. She knew that she had to be made whole before she could help Jonathan in the weeks and months ahead. She knew what would happen to him when the blow finally fell. Then (could it be the first time?) he would truly need her and she wanted to be ready.

As she lay there, her mind feeling strangely detached from her body, the story of Christ's temptation crossed before her eyes and forced her to contemplate that event. She saw and heard Christ and Satan, seated on the pinnacle of the temple. Satan was urging Christ to cast himself down into the throng of worshipers. She noticed that Satan wore a handsome green satin robe. She was surprised at how carefully and eagerly Christ was considering Satan's suggestions. "Forsooth," she heard him say, sounding almost like Jonathan, "I much like your proposal. It has great merit in it. I like the thought of being hailed as Messiah and crowned King of Israel. I truly believe that is God's will for me, by the way. That will speed up the salvation of Israel." In Christ's words, Sarah recognized the logic that she used to deny the presence and power of pride in her life. Could Christ be swayed by pride?

As Christ readied himself for the jump, Sarah saw a sheet coming down from heaven, wrapped around the Northampton chalice which was filled with dark red wine. She heard a voice from heaven, "If you succeed in this way, My Son, who will drink this cup? It contains the price of Sarah Edwards's deliverance from hell, the blood of an innocent Lamb." Christ hesitated. The struggle within himself was obviously furious.

Sarah watched with fascination and terror. She knew that her future and the future of everyone depended on the outcome of the struggle. Pride was the enemy, its force too great even for the Son of Man. Christ threw himself down on his knees, the perspiration streamed from his face like drops of blood. He cried out, "O, my Father, if it be possible, let this cup pass from me." There was silence in heaven about the space of half an hour. The struggle was his alone. Finally, with an agonizing sob, he took the cup. "All this," Sarah heard him mutter, "for Sarah Edwards." As he drank to the dregs, a look of wonderful peace came into his eyes. Not even Jonathan had looked so calm after one of his ecstatic experiences.

Sarah awoke, no longer frightened, but puzzled. She knew the vision was from God, sent to help her in her hour of need. But who was this Christ, so human, so tempted by the kind of pride that Sarah knew? Who seemed to be made in all things like she was made? This was not her husband's sweet, glorious, and all-sufficient Christ, so divine that his death on the cross was only a performance, almost a charade that had not involved him in real suffering.

This was a different Christ, a man who suffered with her, who bore her burdens, a man of like passions who had overcome a great temptation and had united his will with that of his heavenly father. A sense of new peace filled her. She loved this new Christ who knew her so well and still loved her and died for her. She felt that his love had made her clean; she understood in a new way what it meant to be washed in the blood of the Lamb. She knew that tomorrow she would do much better with the help and support of her new Friend. She loved him, at long last. She hummed the words of the twenty-third Psalm to herself as the first rays of the sun brushed her forehead.

Jonathan gave the remaining four lectures, partly because he still believed that God might work through his words, partly because he had inherited a double portion of his father's stubbornness. But now they both knew that the outcome at Northampton had been decided. He would be dismissed. The vote of the congregation, two hundred and thirty to twenty-three, and the maneuvering over the makeup of the district council were

anticlimactic. Jonathan would not stop fighting, though he knew
he was defeated. He found a new source of strength and peace
in Sarah.

The district council assembled on June 19, stacked with a
comfortable majority of Hampshire County men. Joseph Hawley,
young law-trained relative of Jonathan, delivered the main
speech, lashing out at Jonathan in a vicious way. On the 22nd the
council resolved that Jonathan should be dismissed because of
irreconcilable differences in principle between him and the parish.

After the struggle was over, Jonathan disintegrated. It took
him almost a year to reestablish the iron control of his affections.
He begged the parish council for permission to preach during the
vacancy, and they hired him for ten pounds a Sunday. The Root
faction, implacable in its opposition, managed to drive him from
the pulpit by November. They also succeeded in barring his cows
from the common meadow. Still, Jonathan remained in
Northampton, rebuilding himself emotionally and reconstruct-
ing his theological system without change or alteration. He was
convinced that the problem was not in his system, but in the
people's hardness of heart, and that God would vindicate him
and his system at the Great Assize. Sarah hoped and prayed that
Jonathan would not be called to a large parish where he would
again attempt to impose his half-Christ, glorious and unperturbed, upon human beings who needed her whole Christ.

Sarah had rebuilt her foundation and had overcome the crack.
Jonathan applied a heavy coat of whitewash and plaster to the
crack in his own system. Sarah knew the repair job would last if
somehow Jonathan could be largely confined to his study, his
books, and his writing. The call to the Stockbridge Indian mission was God's perfect answer. Dwight and Mather argued that
it was an insult and beneath his dignity. Sarah knew better. In a
hundred little ways she pushed Jonathan to accept it, and things
went reasonably well for them among the Indians.

Sarah never revealed her vision to Jonathan. She made no
effort to introduce Jonathan to her Christ. She knew that his
Christ fitted his iron-willed personality and worked for him. She

knew that his Christ grew directly out of his understanding of God's glory and sovereignty. On that theme he would write four major treatises at Stockbridge. They would, at least, help and strengthen her man. They could not help Sarah, Joseph Hawley, Seth Pomeroy, and the other people at Northampton.

COMMENTARY

The Cameo portrait of Jonathan Edwards (1703—1758) shows him to have been a complex person. His style of pastoral leadership was also complex. In part it was clearly shaped by the influence of Richard Baxter. But it was also shaped by certain conditions in colonial America, and by the personality of the man himself. This seems to be the usual pattern in the formation of pastoral styles. The Edwards Cameo provides an opportunity to explore the way in which theological convictions function against these three other factors.

Edwards based his system of theology and pastoral care on two foundation stones: the first he called "experimental piety" and the second was the sovereignty of God. Edwards defined clearly what he meant by "experimental [or as he also called it "experiential" or "experienced" or even "felt"] piety." That phrase described the emotions that filled the hearts and minds of converted Christians as they thought about God's sovereign glory and grace. Edwards described experimental piety as the vigorous operation of the converted mind in enjoying the contemplation of God's glory and grace after turning from sin. Experimental piety meant to experience God's presence in one's life in an almost physical way so that the person was transformed and filled with unspeakable joy. Edwards himself was often moved to tears as he meditated upon God's goodness. The aim of theology and of pastoral care was to enable people to be filled with experimental piety.

The second foundation of Edwards's system was the sovereign glory and grace of God. In this respect, he followed the Calvinist tradition. He believed that God manifested his sovereignty by controlling all things through the operation of his will. He believed that God sustained all things and kept all things in a descending ladder of spirituality and importance. In government, this meant that the magistrate had the highest rung on the ladder and was entitled to respect and obedience from all below. In the church this meant respect for the pastor, and in the family serious respect for and obedience to parents. In this Edwards followed Baxter's teachings to the letter. God maintained this hierarchy of respect and obedience in a loving way: order, harmony, and respect were the chief marks of God's sovereign will at work in the world. Again the goal of theology and of pastoral care was to help people to experience and to enjoy God's sovereign will, regardless of what it might mean for them.

Like Richard Baxter, Jonathan Edwards wrote a great deal about the person and work of Jesus Christ. But despite the multitude of references, his view of Jesus Christ is difficult to analyze and interpret. People who have spent their lives studying his views of Christ will probably not agree with the interpretation presented below.

In his sermons and writings, Edwards said much about Jesus Christ and sang his praises in many lyrical passages. But he sang chiefly about the heavenly, exalted Christ, and said little about the earthly, human Christ. He spoke of the sweet and all-sufficient Christ who was his lion and who fought against all his enemies. This heavenly Christ was his prophet and teacher. According to Edwards, Christ's work consisted primarily of sharing his divine triumphs and glory with his followers. Christ bestowed salvation upon us out of the infinite riches of glory and power that were Christ's as a member of the holy trinity.

He said very little about Christ's suffering and death. Christ's human mind and body play a secondary role in Edwards's entire system. Christ's suffering and death were not central. It can be observed that Edwards's view of Christ reflects the emphasis of St. John, who stresses his divine nature, rather than the emphasis of Matthew and Mark, who stress his humanity and his suffering and death.

At times Edwards sounds almost like a Docetist. This term

describes one who believes that Jesus Christ only seemed (Greek: *dokein*, to seem, to appear) to be a human being, while in reality he was not. The church has always rejected this view as heretical, and yet it seems that the great majority of Christians find a Docetic view of Christ's person more comfortable than a view that takes seriously his humanity. Edwards's semi-Docetic view of Jesus Christ colored every other aspect of his theology and his pastoral care.

Christ's chief work, then, is not to suffer and die for sinners, but rather to create in the repentant sinner the perfect Christian virtues. Edwards calls these virtues by such Pauline names as righteousness, meekness, joy, and faith. But more commonly he speaks of one fundamental virtue that enables the Christian to see things as they really are. From their new perspective, Christians see that "the essence of beauty consisted in order and agreement." Further, from this new perspective, the Christian understands that it is God's purpose to preserve this beauty of order and agreement and that the Christian is to be God's agent in preserving it. Thus his view of Christ's work as the bestower of this new virtue supported his views of church, society, and family, that were basically hierarchical and authoritarian. Of course, Edwards was convinced that his views were Biblically correct, and he was unable to realize that the new views of society that were emerging in Northampton had doomed the old Puritan order.

Edwards's stress on experimental piety led him to place a great deal of emphasis upon the work of the Holy Spirit. Here, too, he follows the lead of Richard Baxter. One scholar has gone so far as to suggest that the Holy Spirit is really at the center of Edwards's faith, rather than Jesus Christ. In 1734 Edwards preached an important sermon at Northampton, arguing that only one who had been illuminated by "a divine and supernatural light" could think the thoughts of God. He defined this divine and supernatural light as almost equivalent to experimental piety. He maintained this point in order to rule out from the Christian commonwealth those Christians who had not had a personal experience of conversion. At the same time, the person who had experienced the divine and supernatural light understood God's word and will perfectly. Because Edwards had had this experience, he considered himself to be the authoritative interpreter of God's word among the people of God at Northampton. The Holy Spirit's work, according to Edwards, consists in dwelling in the Christian and uniting completely with all the faculties of the Christian soul. The bestowal of the Spirit is a life-changing experience for individuals and should turn them into dynamos of Christian energy.

In keeping with his thoughts on experimental piety, Edwards believed that the conversion experience could be dated and related by the person who had had it. In his writings he described two conversion experiences in his own life, and thought that the earlier one, which did not last, was really the better one. Puritan and revival preachers had worked out detailed manuals on the psychology of conversion so that people would know how to assist the Spirit and would know beyond doubt when they themselves had been converted. The process began with an experience of terror and despair at the presence of sin in one's life and proceeded from there in clear stages. It reached its climax when the individual experienced the intense and transforming glory of the "king, eternal, immortal, invisible, the only wise God."

How do you understand the work of Jesus Christ? What role does emotion play in your Christian life? How do you understand the process of conversion?

According to Edwards, the converted Christian was ready to sign a public covenant of commitment with the gracious God. In the mild form of the covenant that Edwards designed at Northampton, covenanters publicly pledged full obedience to God and committed themselves to walk in the ways of his commandments. Edwards believed that this public pledge would restore and maintain the high standards of discipline that had existed in Puritan congregations a century earlier.

Apparently he had forgotten the history of covenant theology in New England. While it contributed significantly to the first glorious days of the Puritan experiment, it soon became a cause of strife and eventually was generally rejected. In an attempt to solve the covenant principle, a Half-Way Covenant was developed as a substitute. In this covenant, the "unconverted" spouses, that is, those who could not date and relate their conversions, and the children of "mixed marriages," could nevertheless be members of the congregation and even share in the sacraments. Eventually, even the Half-Way Covenant gave way to Solomon Stoddard's insistence that all interested people should be invited to share in the sacraments. Stoddard even described the Lord's Supper as a means for converting people. In view of the history of the covenant theology, it is difficult to understand Edwards's decision to reinstitute it.

Although Edwards never said much in a systematic fashion about the doctrine of the church, he had clear and firm ideas about Christian fellowship at the local level and about the mission of God's people. He viewed the local congregation as a voluntary association of people, and he does not seem to have believed that the Northampton parish had been brought into one body by the activity of God's Holy Spirit. This latter view can be called the sacramental view of the nature of the local congregation. The word "voluntary" is used to cover the principle that a local congregation comes into being because a number of men and women gather together and decide to establish a Christian congregation. Those who hold to the voluntary principle may tend to think that they own the congregation and that the pastor is their employee. They may believe that they can hire pastors today and fire them tomorrow. Those who subscribe to the sacramental view tend to think of the congregation as the body of Christ, belonging to God himself, and of their minister as God's servant and the dispenser of God's grace.

In Edwards's day the great majority of American Christians thought of their fellowship as voluntary. For example, the Brattle Street Church was organized in Boston in 1700 on a clearly defined voluntary basis. They described themselves as "a society of Christians by mutual agreement." This statement leaves little room for the work of the Holy Spirit in creating their fellowship. However, as has been pointed out, Puritans like Jonathan Edwards said a great deal about the work of the Holy Spirit in creating faith in each individual's heart. Or to put the matter in other words, Jonathan Edwards and most of his contemporaries thought of faith as having only a vertical dimension that linked them to God, and did not understand that faith also had a horizontal dimension that linked them with their fellow believers.

Edwards's view of Christ's person and work would mesh with and support this understanding of the church. Since the body of Christ was not important to Edwards, it is not surprising that he says little or nothing about the church as the body of Christ. Because he saw the work of Christ consisting largely in the creation of Christian virtues in the mind of the individual, his view of the church also remained largely individual. In the church, the individuals volunteered to sign a covenant, and thus identified themselves as members of the church.

Can you reflect on your own understanding of church membership by using the adjectives "voluntary" or "sacramental"? Which point of view probably best characterizes the majority of the members of your parish? Do you see strengths and weaknesses in each view?

Edwards's understanding of God, of Christ, of the Holy Spirit, and of faith combined to support his definition of the Christian mission. As he saw it, the mission of God's people was to establish the kingdom of God on earth beginning at Northampton in his own lifetime. The first Puritan settlers in the New World had thus defined their mission, but as time went by this vision faded. These early Puritans and Edwards shared a clear understanding of God's kingdom, which had both internal and external dimensions. According to its internal nature, the kingdom was the vigorous activity of the Spirit in the mind and heart of the individual. This activity was marked by a feeling of terror over against one's sins and a glorious experience of the indwelling grace and love of God. Furthermore, the kingdom brought the virtues of Christ into the person's life, especially that fundamental virtue of seeing all of life from the proper Christian perspective. The presence of the kingdom also meant that the individual could exercise strong and almost complete control over thoughts and actions. It enabled the individual to walk perfectly in the ways of God's commands.

According to its external nature, the kingdom would bring a society marked by perfect order and agreement. This, it will be recalled, was Edwards's definition of true beauty. Each member of the community would occupy a proper place and perform proper duties. Each would be respectful of superiors and submissive to them. No one would step out of line or rebel. The structure of society would be pyramidal in shape. At the apex would be the Christian pastor and the political officers of the community. The kingdom was aristocratic in nature and exclusive in membership. It would include only the truly converted, those who had a datable and relatable conversion, and who had signed the covenant giving God first place in their lives. In the kingdom, the members would care for the poor and needy in the community, even for those who were not members of the church. As a matter of fact, charity would be a central part of their duty. In his own lifetime, Edwards and his wife performed a great deal of Christian charity as one way of bringing about God's kingdom. But more important than charity would be the evangelistic program of the parish. The coming of the kingdom meant that only a little time remained before Christ's second coming. That time needed to be spent in mission work and in bringing in a great harvest of souls. As the Cameo reported, this kind of great awakening spread across New England twice in Edwards's ministry, beginning at Northampton. It is not surprising that he saw in all these things clear signs that the kingdom was indeed breaking in.

The expectation of the kingdom was not nearly as strong in the hearts and minds of Edwards's people as it was in his own mind. They and their fathers had waited in vain and their hope and enthusiasm had grown faint. However, they had been trained in the Puritan theology and knew their hopes should be centered in the kingdom and as a result they had guilty consciences about their own attitude and their own lack of expectation. Thus it is understandable that when Edwards talked kingdom language the members responded either with enthusiasm or with antagonism because of their guilty consciences. But Edwards was completely unaware of the psychological tensions that kingdom talk stirred up in his hearers. Instead, he pushed it with all his force and energy and achieved certain superficial signs of its arrival.

How do the people of your parish define their mission? Does the idea of God's kingdom play a role in your definition of mission?

Edwards's conception that Christ was bringing perfect order and agreement also affected his view of ministerial authority. To a far greater degree than Richard Baxter, Edwards thought of himself as the parish father who carried all the responsibility for the spiritual welfare and earthly conduct of his people. He was obligated by his office to meddle (he used the word himself) in the private lives of his people. The fact that he suffered dire consequences from this "meddling" did not change his paternalistic view of the ministry. As the Cameo indicated, he also believed that pastors by virtue of their calling had to maintain an aristocratic and privileged standing in the community so that they could play their fatherly role with greatest effectiveness. Edwards's view on ministerial authority is not utterly different from Ambrose's thought of the two-compartment or two-tier church.

However, his high view of ministerial authority rested on an insecure foundation because of his conviction that the church was essentially voluntary with respect to members. Edwards believed that the people of the parish had called him and thus had the right to depose him. This he never questioned. In effect he accepted a political view of ministerial authority. The body politic, the congregation, had bestowed on him his powers and they in turn could take them away.

There seems to have been no place in Edwards's system for the idea that he was in some sense called by God to the congregation. This view of ministry is often found in those who hold sacramental views of the nature of church membership. It provides the pastor with a measure of independent authority among the people of God.

Although Edwards felt his authority was essentially political in character, there was a "semi-sacramental" dimension to it. That dimension derived from the authority and power with which Edwards expounded the word of God and brought it to bear on his people's needs. His preaching activity gave him considerable power and influence in the community. Many of the people believed that God spoke to them through him. But this preaching authority, in turn, rested on the degree to which people were prepared to accept his preaching. If his ideas no longer suited the people, whether the reasons were proper or improper, then his preaching authority would rapidly disintegrate. The Cameo suggests that this is indeed what happened at Northampton.

The Cameo shows that two other factors influenced Edwards's thought about pastoral authority. The first was his own nature. By birth he was an aristocrat, and so was Sarah. He possessed a strong and formidable will and a powerful intellect. Some scholars believe that his mind was among the six best that the United States has thus far developed! Apparently he expected that others had or could develop the same kind of will. He was a ruthless self-disciplinarian, a true "workaholic." One psychologist suggests that his relationship with his own father was never fully resolved into a happy one and that Edwards may have compensated for this by loving, adoring, serving, and worshiping his heavenly father who was in no way a potential rival to the earthly father he had trouble liking. Because, the argument goes on, Edwards was unable to give loyalty and obedience to his earthly father, he gave it without reservation to his heavenly father.

Furthermore, it seems that Edwards lent his conception of ministerial authority to a political cause. Cotton and Mather viewed Puritanism as a useful political position to protect them against the new democratic spirit. All three men undoubtedly believed that it was God's will that aristocractic Puritanism survive in the Valley, but, however sincerely, Edwards surrendered the freedom and independence of the gospel to a political cause. This surrender alienated many of the members of his parish.

One aspect of Edwards's thought remains for consideration and that is his view concerning human nature and sin. In a fictionalized way, his views were evaluated through the eyes of Sarah and were found to be seriously inadequate. The power of his own will apparently enabled him to keep sin under control, and he seems to have assumed that others could do likewise. Further-more, his emphasis on Jesus Christ's deity led him to pay little attention to the question of human will and human weakness. Despite all his talk about the terribleness of sins, Edwards's view of humanity really did not go down all the way to understand the terrible power of sin. His limited view of human nature permitted him to remain comfortable with the "half-Christ" that he preached. Because he had developed a carefully expressed and logical system of theology, even his study of St. Paul and *his* views of sin could not correct this weakness. His system was so strong that it permitted him to find in Scripture only what was in agree-ment with his system.

Because he had no deep understanding of sin as lust for selfish satisfaction and rebellion against God, he did not need to preach Jesus Christ as the one who, destroyed by sin, rose again and by his rising broke sin's power. In effect Edwards urged the people to overcome sin in their lives by their own efforts, with some help from the Holy Spirit. The Cameo suggests that the people of Northampton failed in this effort.

In the light of what has been said about Edwards's authoritar-ian paternalism, it is not surprising that the five basic functions of the Christian parish were not balanced at Northampton. As a matter of fact, some of them seem to have been absent. The worship action was present, and apparently adequately effective. The fellowship function seems not to have had any relationship to the church and religious life, although this is a difficult judg-ment to make. It is difficult to make because in Northampton community fellowship was always carried on among the same people who were members of the church. The witness action was, at best, limited because there were few if any non-Christians in the Valley. Of course, there were many who by Edwards's stan-dards were not to be considered Christians, but there is no evi-dence concerning the witnessing that was done for their spiritual benefit. Surviving evidence does not make possible any careful judgments about the kind of service that went on. As the Com-mentary says, Edwards considered the practice of charity to be central to the kingdom program, and so it may have been relatively active. The greatest persistent imbalance existed in the area of Christian nurture, largely because of Edwards's views about his own role. Nurture was the pastor's responsibility, and was carried on chiefly through sermons and instruction. Presumably some nurture was effected in family devotions, but there is no evidence to indicate a consistent program of mutual nurture and edification. Furthermore, the sacraments were of rather limited importance in the nurturing program in Northampton. So much of it centered in the pastor and the spoken word.

This analysis of the theology and practice of Jonathan Edwards serves to underscore an important aspect of parish life. It illustrates that theology, or if you prefer, your beliefs about God and salvation and yourselves, is finally what makes the parish go around. Or, at least, it says that theology should be what shapes your parish life and should also be the source of power for Christian living. If this is indeed true for your parish, it follows that a delicate balance needs to be maintained among the various ideas in your theological system. Edwards's system can be likened to a carefully constructed clock. If one part is working improperly or has been bent out of shape, the entire machine will be affected for the worse. So it also seems to be with parish theology. If one theological principle is wrongly or inadequately understood and/or implemented, the complete program of the parish suffers.

Is the theology of your parish written down somewhere? How can you maintain the necessary delicate balance among the various parts of your theological system?

9.
Francis Asbury

CAMEO AND COMMENTARY

Francis Asbury (1745—1816) established in the United States a unique vision of the church's mission and of the pastoral office. His life and his theology are so inseparably intertwined that the story of his contributions can be best told in his own words which are found in his journal and letters. In the following excerpts, the focus will be on four aspects of Asbury's work: the experience of conversion and the pursuit of holiness, the role of the Methodist Society in the church's life, his understanding of the mission of the church, and the place and work of the minister in the church.

Asbury's understanding of mission and ministry was deeply shaped by his own conversion experience, which he describes in the following words.

> The next year Mr. Mather [one of John Wesley's itinerant preachers] came into those parts [his home in England]. I was then about fifteen; and, young as I was, the word of God soon made deep impressions on my heart, which brought me to Jesus Christ, who graciously justified my guilty soul through faith in his precious blood; and soon showed me the excellency and necessity of holiness. [Francis Asbury, *The Journal*, ed. Elmer Clark, in *The Journals and Letters of Francis Asbury*, 3 vols. (Nashville: Abingdon, 1958), entry for July 26, 1774, I:124–125]

Following his conversion, he felt a strong call to preach which superseded all his other natural obligations. He wrote to his parents in defense of his actions.

> Let others condemn me, as being without natural affection, as being stubborn, disobedient to parents, or say what they please. It does not alter the case, for it is a small matter with me to be judged of man. I love my parents and friends but I love my God better and his service, because it is perfect freedom, and he does not send me away at my own cost, for he gives me to prove, as my day is, my strength is, and it my meat and drink is to do his will. And tho I have given up all I do not repent, for I have found all. [Francis Asbury, *The Letters,* ed. J. Manning Potts, in *The Journals and Letters of Francis Asbury,* 3 vols., letter of October 26, 1768, III:4]

During his career in the United States, Asbury kept a detailed journal in which he recorded his adventures and his inmost personal thoughts. This journal provides a character sketch both of the man and of eighteenth- and nineteenth-century American Methodism, for that was largely his long shadow. In the preface, he gives a brief description of his own spirit and of his career.

> As I have had no certain dwelling-place in America, my manuscripts have frequently been exposed to be lost and destroyed; but, by the permission of Divine Providence, I have collected them together. . . . And as I have been (under God and my Brethren) the principal overseer of the work in America, and have constantly travelled from the centre of the circumference of the Connexion, I flatter myself that reasonable men will acknowledge that I have always had an opportunity of obtaining better information relative to the true state of the whole work than any other man could possibly have. . . . I have attempted to give a simple narration of facts in the integrity of my heart, and in the fear of God. [Asbury, *The Journal,* I:xx–xxi]

From the time he first set foot on American soil, Asbury became an enthusiastic and committed American. Unlike many of his contemporaries in the clergy, he cut his ties with England and opened himself to American influences. One evident result of this openness was that Asbury and his followers understood the spirit of the new country and so were able to function as friends and supporters of it rather than as strangers come to judge or deliver. A second result was that Asbury and his followers were able to develop structures and customs that were uniquely American from the beginning and well suited to the highly mobile people of America. In general, Asbury's lifetime was a period of bubbling optimism, for the frontier seemed to offer a golden future to everyone. People did not want to be burdened by the dreary Puritan emphasis on original sin and human helplessness. On the frontier, people needed to believe in their own ability and power. This was also a time of social mobility and therefore people cherished any experience that would give them at least a temporary sense of belonging to something. In a rich and satisfying degree, the Methodist Society provided this experience of belonging.

Many of Asbury's contemporaries were strongly influenced by the Romantic spirit that was coming to America from Europe and that was influencing all forms of art, life-style, and politics. The Romantics, in general, were in revolt against the established social order and established religion—against established values of any sort. In place of tradition, they craved deep emotional experiences, real or imaginary, provided they were sufficiently intense. Methodist preachers stressed the highly emotional experiences of conversion and the gift of holiness. Asbury's journal is filled with references to tears and weeping on his part and on the part of his people. Furthermore, the Romantics wanted to return to nature and that was again where the Methodists were strongest. The Methodists often found the city hostile to their message, and they followed the Romantics to nature, to the wilderness. The Romantics wanted to return to the values and traditions of the past Golden Age. The Methodists tuned into this desire with their emphasis on a return to the values and organization of simple New Testament Christianity. (This description of Romanticism is taken from H. W. Janson, *History of Art* [Englewood Cliffs, N. J.: Prentice-Hall; and New York: Harry N. Abrams, 1969], pp. 453ff.)

At the center of Asbury's life was his own conversion and the subsequent spiritual gift of holiness. He had learned these things from John Wesley, the founder of English Methodism. John Wesley, in turn, had been strongly influenced by Jonathan Edwards's sermons and tracts on the importance of the individual's conversion experience. Wesley's own spiritual life began with his well-known experience of conversion in the chapel at Aldersgate in

London. The followers of Wesley believed that their own life began with such an experience that could be "dated and related," exactly as Jonathan Edwards had taught. Asbury's journal and the writings of other Methodists are filled with detailed accounts of their own conversion and the desired gift of holiness or perfection. To understand Methodism, including its approach to mission and to pastoral care, one must understand the nature of conversion and the gift of holiness.

A detailed description of the experience of the new birth is found in the writings of Philip Gatch, a contemporary of Asbury. Gatch reports that he was on the verge of despairing because he had not received the gift of holiness when

> the Spirit of the Lord came down upon me, and the opening heavens shone around me. By faith I saw Jesus at the right hand of the Father. I felt such a weight of glory that I fell with my face to the floor, and the Lord said by his Spirit, "You are now sanctified, seek to grow in the fruit of the Spirit." . . . This work and the instruction of Divine truth were sealed on my soul by the Holy Ghost. My joy was full. I related to others what God had done for me. This was in July, a little more than two months after I had received the Spirit of justification. [Cited in Emory Stevens Bucke, ed., *The History of American Methodism* (New York: Abingdon, 1964), vol. 1, p. 303]

William Thatcher, a Methodist storekeeper, had a full experience of holiness in the spring of 1793. In his diary he first confesses the deep sense of his own sinfulness, and then describes the gift of holiness.

> O what a view of the fullness of Christ I then had! The all-sufficiency of the infinite merits of our Savior was then spread before me; my soul was all imprisoned by his love; my unbelief gave way; faith grasped the prize! The witness of full sanctification was given, O astonishing love Divine! Redeeming love! Glory be to God, I now know that the blood of Jesus Christ cleanseth from all sin. . . . Humbled in the dust, my heart could say, "To me, who am less than the least of all saints is this grace given." [Cited in *The History of American Methodism,* vol. 1, p. 304]

The experience of sanctification or holiness or perfection did not mean that the believer became perfect and was delivered from all problems and the power of Satan. That kind of perfection would have to wait for judgment day. But sanctification was a transforming experience of the depth and sufficiency of God's love. This description is identical with the descriptions that are found in the diary of Jonathan Edwards. Twice-born persons had experienced God's indwelling love in Christ to such a degree that they could almost always match that experience of love against all the doubts and temptations that assailed them. This experience of God's love was radical, and its consequences in the life of the individual Christian were radical. The experience of holiness provided the chief dynamic for the exemplary life-style of the Methodists. In simple language, the stress on holiness made a difference; lives were radically changed.

Some of the deep ecstasy and anguish that characterized a person who had received the second birth is reflected in passages from Asbury's journal and letters.

> Since I have been ranging through Virginia, toward the Alleghany [sic], and Maryland, Pennsylvania and East and West Jerseys, and the Peninsula, I enjoy more health than I have for twenty years back. I travel 4,000 miles in a year, all weathers, among rich and poor, Dutch and English. O my dear Shadford, it would take a month to write out and speak what I want you to know. The most momentous is my constant communion with God as *my* God; my GLORIOUS victory over the world and the devil. I am continually with God. I preach frequently, and with more enlargement of heart than ever. [*The Letters,* letter of August 1783, III:29]

But he also had times when his experience of holiness was weak. On October 28, 1774, he wrote: "I do not sufficiently love God, nor live by faith in the suburbs of heaven." (*The Journal,* I:136) And on August 19, 1775, he wrote:

> My body is weak; but this does not concern me like the want of more grace. My heart is too cool towards God: I want to feel it like a holy flame. [*The Journal,* I:162]

And on March 2, 1796, he wrote:

> For my unholiness and unfaithfulness, my soul is humbled:
> were I to stand on my own merit, where should I be or go,
> but to hell? [*The Journal*, II:79]

In his pursuit of holiness, Asbury watched his every thought
and emotion. His extremely sensitive conscience is revealed in
journal entries like this: "I felt some conviction [of sin] for sleeping too long." (*The Journal*, entry for August 15, 1774, I:128) Or
again: "Unguarded and trifling conversation has brought on a
degree of spiritual deadness." (*The Journal*, entry for November
18, 1774, I:138) And on February 1, 1779, he wrote:

> My conscience smote me severely for speaking an idle word
> in company. O! how frail is man. It is very difficult for me to
> check my rapid flow of spirits when in company with my
> friends. [*The Journal*, I:295]

But his more usual mood is reflected in the entry for Monday,
January 20, 1806: "I have been greatly afflicted with cold, but
exceedingly happy in God—I live in love." (*The Journal*, II:494)

The importance that he ascribed to this doctrine of holiness
is clearly indicated in a journal entry for March 7, 1803:

> I find the *way of holiness* very narrow to walk in or to preach;
> and although I do not consider *sanctification—Christian perfec-
> tion*, commonplace subjects, yet I make them the burden,
> and labour to make them the savour of every sermon. [*The
> Journal*, II:383]

*How necessary do you think it is that a person can "date and
relate" his or her conversion experience? Have you experienced the
gift of sanctification (or holiness or perfection)? How do your answers
to either of these questions affect the way in which you go about your
mission?*

The doctrine of holiness made enormous demands on the
total life of the Methodist. And, therefore, the practice of holiness
could be carried on only in an effective small support group. It
was the genius of American Methodism that these support
groups, called either Society (the larger circle) or Class (the

smaller, more elite group), were the central organizational structure of the movement.

Billy Hibbard, another contemporary of Asbury, provides a
classic description of the effectiveness of the Society in his *Memoirs.*

> I went to the Methodist meeting, seven miles off. The first
> I had been at for eight months. The meeting had begun
> when I came in. On seeing my old Methodist friends, I was
> exceedingly affected; tears ran down all the time of meeting;
> and after preaching, I stayed in class, and a most melting,
> loving time we had. The preacher at the close of the meeting,
> asked if anyone desired to join the class. I arose and said, "I
> feel myself unworthy to be a member of any church, but I
> believe the Lord has blessed me, and if the brethren think
> it is proper, I wish to be a member." They accepted of me,
> and I was very happy in God and with my brethren. [Cited
> in *The History of American Methodism,* vol. 1, p. 310]

Even more dramatic was the impact of the Society or Class
experience on Hibbard's wife. She was not a churchgoer, and one
evening as Billy was preparing to go to a prayer meeting,

> as my wife had so repeatedly said that she would not be a
> Methodist, or go with me to my meetings, I said nothing to
> her. But now she said, I have a mind to go along with you,
> if you will carry the child. I said, "O yes." So for the first
> time, she went with me to a prayer meeting. After we re-
> turned home, and I was kindling a fire she sat holding the
> child, I said, "how did you like the meeting?" She said noth-
> ing, I blowed up the coals, and got the fire blazing: then I
> asked her again . . . and turning to her I saw tears running
> down her face. Seeing this, I renewed my question in a softer
> tone. She answered, *"O how they love one another, I never saw
> such love in all my life."* I said, "my dear, that is our religion."
> "Well, I believe it is a good religion," said she. [Cited in *The
> History of American Methodism,* vol. 1, p. 308]

Ezekiel Cooper, who became an influential Methodist
preacher, stressed the importance of the Society in equally strong
terms.

> O how I needed the help arising from Christian communion!
> But I had it not. I resolved to form acquaintance with the

> Methodists, and to join [the] society . . . ; to open my mind
> to them, hoping to be fully satisfied, yea or nay, when I heard
> their experience of the work of grace upon their souls. [Cited
> in *The History of American Methodism,* vol. 1, p. 308]

Asbury explained the function of the Society in a letter he
wrote in July 1790 to a Quaker friend, encouraging him to begin
the Class system.

> Would it not be well to have a congregation and a Society
> —an outward and an inward court? In the former let children
> and servants, and unawakened people come; in the inward
> let mourners in Zion come. . . . If this inward court or Society
> were divided into small bands or classes, and to be called
> together weekly by men and women of the deepest experi-
> ence, and appointed for that work, and asked about their
> souls and the dealings of God with them, and to join in
> prayer, one or two or all of them that have freedom, I think
> the Lord would come upon them. [*The Letters,* III:86]

Thus the Societies were distinct from congregations and
maintained a separate existence. It may be that this separation
from the congregation proved to be a liability more than an asset
to the entire movement. The separation could and sometimes did
create in the minds of the Society people the idea that they were
somehow better Christians. Occasionally tension and jealousy
would develop between those who were members only of the
congregation and those who were members of the Society.

However, the general contribution of the Societies was
strongly positive. In those groups, the members engaged in Bible
study together, hymn singing, prayer, and mutual counsel and
forgiveness. Here they found the encouragement they needed to
pursue holiness; here they offered their strength to others to help
them walk that way. Here they found the strength in fellowship
to stand together against an often hostile and threatening world.
The practice of holiness probably would have been unthinkable
apart from the Societies, and the Societies fill no real need or
make little sense apart from that central doctrine.

In many ways, the structure and the spirit of the Methodist
Society remind one of the structure and the spirit of the early

Christian communities. One must avoid the temptation to romanticize either the Society or the early Christian communities, but there does seem to be a persistent connection between individual and personal Christian vitality and the size of the group.

Have you participated in an experience similar to the Methodist Society? Do you think that there would be a useful place for that kind of experience within the structure of your congregation?

The Societies selected their leaders, men and women, from within the group. These leaders had proven themselves to the members to be understanding, reliable, and spiritual people. In many cases, the male leaders of Societies or Classes frequently became circuit riders. Thus many Methodist clergy were selected by the people, who in turn believed themselves to be guided and inspired by the Holy Spirit to make that choice. The clergy had proven themselves to be people of the Spirit before they were certified for the public ministry.

Though the American Methodists were intensely democratic in their structure and philosophy, they nevertheless had a high regard for the ministerial office. This was in large measure the legacy of John Wesley. Wesley had been trained as an Anglican clergyman, and in all of his writings throughout his life he preserved a deep understanding of the importance of the pastoral office and a high respect for it.

But the respect accorded to clergy in the Methodist Connexion seems to have been of a different character from the respect given Anglican, Episcopalian, or Roman Catholic clergy. In the latter cases, the people are often taught to respect the clergy because of the office they hold. In Methodism the emphasis is upon respect for the clergy because of the work they do. The ideal attitude of respect seems to exist when these two can be blended. But the history of the pastoral office indicates how difficult it is to maintain this blend, particularly as the congregations become rather large. In every case, it is true that the pastor is the hinge, the person who is the successor to Jesus Christ in a unique way and who provides to the congregation an example of Jesus Christ to be imitated. As indicated in earlier chapters, the problem of respect and authority arises when the pastor is not only hinge, but also chief administrator and ruler in the congregation. Then the hinge function seems to become more difficult and a ruling administrative function becomes more important. It seems that in the small Methodist Societies and in their small frontier congregations this administrative development was frequently not present.

Asbury had his own peculiar way to retard the development of an improper attitude toward the pastoral office. He did this by insisting that the Methodist ministry be mobile and that no pastor remain for long with any established group. He believed that a stationary or localized ministry would quickly become soft and self-serving, would lose its concern for the universal church, and would substitute for that a paternalistic care for the needs of the local group. In his journal for November 19 and 21, 1771 he wrote these words during his first winter in North America:

> *Tuesday,* 19. I remain in New York, though unsatisfied with our being both in town together [another minister named Pilmoor was also in New York]. I have not yet the thing which I seek—a circulation of preachers, to avoid partiality and popularity. However, I am fixed to the Methodist plan, and do what I do faithfully as to God. I expect trouble is at hand. This I expected when I left England, and I am willing to suffer, yea, to die, sooner than betray so good a cause by any means. [*The Journal,* I:10]

> *Thursday,* 21. My brethren seem unwilling to leave the cities, but I think I shall show them the way. I am in trouble, and more trouble is at hand, for I am determined to make a stand against all partiality. . . . I am come over with an upright intention, and through the grace of God I will make it appear. [*The Journal,* I:10]

Asbury translated this idea into his own life, and to his dying day, literally, Asbury refused to locate in a fixed spot, but continued as a circuit rider. Throughout his life, he accepted localized clergy only with reluctance and, although he granted that this was a legitimate form of ministry, he always considered it non-apostolic and secondary in value. The early Books of Discipline reflect this same attitude. Asbury believed that the apostolic ministry had been a circulating ministry and, therefore, in the spirit of the Romantic age, believed that that form should be reestablished for his time. But Asbury supported the circuit-riding ministry for another very good reason: it provided a mobile ministry to keep up with a mobile population. The circuit rider was the key to the Christianization of the western United States and was in large measure responsible for making the nineteenth century in America a Christian century. Circuit riders rank with the greatest Christian heroes of all ages. Often they were the only link with civilization, the only source of outside news, the only people of any educational achievement that a frontier family would see for months at a time. The most moving paragraphs in Asbury's journals are the reports that he gives concerning his own circuit-riding schedule. A few samples follow.

Saturday, April 1. [1786] Rode through the rain twenty-four miles to the Widow Bedford's, where but a few, besides the Society, came. I met the married men and women apart, and there were tenderness and tears, greatly felt, and copiously shed, among them. [*The Journal,* I:511]

Monday, [January] 20. [1794] I reached the city of Charleston. Here I began to rest: my cold grew better. . . . The kindness of sister Hughes was very great. I have ridden largely to the West, . . . and [the] great rains, swimming the creeks and rivers, riding in the night, sleeping on the earthen floors, more or less of which I must experience, if I go to the Western country, might at this time cost me life. I have only been able to preach four times in three weeks. [*The Journal,* II:4]

Sunday, [March] 4. [1810] I held forth to about one thousand attentive souls in Weems's chapel on "the great salvation." I lodged with David Weems: his wife is in glory, his daughters in the Church, and his sons in the world. On *Monday* we rode fourteen miles through damps and thick woods to Samuel Maccubbin's. I was done over. I blistered for a severe inflammation in the face. *Tuesday morning,* sick and suffering, I rode sixteen miles and filled an appointment at Bicknell's chapel. I hasted on to Baltimore on *Wednesday. Thursday,* very sick: I need bleeding and medicine. I was scarcely able to sit

in conference on *Friday.* Day of fasting and humiliation to all
the members. *Saturday,* busy. [*The Journal,* II:631]

Frontier people, sometimes against their will, came to believe
that the circuit riders had a special nose for locating people.
Richmond Nolley, a circuit rider, reported a conversation he had
with a new settler in the Mississippi territory. Nolley had found
the man by following a fresh wagon track!

> What! Have you found me already? Another Methodist
> preacher! I left Virginia to get out of reach of them, went to
> a new settlement in Georgia, and thought to have a long
> whet, but they got my wife and daughter into the Church;
> then, in this late purchase (Choctaw Corner), I found a piece
> of good land, and was sure I would have some peace of the
> preachers, and here is one before my wagon is unloaded.
> [Cited in *The History of American Methodism,* vol. 1, p. 502]

Inspired by Asbury's own example, the circuit riders themselves offered examples of self-discipline and self-sacrifice to
Methodist Christians throughout the west. The minutes of the
1794 conference report on the work of circuit rider Henry Bir-
chett.

> Henry Birchett, from Brunswick county, state of Virginia;
> between five and six years in the ministry:—a gracious,
> happy, useful man, who freely offered himself for four years'
> service on the dangerous stations of Kentucky and Cumber-
> land. He might have returned at the Kentucky Conference,
> 1793, but finding there was a probability of Cumberland
> being vacated by the preachers, notwithstanding the pain in
> his breast, and spitting of blood, the danger of the Indians,
> and prevalency of the small pox, he went a willing martyr,
> after asking the consent of the bishop and the Conference.
> We hoped his life would have been preserved, but report
> saith he departed in peace at Cumberland, on the western
> waters, in February 1974. [Cited in *The History of American
> Methodism,* vol. 1, p. 320]

Another descriptive paragraph is found in the journal of superintendent Thomas Coke.

> Brother *Hawes,* one of our Elders, who last year was sent with
> a preacher to *Kentucke,* on the banks of the *Ohio,* near the

Mississippi, wrote to us a most enlivening account of the prospect in his district, and earnestly implored some further assistance. "But, observe!" added he, "No one must be appointed for this country, that is afraid to die! For there is now war with the Indians, who frequently lurk behind the trees, shoot the travellers, and then scalp them: and we have one Society on the very frontiers of the Indian country." After this letter was read, a blessed young man brother *Williamson* offered himself as a volunteer for this dangerous work. [Cited in *The History of American Methodism,* vol. 1, pp. 387–388]

To help the circuit riders work with maximum efficiency, Asbury instructed them in the art of pastoral care. In the Books of Discipline he provided sermon outlines. He insisted that they visit the members in their homes as much as they could, and in this respect he himself set a good example. In these visits, the preachers inquired after the spiritual health of the individuals and also asked about their progress in Bible reading, praying, and, above all, in holiness or perfection. The circuit rider was also the bookseller on the frontier and the people eagerly spent the few pennies that they had in cash for those items. Bonds of real affection existed between circuit riders and the lonely people they visited, and frequently these ties lasted for many years.

In a letter to Ezekiel Cooper on December 24, 1788, Asbury laid out his understanding of pastoral care.

I wish you to be blessed with health to do your duty. If possible visit from house to house, and that regularly once a fortnight for no other purpose than to speak to each in the family about their souls, that they may be ready for your help. Appoint preaching every other night, if able visit the Classes every other week. Take some one of the poor Negroes and also the children. Remember the sick. The pastoral charge is very great. Whether our circle is large or small we may find work. The Society should be put under bands. I wish something might be done to revive the work in town and keep it in motion; these people I know, I feel, will settle on their lees. Sermons ought to be short and pointed in town, briefly explanatory and then to press the people to conviction, repentance, faith and holiness. [*The Letters,* III:66]

In his journal for May 24, 1795, Asbury describes his own style of pastoral care.

> I spent part of the week in visiting from house to house. I feel happy in speaking to all I find, whether parents, children, or servants; I see no other way; the common means will not do; Baxter, Wesley, and our Form of Discipline, say, "Go into every house": I would go farther, and say, go into every kitchen and shop; address all, aged and young, on the salvation of their souls. [*The Journal*, II:51]

As mentioned several times, there is a close connection between the view Christians have of ministry and their understanding of the church. In both England and the United States, the Methodists did not think of themselves as a church or wish to become one. In England they remained members of the Anglican church for as long as they could. The situation in America was different, because with the coming of the Revolution the Anglican church lost its appeal among most Americans. Thus the American Methodists were forced to establish themselves as a church, against their will.

This action caused two developments that affected the Methodist understanding of the church. The first and less important one was that they were deprived of the use of liturgically oriented church buildings furnished with beautiful symbols of the church's antiquity and grandeur. Instead they worshiped in plain chapels and homes, and were thus deprived of the architectural experience of the meaning of the church. But the separation from the Episcopalian church also drastically altered the role of Methodist ministers and the nature of their authority. They were changed from aloof and slightly mysterious sacramental officers with a college education into mud-spattered and frequently uneducated people who shared the board and frequently the bed of those they served, while also sharing with them the secrets of their own innermost thoughts. Ordination was really not practiced among the Methodists; at least it was not viewed as an awesome act that united the candidate with an ancient priestly succession and bestowed awesome sacramental powers. Instead it was viewed as a form of licensing that was fairly easy to come by.

From the beginning, the Methodist Church was bothered by the absence of ordained clergy. No American preacher, including Asbury, had received ordination from an Anglican bishop. Therefore, according to their understanding of the church, no American could celebrate the sacraments. Before the Revolutionary War, Methodists had been permitted to receive the sacraments in many Episcopalian churches, but after the War this privilege was denied them. However, by that time, Wesley had restudied the practice of ordination in the early church and had become convinced that elders or pastors in the church had the same power to ordain as bishops had. Since he was an ordained elder or pastor, he ordained Asbury and Thomas Coke as superintendents of the American Connexion, with power to ordain others for the full sacramental ministry. After this, almost every major Conference ordained a few brothers to the full ministry, but only after they had given ample evidence of their fitness. The common-sense approach to ordination that Wesley followed is set forth in a letter that he wrote on September 10, 1784 to "Our Brethren in America," with the news that Coke and Asbury had been ordained as superintendents or bishops. Here are parts of Wesley's letter.

2. Lord King's Account of the Primitive Church convinced me many years ago that bishops and presbyters are the same order, and consequently have the same right to ordain. . . .

3. . . . in America there are none [no bishops], neither any parish ministers. So that for some hundred miles together there is none either to baptize or to administer the Lord's supper. Here, therefore, my scruples [about ordaining clergy for America] are at an end; and I conceive myself at full liberty, as I violate no order and invade no man's right by appointing and sending labourers into the harvest. . . .

5. If any one will point out a more rational and scriptural way of feeding and guiding those poor sheep in the wilderness, I will gladly embrace it. At present I cannot see any better method than that I have taken. [Here Wesley reflects the calm and evangelical approach that Richard Baxter took to the practice of ordination in his day.] [*The Letters,* III:38]

Despite the introduction of the practice of ordination, the nature of pastoral authority within the Methodist communion remained different from that usually granted in the Anglican churches. Some of the reasons for this unique development have already been indicated in this chapter. At this point it needs only to be emphasized once more that Methodist elders or pastors derived their authority more from what they did for the people than from what the people had done to them in ordaining them. This is both a good development and a bad development. It is good in that it rightly stresses the pastor's servant role and complete equality with the people. The pastor is one of them, sharing in their strengths and weaknesses and in their joys and sorrows. It is an unhealthy development in that it denies pastors some of the authority that God wants them to have. For example, it makes it difficult for Methodist pastors to say that they have received from God the authority to forgive the sins of their people. In other words, though there is much to be said for the Methodist approach to pastoral authority, it is not the perfect answer to this crucial problem.

All that the Methodists did, whether in the practice of holiness, in the development of the Society, or in the practice of ministry, was intended to help them discharge the mission that God had given them. They knew exactly what this mission was. God had called them to bring salvation to every individual on the continent, and to introduce into this western world the fundamental Christian virtues. The Methodists prosecuted that full mission with enthusiasm and remarkable success.

Asbury himself was possessed by a deep love for the future prospects of a Christian America. In a letter written in August 1783 he expressed this love.

> O America! America! It certainly will be the glory of the world for religion! I have loved, and do love America. I think it became necessary after the fall that Government should lose it [he has in mind the British government and the Declaration of Independence]. Your old national pride, as a people, has got a blow. You must abate a little. O let us haste in peace and love, where we shall know, love, and enjoy God

and each other, and all the differences in Church and State, and among private Christians, will be done away. [*The Letters,* III:29]

The work of the circuit riders in bringing the gospel to every remote cabin and hamlet on the frontier has already been described. One assumes that lay Methodists were engaged in spreading the gospel with that same fervor and determination. Furthermore, the Methodists made effective use of camp meetings in spreading the gospel and in bringing thousands of people under the influence of the Spirit of God. Asbury himself was completely committed to camp meetings as a major part of the Christian mission program. He encouraged his preachers to hold them as often as possible. The phenomena that frequently accompanied camp meeting experiences did not bother Asbury or his fellow leaders. At the same time, contrary to many popular reports of camp meetings, they were disciplined and policed quite closely, and excesses were rather rare.

Richard Whatcoat, one of Wesley's first ordained pastors to come to America, described a camp meeting in the Baltimore area. He observed that some things

> appeared of an extraordinary nature: while many were suddenly struck with convictions, and fell to the ground, roaring out in the disquietude of their spirits, or lay in a state of apparent insensibility, after a while starting up and praising God, as though heaven had come into their souls; others were as much concerned with a clean heart, and as fully delivered. [Cited in *The History of American Methodism,* vol. 1, p. 299]

Thomas Coke, Asbury's associate as superintendent and a reserved Englishman, was at first offended by such outbursts. But as he reflected on their meaning, he changed his mind, and wrote:

> All the shouting seasons, in spite of my proud reluctance to yield to them at first, were a matter of great praise and rejoicing to me very soon: and I shall defend them, both from the pulpit and the press, throughout the European part of our connection. [Cited in *The History of American Methodism,* vol. 1, p. 300]

The Methodists were sustained and driven on by a vision of conquering the continent for Christ. In a letter written from Ireland in 1795, Ezekiel Cooper expressed this hope and outlined the strategy for achieving it.

> . . . (if) Methodist preachers keep close to God they will be the chief instruments of bringing about this most desirable state of things. Let us be a praying, preaching, self-denying, mortified, crucified, zealous set of men . . . and we shall carry the world before us.

The Society contributed immensely to the development of a Christian spirit in American life. The good that was done for individuals in Society meetings is beyond calculation. Regular participation provided a vision, zeal, and courage that enabled the Methodists to be about their mission. For many frontier people, participation in a Society gave them rudimentary experiences in democratic processes, which they then transferred to the secular political world. In the Society, they experienced a unique degree of democratic equality. The poorest had great spiritual gifts to share with the wealthiest, who in turn shared their material possessions with the poor. In the Society many Americans received the only formal education available to them. Through Bible study they learned much about their souls, but they also learned much about ancient times and other people. Here they practiced their speaking and leadership skills. Here they developed the courage to stand against the evils that they saw about them in American life.

Thus Methodist farmers supported the first temperance movements, even though they knew that the success of that movement would cut deeply into their profits because it would increase the cost of transporting grain across the mountains to market. Grain, in the liquid form of alcohol, could be transported much more cheaply than in dry bulk. In like manner, the Methodists fought against cursing, insisted upon proper honor and respect for women, on honest business principles, and extended to every person a second and a third chance. In communities where Methodists predominated, these gospel emphases served to create a life-style that was different and that became an essential part of the American life.

In Society meetings, Methodists learned about God's kingdom and became convinced that it would be finally established in the United States through their efforts (probably in the western parts around Cincinnati). They were convinced, in the tradition of Jonathan Edwards, that America was a great experiment in holy living and they implanted that conviction deep into the lifeblood of America, where it shaped political dreams, rhetoric, and reality, until the Watergate era. The New Deal, the Fair Deal, the New Frontier, and the Great Society are all legitimate offspring of American Methodism.

Is there place or need in American life today for the double-barreled mission strategy of the early Methodists? What in your judgment needs to happen to enable Christians to be about their Father's business as these people were?

This study of Francis Asbury can best be concluded with several longer quotations from entries that he put into his journal and letters toward the end of his long life. On August 5, 1813 he wrote:

> You know, my brother, that the present ministerial cant is that we cannot now, as in former apostolical days, have such doctrines, such discipline, such convictions, such conversions, such witnesses of sanctification, and such holy men. But I say that we can; I say we must; yea, I say we have. And can men claim the rights and privileges of apostles if they are impostors and not true ministers of the holy sanctuary? Instead of going to preach, they stay to preach. . . . Again it may be said, This man speaks well; he is a scholar! But you are mistaken. He has only a common education—a plowman, a tailor, a carpenter, or a shoemaker! Then he must be taught of God, if he is not taught of man. Then we may rationally conclude that learning is not an essential qualification to preach the gospel. It may be said no man but a fool will speak against learning. I have not spoken against learning. I have only said that it cannot be said to be an essential qualification to preach the gospel. [*The Letters*, III:476, 481]

And to the General Conference about the same time he said:

> Be rigidly strict in all things. Examine well those who come
> as candidates for the ministry. It is ours to plead, protest, and
> oppose designing men from getting into the ministry. It is
> the peculiar excellence of our church and the superinten-
> dents' glory and stronghold that the character of every min-
> ister among us must undergo a strict examination once a
> year. Put men into office in whom you can confide. If they
> betray your trust and confidence, let them do it but once. Of
> all wickedness, spiritual wickedness is the greatest; and of all
> deceptions, religious deception is the worst.

Finally, in a letter written to Joseph Benson on January 15,
1816, Asbury described the typical Methodist bishop. Unwit-
tingly, he drew his own portrait and wrote his own epitaph.

> With us a bishop is a plain man, altogether like his brethren,
> wearing no marks of distinction, advanced in age, and by
> virtue of his office can sit as president in all the solemn
> assemblies of the ministers of the gospel; and many times,
> if he is able, called upon to labor and suffer more than any
> of his brethren; no negative or positive in forming church
> rules; raised to a small degree of constituted and elective
> authority above all his brethren; and in the executive depart-
> ment, power to say, "Brother, that must not be, that cannot
> be," having full power to put a negative or a positive in his
> high charge of administration; and even in the Annual Con-
> ference to correct the body or any individual that may have
> transgressed or would transgress and go over the printed
> rules by which they are to be governed, and bring up every
> man and everything to the printed rules of order established
> in the form of Discipline of the Methodist Episcopal Church
> in America.
>   It is an established maxim with us that if a man is not well
> taught and practiced in obedience to know how to serve, he
> will never know how to handle command or be fit to take any
> office in the Church of God, and that stubborn, disobedient
> men must be mended, though it will take much time and
> more labor. [*The Letters,* III:544–545]

10.
Wilhelm Loehe

CAMEO

Wilhelm Loehe (1808—1872) offers an understanding of church, congregation, mission, and pastoral care that seems in many ways to be helpful for present-day American church life. Though he was a convinced conservative Lutheran, his ideas can be studied with profit by members of almost any Christian denomination.

He was born on February 21, 1808, into a middle-class family living in the small town of Fürth, a few miles from Nuremberg, Germany. The Loehe home was marked by the practice of regular churchgoing, family devotions, and the practice of personal piety. Almost from the beginning, Wilhelm Loehe was interested in studying for the Christian ministry. His father opposed the idea on the grounds of cost, but he died when Loehe was eight years old and his mother shared her son's dream. She was a very religious person, praying daily at great length, and consenting to go to communion only after several days of sincere preparation. Concerning his mother's support, Loehe wrote later

> When my father died she did what she thought was right. Her love for the ministry and the church led her, although she was a widow, to let me choose such a life's calling. I owe her a thousand thanks. Who knows whether I would have become a Christian if I had not become a pastor. [Cited in Wilhelm Loehe, *Three Books About the Church,* trans. James L. Schaaf (Philadelphia: Fortress Press, 1969), pp. 2–3]

From the family practices, Loehe developed the habit of regular Bible reading and study. The family patterns also led him to stress practical Christian living. From his mother's arms, he also learned to cherish the conviction that God was gracious to him, a sinner, for the sake of Jesus Christ.

As he moved from school to school, Loehe was fortunate in his teachers. In the high school in Nuremberg he came under the influence of Rector Karl Roth, who kindled in him a love for the old songs and the Lutheran liturgy and involved him in the active life of local circles of particularly pious Christians. At the University of Erlangen, Loehe was strongly influenced by a Reformed theologian, Christian Krafft. Though himself Reformed, Krafft awakened in Loehe a strong conviction concerning the importance of the Lutheran Confessions and the necessity of remaining loyal to them at all times. At the same time, Krafft undergirded Loehe's lifelong interest in Bible study. He drilled into the young man the principle that the Word of God as found in the Bible is the only center of the church's life and the only center for the life of the Christian. Also at Erlangen, Loehe came under the influence of G. F. A. Strauss, who further developed his ardor for the Confessions and also alerted him to the dangers of the then common idea that the strength of one's faith was in direct proportion to the good feelings that one experienced. Following his graduation Loehe served some twelve congregations in a period of six years. Sometimes the short pastorates were due to Loehe's effective opposition to the indifferent spirit that marked many Christians at that time. Through earnest preaching and Bible study, Loehe succeeded in generating a new approach to Christian living, and this new approach often put him in opposition to prominent local persons. Sometimes his preaching about ethical behavior offended local citizens. At other times the short pastorates were simply due to the fact of temporary vacancies or some other local problem.

In 1837 Loehe received a call to the small farming community in Bavaria known as Neuendettelsau. At Neuendettelsau Loehe further developed his theological understanding and his pastoral abilities. He is described as possessing a powerful voice, piercing eyes, and an imposing physique. He was so highly regarded as a preacher that people traveled miles to hear him and were content to listen to him for hours at a time. At Neuendettelsau, at the request of the congregation, he instituted weekday prayer services and organized Bible study groups, missionary societies, and prayer cells. He worked for thirty-five years at Neuendettelsau, the place that he called "this quiet wilderness." Even though he applied four times for city pastorates during this period, he regarded it as a blessing from God that he received none of them.

In addition to his preaching and Bible study, Loehe was also a master of the art of caring for people in their spiritual, emotional, and physical needs. He was especially effective in the care of the sick and the dying, usually remaining with the dying until the final moment. He centered his practice of pastoral care on private confession and absolution. In his sermons and writings he devoted considerable time to this ancient institution, seeking to rescue it from the bad reputation that it had gained in Roman Catholic and in some Protestant circles. The people at Neuendettelsau responded to his emphasis on private confession and absolution and they stood in long lines waiting to unburden themselves to their pastor. In this connection, Loehe also placed considerable emphasis upon church discipline. He believed that it was an important part of the pastor's duty to bar from holy communion sinners that the pastor judged to be unrepentant. This practice created some disturbance in Neuendettelsau and was frequently criticized by pastors in other German cities. Some argued that the practice itself was improper, while others argued that as pastor Loehe was taking too much power and authority to himself. But Loehe was adamant and the discussion over the use of confession and absolution raged throughout the time of his ministry.

Loehe also believed that the public worship of the congregation was of greatest importance. Concerning participation in public worship he wrote:

> In holy, childlike innocence which only a child's innocent heart understands properly, the multitude of redeemed,

sanctified children of God dances in worship around the universal Father and the Lamb, and the Spirit of the Lord of lords guides their steps. The spiritual joy and heavenly delight enjoyed by those who take part in this sort of liturgy cannot be described. [*Three Books About the Church*, p. 177]

In order to make the liturgy as spiritual and helpful as possible, Loehe devoted a great deal of time to liturgical research. He pored over more than two hundred agendas, or orders of service, from the past, including both Lutheran and Roman Catholic, and on the basis of this research he prepared a liturgical pattern that was to have great influence both in Germany and in the United States. As he prepared this liturgy, Loehe, like Luther before him, tried to preserve all that was good and useful from the past, rather than rejecting it because it bore the label of Roman Catholic. His second liturgical principle was that the liturgy must place the central focus on the preaching and the reading of the Word of God. Of course, he insisted that the Word of God be read and preached according to the Lutheran understanding of it.

Unlike some of his contemporaries who either opposed any form of church union or simply proposed church union without any questions asked, Loehe pursued church union in a careful and disciplined way. Again his study of the past helped him, as it had done in the preparation of the liturgy. He argued that the Lutheran confessional writings represented the true understanding of God's Word, and should also be the center for church union. But he avoided the charge of Lutheran parochialism by maintaining that the Lutheran Confessions represented the position of the New Testament and of the majority of the fathers of the church. To prove his point, he quoted at some length from church fathers where they agreed with the Lutheran confessional teachings. Thus he tried to make the Confessions a bridge toward church unity, rather than a wall that shut Lutherans off from other Christians.

But the real contribution of Wilhelm Loehe to the life of the Christian church is in the area of mission. He developed and took with utmost seriousness the motto: "Mission is nothing but the one church of God in motion!" Thus he insisted that the church, by definition, had to be in mission or forfeit its right to be called church. He also insisted that mission was the work of the whole church, rather than the responsibility of individual and often independent mission societies. These independent mission societies were springing up all over Germany and Loehe had been a member of one or more in his earlier days. But as he matured he discovered that these societies represented a negative, rather than a positive, contribution to mission. The societies were sometimes indifferent to their churchly connections, and sometimes were actually opposed to the church. Loehe believed that this separation of mission from church could only lead to the ruin of both. So at Neuendettelsau he developed a churchly mission complex that continues to this day to be a major factor in the church's mission. He transformed Neuendettelsau into a complex of charitable and mission institutions that became so well known that people thought of the town as the "university of mercy." Over the years he founded a deaconess house, a house of rescue, a home for the mentally ill, a home for fallen girls, a hospital for men, a hospital for women, a seminary for missionaries to America, and a seminary for school teachers. From Neuendettelsau through these institutions and the people who were trained there, the influence of Loehe left a permanent impress on religious life in Europe, North America, and Australia.

During Loehe's own lifetime, North America was the chief object of his concern and the Lutheran church in North America owes a great debt of gratitude to him. Late in 1840 he happened to read a pamphlet from North America, written in German, containing appeals for help from the overworked pastors who were trying to minister to the flood of German immigrants. Stirred by this pamphlet, he wrote an article in a local paper, which contained the following paragraph:

> Our brethren are living in the wildernesses of North America —without food for their souls. We sit on our hands and forget to help them. So much more eagerly do the followers of the pope and the adherents of the sects approach them. And their love appears holy; they do not turn away from those who are suffering. To thirsty men the muddy, impure,

unhealthy water always seems preferable to death from thirst. Shall we not help? Shall we simply look on while our brethren in the faith are led astray because of a lack of shepherds, merely observe while the evangelical church in North America disintegrates? Shame on us if we here do not do what we can! Will we support our church's missions among the heathen, yet let already established congregations go under? Shall we let thousands starve while we devote so much attention to win individuals? We pray that the Lord will gather one holy church among the heathen, and are we then to let established congregations fall prey to this temptation? We forget those who are so near to us while we stretch out to those who still serve idols. We should not do one and forget the other! Up, brethren, let us help as much as we are able! [*Three Books About the Church,* pp. 18–19]

Loehe's words sparked a great missionary fervor throughout Germany, although the hub was always located at Neuendettelsau. From Neuendettelsau Loehe sent forth a number of pastors and teachers, poorly trained by modern standards, but devoted to the work of gathering together the scattered German Lutherans in the New World. Within twelve years, Loehe had sent eighty-two ministerial prospects to North America. These men in turn profoundly influenced the development of the Lutheran Church—Missouri Synod and of several synods that now belong to the American Lutheran Church.

Unfortunately, some of Loehe's theological principles led to conflict between himself and the Missouri Synod leaders, and to eventual division. The concept of ministerial authority was a particularly sensitive area. Loehe believed that the pastor was called directly by Christ and placed by him into the congregation. Because of this view, Loehe encouraged his pastors to play the dominant leadership role in the congregations. Loehe ran his own congregation in a somewhat authoritarian manner, insisting upon his personal right to bar people from the Lord's Supper. In contrast to this, the members of the Missouri Synod had a strongly democratic view of pastoral authority. Because of their own painful experiences in the New World, the pastors believed that the authority to preach the Word, to forgive sins or to refuse to forgive sins rested with the members of the congregation. The members called the pastor and they transferred to the pastor their own spiritual rights and authority, to be administered for as long as that person was pastor. The Loehe pastors and the Missouri pastors were unable to reach agreement on this crucial point, and so they separated. However, despite the separation, Loehe's influence upon the Missouri Synod in respect to preaching, the instruction of children, and the art of worship was enormous.

While Loehe's first mission interest was directed to the German Lutherans in North America, the condition of the Indians also caught his attention. He developed a radical approach to Indian mission work. He organized a complete town of immigrants in Germany and then sent them over as a unit into the wilds of Michigan, there to found such towns as Frankenmuth, Frankentrost, and Frankenlust. In these towns they were to live their normal lives and from these towns let the influence of the gospel spread to the neighboring Indians. The mission experiment could not be properly evaluated, because shortly after the establishment of Frankenmuth the government moved all the Indians to the west.

Through his American representatives, Loehe also came into conflict with a large group of eastern Lutherans, led by Samuel S. Schmucker. Schmucker argued that the mission needs of North America indicated that Lutheranism should modify its confessional position so that unity might be established especially with Reformed congregations. To achieve this end, Schmucker cut out from the Lutheran confessional writings their unique doctrine concerning the real presence of Jesus Christ in the Lord's Supper, and also rejected other fundamental Lutheran teachings. At the same time, Schmucker and many of his influential colleagues adopted pastoral techniques that were then known as "New Measures." These "New Measures" were largely borrowed from the Methodists and included such things as the anxious bench, the necessity for the second birth (in this book the second birth is discussed at length in the chapters on Jonathan Edwards and Francis Asbury), camp meetings, and extended revivals. Loehe strongly objected to the "New Measures," as did some of the other American Lutheran leaders. Loehe believed that the "New Measures" placed all the emphasis on human emotions and feelings, and took the emphasis away from the power of the Word of God and the solid and trustworthy character of God's promises as recorded in the Bible. He spoke of the "New Measures" as steamrollers that would eventually destroy Christian faith. Following a bitter battle that went on for a decade or more, the position of Schmucker was eventually rejected and the Lutheran church in America returned to its more traditional confessional practices. The influence of Loehe in this reversal was of paramount importance.

On January 2, 1872 at 5:45 P.M., following a brief illness, Loehe died. His influence on the mission of the church and the practice of pastoral care was great in his own lifetime. It now appears that in the Lutheran church there is a noticeable revival of many of the ideas that Loehe set forth a century ago. This revived interest in Loehe centers on the practice of private confession and absolution, on the principle that the entire church is mission, and on his insistence on liturgy and worship. In these ways, the spirit of Wilhelm Loehe is again making its presence felt in American Lutheranism.

COMMENTARY

Four aspects of Loehe's thought will be stressed in this Commentary, namely his ideas about the church, the Word of God, mission, and pastoral care. In all four of these areas, Loehe's thought is sharp and clear and provides perspectives for Christian congregations today.

With respect to the idea of the church, Loehe reflected the attitude of many church fathers who preceded him in that he was hopelessly in love with the church. He said that nothing was lovelier or more lovable than the church. He thought of the church as Christ himself being present on earth, and this idea helps to explain his great love for it. He often repeated the motto that where Christ was, there was the church; and where the church was, there was Christ. From this understanding, it followed that Christ through his Spirit was the creator of the church and thus also of the local congregation. In this sense, Loehe had a sacramental view of the church rather than a voluntaristic view. That is, he did not believe that the church comes into being as a group of individuals covenant together to form a congregation. Rather, the congregation is always the creation of God's Spirit, who carefully brings together a group of people who have precisely the right gifts so that they can mesh their talents and their abilities to form the Christian congregation that the Spirit needs for his mission in that place at that time. This sacramental view exalts the nature and character of the local congregation and provides it with a glue and a foundation that does not exist in the voluntaristic understanding of the church.

One of Loehe's major contributions to the thought about the church is his stress on the church as fellowship. He provided a profound theological basis for this idea of fellowship, teaching that all people are born both with a restless desire for God and also with a restless desire for human fellowship. He said, "For just as the Lord did not create an earth for only one man, so he also did not create a heaven for just one man." Augustine, the great fourth-century church father, had maintained that people were created for God and that they were restless until they found rest in him. To that Augustinian idea, Loehe added that people were also created for each other and that they would be restless until they found meaningful human fellowship.

In Loehe's time in Germany, other thinkers were placing great emphasis on the importance of the individual and encouraging individuals to stand up and to assert themselves. In opposition to this principle, Loehe taught that the individual exists only as a being in organic relationship with the whole. Furthermore, Loehe taught, living Christians constitute a fellowship with those who have already died in the faith and with those who are yet unborn. Thus Loehe viewed the church as a fellowship that extended throughout the world and throughout time. It was an exciting view of the church then, and it remains so now.

Some professors of theology in the years before Loehe had

destroyed the concept of fellowship by dividing the church in two, giving it a visible and an invisible existence. They taught that in the invisible church all Christians were indeed one, but that this had not happened and need not happen in the visible church. Loehe had to attack this distinction before he could build his concept of fellowship. He did this rather poorly, by defining the visible church as consisting of all those whom God calls, while the invisible church consists only of those whom God has chosen from all eternity. He was aware of the fact that no one could tell with absolute certainty who were the called and who were the chosen. Some of the difficulty that existed in his own mind comes to the surface in another of his statements when he said that the visible and the invisible church are identical. Perhaps that latter statement is a better reflection of the depth of Loehe's thought about church and fellowship.

One development that was threatening the fellowship and unity of the church in Loehe's day was the growth of small groups of believers that were often called conventicles. Christians gathered in conventicles because they were disappointed with the lack of spiritual vitality in larger congregations. In these conventicles, they spent a great deal of time in Bible study and in prayer, waiting for the direct outpouring of the Holy Spirit. As a consequence of their conventicle experiences, they often thought of themselves as better Christians, more devoted to the mission of the church. As a result, conventicles often became disruptive and divisive in the nineteenth-century German church. Thus Loehe was understandably opposed to such anti-churchly gatherings. Instead, he stressed the public gathering of the people of God around the spoken and read Word and the sacraments, gathered together in worship and experiencing the fellowship with each other that the Spirit had given them.

To nurture the fellowship of the church, Loehe taught, God had instituted the public ministry. The Cameo briefly described some of the difficulties that existed among nineteenth-century American Lutherans with regard to the authority of the congregational pastor. This is also a crucial question among many Christians today. By no means has the question of ministerial role or authority been resolved, as has been indicated at several places in this book. There is much to be said for Loehe's high view of ministerial authority. There is surely a sense in which the pastor is called by Christ to minister to a specific group of people who gather around Word and sacraments at a fixed place and a fixed time in history. But this high view also has problems built into it, for it can frequently lead to an oppressive practice of ministerial authority. Pastors become so solicitous and conscious of their authority that they deny the people the right to participate in the mission of the church and the right to grow in grace and into the stature of Jesus Christ.

But the democratic view of ministry as represented by the Missouri Synod also has problems built into it. For one thing, it can lead to the people viewing the pastor as their creation and therefore subject to their control. This is a situation as unhealthy as the oppressive situation described in the preceding paragraph. There is a sense in which people must be conscious of the special authority that pastors have as they preach God's Word and as, in the name of Jesus Christ, they announce God's forgiveness to the people or withhold it. The dilemma was neatly posed by Gregory the Great almost fourteen hundred years ago. Gregory said that the pastor must be "near neighbor" to all the good people in the congregation, while retaining a priority of authority in order successfully to rebuke sinners.

Part of the difficulty for Lutherans lies in the fact that sometimes they confuse what Martin Luther called the universal priesthood of all believers with the office of the public ministry. Luther taught on the basis of 1 Peter that each Christian is a priest. As a priest, each had the right to go directly to God in prayer and the right and the duty to offer priestly sacrifices to God, whatever the Christian's calling in life might be. At the same time, Luther stressed the importance of the called and ordained public minister, who took care of all the public worship requirements of God's people. While the idea of the universal priesthood and the public ministry seem to be in tension and even conflict, they need not be. Luther's twofold concern was to set people free from the priestly tyranny that he believed they were living under in his day while at the same time to preserve a proper public preaching of the Word and administration of the sacraments. Against certain Roman Catholic ideas, Luther stressed the authority and the dignity of the individual Christian with respect to the right to preach, to teach, and even, in emergency, to administer the sacraments. At the same time, he wanted to make it plain to Christians that they were all priests, called by God to offer spiritual sacrifices. Perhaps one way to resolve the difficulty that Loehe and others were unable to resolve in the nineteenth century is to think of the call to ministry as coming from Christ but through the calling action of the local congregation. In this view, the rights of both the congregation and the minister are adequately protected. That I have solved an ancient and critical problem with this simple suggestion is highly unlikely.

How do you experience human fellowship in your congregation? Is it effective and satisfying? Will you try once more to work on your understanding of the relationship between pastoral authority and the rights and privileges of each Christian?

The second aspect of Loehe's thought that should be emphasized is his view about the place of the Word of God and preaching in the life of the Christian congregation. The point received some stress in the Cameo, and not much more needs to be added here. As a cure for the emotionalism rampant in the Germany of his time, Loehe maintained that apart from the foundation of God's Word faith can only evaporate into a fog and a mist. As one witnesses similar outbreaks of emotionalism in our day, one appreciates Loehe's emphasis upon the objective reality of the promises of God located in his Word. At the same time it should be pointed out that Loehe's emphasis on the centrality of preaching is directly linked to his emphasis upon the church as the presence of Christ. Loehe maintained that the only action that brought the church into being was Christ present in his Spirit. Because it is Christ acting through his Spirit that calls the church into being the church is bound to the Word, for Christ's Spirit works only through the Word. He speaks of the church always as a miracle of God, created through Word and sacrament.

While one appreciates Loehe's emphasis, the way he puts it can create a problem in people's understanding. When Loehe speaks of the Word as the power that creates the church, he really means to say that it is the Spirit working through the Word that creates the church. However, many people fail to see this distinction. They apply to the Word those properties and powers which strictly speaking can be applied only to the Holy Spirit. Lutherans say that the Word is a means through which the Spirit achieves its work. However, many persons misunderstand this idea and give to the Bible the worship and honor that should be reserved for the triune God God alone. This is called Biblicism, and is the source of a great deal of misunderstanding and unrest in many denominations and congregations today.

Loehe's stress on the centrality of the Word emerges clearly in the following quotation:

> The church is one in truth; it is the truth which draws all children into one community. . . . By the truth, which is the uniting force of the church, is to be understood nothing else but God's Word. . . . The truth which unites all and creates one church of believers in all generations and nations is the Word of the apostles. [*Three Books About the Church,* pp. 61–62]

Because the Word was central to him, Loehe also stressed that the Word of the apostles is "clear and understandable to all. This is the most important point in the doctrine of the church." (*Three Books About the Church,* p. 65) While he granted the need of the Spirit's enlightenment to understand the Bible, he argued that this enlightenment is equally available to all. There is no difference among interpreters of the Word. He further said that the obscurities which some allege to be in the Scriptures are "not really sunspots in the heaven of the Scriptures but are spots in the hearts of men and in their own eyes." (*Three Books About the Church,* p. 71)

Like all the pastors who have been studied in this book, Loehe affirmed that preaching was the most important responsibility of the pastor. It occupies the first place among the means that the church uses for the salvation of people. According to Loehe, preachers are so to saturate themselves in the text that when they preach they make the Word of God visible and, Loehe says in paradoxical fashion, the Word of God also makes the preachers visible. They both appear together in the pulpit.

Next to preaching as the best means for the salvation of people, Loehe placed the sacraments of baptism and holy communion. While baptism makes a person a member of the body of Christ, the celebration of the Lord's Supper is the highest spiritual experience. Furthermore, in the eucharist, the church of all the ages is present. Likewise in the eucharist, we partake of the same body of Christ that the saints in heaven are now gazing on in adoration.

Do Loehe's ideas about the centrality of the Word have anything to say to your parish life and your family life today? Are emotionalism and subjectivism problems for people today? What does the phrase "the objective nature of God's promises contained in the Bible" mean to you?

Loehe's teaching about the mission of the church is the third aspect of his thought that may prove important for contemporary Christians. The Cameo paid considerable attention to his ideas in this area, and so only a few other emphases need to be made. In Loehe's day the church was inactive as far as social problems were concerned and was rather inactive in the general field of mission. In both areas, Loehe made significant contributions. In the area of social concerns and daily life, Loehe revived Luther's teaching that each Christian had a direct calling from God to fulfill in daily life. It made no difference at all whether one was a preacher or a housefather, housemother, farmer, or worker. Loehe taught that there was no longer a distinction between the religious and the securlar life, nor, in Christ, was there any difference between the common and the uncommon life. Rather, the important point for Christians was that they were filled with an uncommon love that worked itself out in their common life. All Christians alike were called to the same manifestation of holiness. Everyone's place, said Loehe, is that person's altar, the place where God's name is glorified and his holy love is revealed! Perhaps Loehe had Ambrose of Milan in mind (see the chapter on Ambrose and his teaching about the difference between commands of God and evangelical councils) because he specifically affirmed that in Christ there is no distinction between command and council, between monks and secular people, between clergy and laity. The history of the church seems to indicate that each generation and each individual Christian needs to recapture this idea of vocation and then to apply it in personal daily living.

The idea of vocation is so radical and compelling that it cannot be pursued apart from the fellowship of God's love, that is, the church. It is extremely demanding to live the Christlike life in one's work. It can be very costly to seek to imitate Jesus Christ every hour of the day. The demand and the cost are too much for individual Christians. However, in the communion of fellowship, Christians can find the strength, the encouragement, and the guidance they need to be faithful to the vocation they have received from God. Thus, here again Loehe's thought about the church is at the center of his teaching about vocation. Wherever one plumbs his thought, one finds the church, the communion of saints, at the center.

In addition to Loehe's mission contributions described in the Cameo, he deserves credit for the reestablishment of the Protestant deaconess movement. One of the major foundations at Neuendettelsau was the deaconess institution in which hundreds of women were trained for Christian service not only in Germany but throughout the world. For the deaconesses, Loehe wrote a creed or pledge which not only serves well as his own model, but becomes a challenging pledge for all Christians.

> What do I want? I want to serve. Whom will I serve? The Lord in his suffering and poor. And what is my reward? I serve neither for reward nor thanks but out of thanks and love; my reward is that I may serve. And what if I perish in doing it? If I perish, I perish, said Esther [Esther 4:16], who knew not Him out of love to whom I am willing to perish and who will not let me perish. And what if I grow old in doing it? Then shall my heart flourish as a palm tree, and the Lord will satisfy me with grace and mercy. I shall depart in peace and be anxious for nothing. [*Three Books About the Church*, pp. 26–27]

Do you think of yourself as having a calling from God in your daily life? How would you define your calling? Have you found the fellowship of saints helpful to you in carrying out your calling?

The final aspect of Loehe's thought relates to his understanding of pastoral care. Unlike many pastors, he developed a comprehensive theology for pastoral care and on the basis of that theology he performed the daily functions. Frequently, pastors perform their daily functions and never have the time to work out the theological understanding and rationale which undergird those functions. Loehe believed that pastoral care was the mainspring through which God's Spirit accomplished his objectives. While he believed that all Christians were called to practice pastoral care for each other, chiefly by forgiving each other, his main focus was on the care of souls provided by the called public minister. As the Cameo indicates, he stressed the practice of confession, absolution, and church discipline as crucial in good pastoral care. Some of his comments about confession indicate that he faced some of the same problems that preachers face today when they talk about restoring confession. Once he said:

> The main difficulty [in renewing pastoral care] is that men overlook what is central in pastoral care: the confessional. . . . [Pastor and penitent[were almost embarrassed as they tried, the one to apply God's Word to only *one* person and the other to accept the pastor's word as God's Word to only *one* soul. We learned what an important thing it was to have an ancient, fixed, and generally respected institution for the care of souls. We had literally tried to rob this institution of its divine establishment, and now even those who approve of it are haunted with doubts about its divine origin. There was never a greater sin against the care of souls than when unjustified conscientious objections of some confessors, unfamiliar with their duties and rights and with the method of absolution, were used as the reason for taking away from the pastor his right to examine and for taking away from the penitent the benefit of private confession and absolution. [*Three Books About the Church,* p. 174]

Loehe related church discipline closely to confession and absolution. He wrote:

But private confession is only a half-measure if the power to bind [that is, refusing to forgive unrepentant sinners] is not also given to the man who has the power to loose. Refusal of absolution and denial of the Lord's Supper must be in the hands of the individual pastor . . . although he must remain accountable to the church for his action. . . . Easy care of souls is worthless; its very love is to be doubted. There is no such thing as care of souls without training and discipline. [*Three Books About the Church,* pp. 175–176]

But undoubtedly Loehe's chief contribution to the art of pastoral care lies in his insistence that pastoral care includes almost everything that the pastor does. The chief aim of pastoral care is to apply God's boundless love to the needs of each individual as that individual seeks to live out a vocation. Therefore, preaching, the sacraments, liturgy, worship, and prayer are all crucial elements of pastoral care. Loehe reacted negatively to Richard Baxter (see his chapter in this book) for misunderstanding this fundamental point. The trouble with Baxter, according to Loehe, was that he stressed all the duties and responsibilities of the pastor as a person of action, and almost completely neglected the pastor's responsibility to preach, to administer the sacraments, and to lead in worship and prayer. Loehe may not have understood Baxter's view of pastoral care accurately, but his basic point remains valid. The important principle that Loehe stressed was that the pastor should focus on "not many, but much." In other words, the pastor's first and overriding responsibility is to "the much." By this phrase, Loehe meant that which was central in his understanding of the church, preaching and the sacraments. He wrote:

It is through alternating periods of withdrawal and public appearance, stillness and publicity, through persistent use of Word and sacrament, through giving of a quiet but full measure, through modesty and steadfastness that the Lutheran Church attains its goals. [*Three Books About the Church,* p. 166]

Elsewhere in his writings Loehe observed that for a time there was a great and unsatisfactory "running and racing and caring of souls." He went on to say that "it was forgotten that preaching, sacrament, catechization [the education of the young], and also the liturgy take care of souls in a truly magnificent way."

The contemporary revival of interest in the ideas of Wilhelm Loehe is undoubtedly due to the fact that Christians today confront many of the problems that confronted him. Many people have lost Loehe's confidence in the power of God's Word and in the sacraments of baptism and the Lord's Supper. Many people today long for the kind of fellowship that Loehe described so beautifully with respect to the church. Again in our day each person has been cast loose to make it or to fail to make it alone. The very individualism that Loehe contended against is with us again. The satisfying of emotions, a satisfying that never lasts, has again become a dominant characteristic of our age. Perhaps many pastors and congregations will find in Loehe stimuli for dealing with these problems with increasing success.

How do you react to Loehe's insistence on the central place of private confession in Christian life? Do you agree with his broad and inclusive definition of pastoral care, or do you prefer a narrower one?

11.
Henry Ward Beecher

CAMEO

From the day that he arrived in Brooklyn, Connie sensed that Henry Ward Beecher was fashioning a brand new American style of Christianity, and from everything that he saw and heard, Connie was excited about it. Reverend Beecher's sermons never failed to challenge Connie to do something with his faith, and they never failed to broaden and deepen his understanding of the Christian faith. Furthermore, wherever you went in Brooklyn, Beecher's understanding of Christianity was the subject of talk. How different from the small Connecticut town where Connie had grown up!

In fact, Connie had moved to New York to get away from his parents and their religious style which had been shaped by Lyman Beecher, Henry Ward's father. He had had enough of law and sin and total depravity and hell and God's supreme goodness. There was in him too much appreciation of life and too much concern about what was happening to his nation to tolerate Lyman Beecher's dry harangues about original sin and damnable Arminian errors.

In Brooklyn his uncle, Henry Bowen, offered him a job as a reporter on the *Brooklyn Eagle* and Connie did some writing for the *Christian Independent,* also owned by his uncle. Henry Ward was a regular contributor to the *Independent,* and his columns never failed to stimulate excited discussion, not only in Brooklyn, but increasingly throughout the United States. Beecher's stand on slavery was a particular object of controversy. He was an abolitionist who refused to support the Abolitionist movement; an anti-slavery man who favored the ownership of slaves "for a time"; a man of peace who smuggled rifles into Kansas to thwart the slave owners' plans to make Kansas slave!

Connie and Henry Ward became good friends almost immediately, and the preacher seemed always to have time to talk with the cub reporter. Connie was amazed at the seemingly endless resources of energy that Beecher possessed and that he placed without stinting at the disposal of the members of Plymouth Congregational Church.

Connie asked him about this once, and Beecher launched into an animated answer. It seemed, Connie thought to himself, that everything he did was animated, almost as if he were always on the stage, performing. As usual, he shared himself completely with Connie, revealing his inmost thoughts and experiences.

"You know, Connie, I learned most of what I know by rejecting almost everything my father said and did. Oh, he was powerful, and he thought he was warm. But really, nothing but a bundle of cold theological truths stood where his heart should have been. The only thing that kept me from losing my mind was my mother's warmth and love for me, even though I was only two when she died. Well, my father sure tried to make me into his kind of person. But God kept it from happening to me. How well do I remember those months and years in Indiana as God was pleased slowly to reveal to me such a view of Christ as one whose nature and office it is to have infinite and exquisite pity upon the weakness and want of sinners. I had not known him in that light before. In my childhood home, Christ had been only the Judge, the great spoilsport. He was against everything that was fun." The memory of his own childhood experiences brought a sheepish grin to Connie's face.

"Gradually I came to see that Christ had compassion upon people like me *because* we were sinners, not in spite of that fact. I discovered that he wanted to help me out of my sins, not punish me because of them." Henry Ward's eyes were glowing as he went on. "There rose up before me a vision of Jesus as the Savior of sinners—not of saints, but of sinners unconverted, *before* they were any better—because they were so bad and needed so much from him; and that view has never gone from me.

"This new understanding of Christ helped me greatly because I have always had a desperate need to be loved. I was a clown and a dunce in a family of brilliant brothers and sisters. The only way I could get attention from anybody, including my father, was by making a fool of myself. When I discovered that God loved me, dunce that I was, and had sent his Son into the world for me, I discovered the central importance of love. I also discovered that if I tried to love people the way God loved me, no strings attached, they responded. And my life has become a life of love and peace from that moment on."

Connie saw, or thought he saw, a shadow pass across Henry Ward's eyes, and Connie attributed this shadow to the painful and loveless relations that existed between Reverend and Mrs. Beecher. She was known throughout Brooklyn as a cold shrew, and almost everyone in the borough tried to reach out to Beecher and give him back the love and warmth that he gave them without measure, but that he was denied in the most important core of his own being. Beecher put his arm around Connie's shoulders and led him into the dining room to have a cup of tea with Mrs. Beecher.

The beautiful relationship between Henry Ward and himself was almost ruined by a sermon on the Bible preached by Beecher to the usual packed house in Plymouth Church. Beecher chose 2 Timothy 3:15–17 as his text and he began by referring to the numerous articles that were being written about how the Bible contained errors, about how the first five books of the Bible had not been written by Moses, about how Jonah had never been swallowed by a fish, and about countless scribal errors in the early manuscripts.

As an expectant hush settled over the huge crowd, he warmed to his subject. "Of what use," he began, "is a book which learned men are in utter uncertainty about? What is the use of a book to guide us when scarcely two of those who take it as a guide agree as to its guidance?" Connie began to relax; he knew what would come next as Beecher would reaffirm the reliability and trustworthiness of his childhood book. But, as usual, Beecher did not take the expected route. "Yes," he thundered, "the Bible is reliable, but it is so only in the one very essential particular for which it was designed! I hold that the Word of God as a guide in the formation of dispositions, in the regulation of conduct and character, in the founding of hope for this life and for the life which is to come, is a reliable guide, is a sufficient instructor, about which all honest men do in the main agree. But if you undertake to erect a cosmogony, and to say that the Bible lays down a perfect system, a complete scheme of philosophy; if you go beyond that, and claim that it prescribes a definite plan for a church, a church order and a church government; and if you include in its economy moral philosophy in the form of theology, I say that the Word of God is not sufficient for these things; and men disagree about the Bible because they are undertaking to do with it what it was never intended to effect!"

Beecher had the audience's full attention, and as usual, he thrived on that knowledge and became more emphatic and dramatic as he went along. "The external history of the Bible is beyond our reach, but the internal part of the Bible we can know; it points us to Jesus Christ as our Example and the Captain of our salvation and the source of the love we share with each other. It is our fault if we do not know and practice that! But I do not like the person who intends to cure doubts about the external form of the Bible by refusing to doubt or question anything about it; who believes with an indiscriminate all-credulous disposition; who denies himself the use of his God-given reason, and wants to deny that use to others to protect himself; who says 'If you begin to question, there is no end,' who says, 'If you once undertake to apply philosophy to Scripture, you never can tell where you will come out'; who says, 'You must take the Word of God just as it is.' That man is the rationalist; that man is the one of little faith!"

Connie was surprised at the fierce anger that he felt welling up within himself as Beecher went along. The ghosts of Lyman Beecher and his own parents were at that moment proving far stronger than the present influence of Henry Ward. Connie was being threatened at the foundation of his faith, and he vented his anger on Beecher. He felt an irresistible moral need to confront Beecher and to demand that he recant or resign. The next few nights passed without sleep for Connie as he mulled over in his mind how he would confront Henry Ward. He memorized more Bible passages than he could ever use. He tried to prepare himself for every strategem that Beecher could employ. Finally, fortified by two glasses of port wine, Connie presented himself at Henry Ward's third-floor study.

Beecher listened calmly to Connie's tirade and to his demand that he recant or resign. When Connie had finished, Beecher permitted a faint smile to play across his lips. Then he reached out and grabbed Connie's hands in his own, to Connie's obvious embarrassment. "Connie," Henry Ward began, "you're about the hundredth member of Plymouth to make that speech to me and to demand that I withdraw my remarks or resign, so I have had more practice with my speech by far than you have had with yours. And I'm going to say these things from the pulpit on Sunday, but let me share them with you now to help you with your pain, and because I love you like a son." Connie struggled to maintain his original level of anger and resentment, but it was difficult to do so in the face of Beecher's own quiet confidence and affection.

"I've already given you part of my answer, Connie, when I revealed to you my own spiritual development in Indiana. As my father taught me to understand the Bible, it was a book of laws and judgments directed against almost everything that I did. Jesus was himself the chief judge. I respected the Bible, and I feared it, but I didn't love it and I didn't care to study it. But when I slowly discovered that the Bible was really nothing but a hymn of praise to God and to Jesus, the Example and the Captain of our salvation, I began to fall in love with the Bible. I wanted to find the spiritual riches that the Spirit had placed in every verse. I found the Bible to be a tower of strength for me, and I found myself unperturbed and unaffected by all this modern criticism of the Bible. So I concluded that I was on the right track and that my people would be helped if I shared my understanding with them. Would you put me out of the church for risking my life in love for the good of my people?"

Henry Ward paused for breath, obviously not expecting an answer from Connie. Then he went on. "And another thing, Connie. The way my father taught me the Bible, all it cared about was my sin, God's anger, Jesus' judgment, and eternal life. That's all. The Bible had little or nothing to say that helped with my daily life. But when I started reading it the other way, I discovered that Jesus was altogether concerned with the way I think and live from day to day, with my role as father, citizen, what have you. I discovered that the Bible was God's guide for moral living by Christian people. It was a shock for me to discover how much my own father misunderstood and misused the Bible, but once I got it straight, I have been preaching that to the people ever since. And they love it!"

That was usually Beecher's final defense: it worked and the people were helped by it. In this case, as in most other instances, Connie couldn't argue with him. He personally liked and appreciated Henry Ward's insistence that religion applied seven days a week. He liked the fact that a church leader like Henry Ward spoke out on current issues and was deeply respected for his views by almost everyone. Connie muttered a few confused words of apology and then fled down the steps and out the door.

He was pleased to discover that Beecher's view of the Bible gradually became his own. With it came an experience of joy and peace that he had not had before. With it came an ability to use the Bible as a guide for daily living. It occurred to Connie that his personal faith had shifted from the Bible to Jesus, with a great deal of enrichment.

About a year later, Henry Ward invited Connie to lunch at Delmonico's to talk with him about a proposition. Finally, over coffee, Beecher proposed that Connie leave his work at the *Eagle* and join the Plymouth Church staff as business manager and administrative chief. Connie was flabbergasted, but immediately excited and interested. Henry Ward told Connie that he wanted to rid himself of all management responsibilities in order to devote full time to the Sunday services and the Friday night prayer meetings. He pointed out that the prayer meetings were the real heart of Plymouth Church, the real power that united them to do God's work. "What goes on on Sunday morning," said Henry Ward, "is more of a public show where I'm the chief actor. I enjoy it, the people are helped, and it goes a long way toward paying our expenses. But the real heart of the parish is nurtured at the Friday meetings. Connie, I want you to understand the crucial importance of prayer. If it doesn't happen on Friday night, it isn't going to happen in the parish. Thus in freeing me to concentrate more on Friday night, you're performing an essential service for the parish."

Henry Ward stopped, swallowed a cup of coffee, and then launched into a description of the second phase of the proposed job, and Connie found himself even more interested. The job description, in typical Beecher style, turned out to be a theological lecture on parish unity, but that was the way Connie preferred to approach all church needs, anyway. "You see," Henry Ward began, "most preachers do not understand their jobs, and as a result, not much happens in their parishes. They think that preaching is all that really matters. Now, of course, it's important, but much more needs to go on. Another primary task of the minister is to drill a body of Christian people to think and work together so that, individually and collectively, they will be a witnessing and ministering body in their community. Thus Christians need to be organized for service and for mutual nurturing so that they can encourage each other to be about their Father's business. The unity of the congregation is very important, and it doesn't just happen. Structures need to be created and opportunities for experiencing unity and fellowship must be offered. Most preachers work only with individuals. That's important, but the group, the body of Christ, must also be nurtured. And that would be your second responsibility. This fellowship and unity doesn't happen automatically. It's got to be worked at. I used to think that my sermons and my leadership would do this. But I slowly discovered that for the first time in my life I was wrong again." Beecher chuckled at his well-worn witticism, and Connie grinned obediently. "I suppose, as I look back over my years here, if I had truly believed it was up to me, I would have worked myself to a frazzle and would have been dead ten years ago. But the Spirit does it, Connie, and it's a beautiful thing to watch. Somebody has to grease the ramp so that the Spirit can work without interruption. That's your job."

Connie noted that Henry Ward was assuming that he would take the position, and he had no hesitation in agreeing to the proposition. Henry Ward, again as usual, had no specific directions for Connie; he simply urged him to keep the ramp greased. Connie knew that Henry Ward would give him a largely free hand, and he set to work creating a program that would facilitate the development of fellowship and unity for the members of Plymouth Church.

The program went well; Connie enjoyed his work thoroughly . . . until the rumors about Henry Ward's adulterous relationships passed beyond the level of rumor and became apparent fact in the confession of Lib Tilton. Everyone in Brooklyn talked about the amount of time that Beecher had been spending with Lib Tilton, ostensibly because she was helping him write his first novel. But the whole thing came to a head when Lib confessed to her husband, Theodore, that Beecher had forced his attentions on her several times. Theodore took the confession to Connie, and together with a group of Plymouth leaders, they decided that Beecher would have to be confronted. They designated Connie for the task. This time it had taken three glasses of port and another battery of memorized Scripture verses to toughen him for the ordeal.

Connie plunged at once into the matter of Lib's confession of relations with Henry Ward, and then began to quote some of the Scripture passages. But Beecher interrupted him in a strangely soft voice. "Oh, yes, Connie, I love her; I love her like a daughter and I have kissed her as I would my daughter. I love her children almost as much as my own, perhaps more." Beecher paused, his eyes becoming moist. Then he continued in that same voice. "She is everything I could ever desire in a wife." That was the only time that Connie had heard Beecher speak even indirectly to what everyone knew about his own marriage. "If I were a free man, I would pursue her with all my energy. But, Connie, there is nothing more than that between us. Shall I be damned because I love a person in a proper way?"

They talked on. Beecher told Connie about Lib's impulsive and unstable nature, something that Connie had been unable to see because of his friendship with Lib and Theodore and becuse of his own half-admitted infatuation with her. "She needed me in order to survive Theodore's own scandalous conduct with Victoria Woodhull. And, frankly, I derived enormous personal satisfaction from our visits."

Connie rose to excuse himself and leave as quickly as possible, but Beecher stopped him as his hand reached the doorknob. "Connie, you have not said everything you came to say, have you? I think you came once again to ask me to resign because in your judgment I was a sinful man. Am I correct?" There was no anger in Beecher's voice. Connie could only nod his head in agreement. "Then sit down, Connie. Perhaps I can help you. For many years now, I have loved you like a son. I shared with you my understanding that God is our loving Father who delights in forgiving and helping sinners. But tonight you came as a messenger from my father's just and angry God. Connie, in a moment of great crisis, you abandoned that one thing that made your life worthwhile. Are you still a disciple of Lyman rather than of Henry Ward?" Connie knew again that no answer was called for and he offered none. He also knew that Henry Ward was giving him an insight into himself that would help him to grow in Christian grace. In Beecher's moment of crisis, he emerged as the strong man of faith, trying to help a weak and struggling Connie.

"Well, Connie, let me try once more to open to you the proper understanding of God's heart. Let me once more point you to your loving, heavenly Father, who loves sinners because they are sinners. Let's suppose for a moment that Lib's charge is true, something I deny completely. Suppose that I had sinned once or twice. Would that damn me forever? Is there no forgiveness for me? And if there is forgiveness for me from God, shouldn't the people of Plymouth also forgive me? I would without a moment's hesitation offer you God's forgiveness."

Connie knew that Beecher would, but he was not satisfied with Beecher's logic. "But, Henry Ward, you're a minister. With you it's different."

Beecher pounced on the statement. "Oh, Connie, I'm no different from my people. I'm a sinner. I need forgiveness; I need their understanding and love as much as they need and have mine." After a few more comments, Connie apologized deeply and left.

As he walked back to his room, he wept unabashedly. At the same time, he felt strangely clean and deeply in love, although he was not sure whether he was in love with God or with Henry Ward Beecher. Truly, he was one of God's great people!

In the long drawn-out and sensational trial that followed, Connie remained convinced of Henry Ward's innocence. Despite a series of damaging charges and pieces of circumstantial evidence, Connie's confidence did not waver. He let Henry Ward know of his support and devoted much of his time to maintaining the programs of Plymouth Church during the months of Beecher's inactivity. When he was finally cleared, almost all the members of Plymouth welcomed him back with open arms. It pained Connie to see that Henry Ward had been so exhausted by the trial that he would never again be the same leader who could give himself without stinting to every member in every need. Connie tried to make up for some of this, almost becoming an associate pastor. He had never found more satisfaction in life than now, as he tried to love even as he had been loved by God and by Henry Ward.

COMMENTARY

Henry Ward Beecher (1813—1887) was the most influential Christian pastor of the nineteenth century, as well as one of the most important American citizens from 1860 until his death.

During the course of his long career as pastor of Plymouth Church in Brooklyn, New York, he created a new style of pastoral care that shaped the thinking of uncounted thousands of pastors and lay people until the end of World War II. Much of his success and importance stem from the fact that he happened to be the right man in the right place at the right time.

As has been noted in this book, the style of pastoral care adopted by Christian pastors is usually strongly influenced by the conditions of the times in which they live. It is often impossible to understand a given pastor's style without that information. This is particularly true of Henry Ward Beecher. He lived at a time of great transition in American culture and values, and his style of pastoral care reflects the fundamental changes that were taking place in American religious and societal life. Beecher was personally involved in fomenting and directing many of these changes.

For example, the older New England style of theology and pastoral care, in this book represented by the work of Jonathan Edwards, had outlived its usefulness. The New Englanders, including Beecher's own father, Lyman, had drained all the vital juices out of Calvinistic religion and had reduced it to a rather dry and dull system of theology. The system was logical and comprehensive, but had little appeal for the average person. The New England theology had built on the principles of the sovereignty of God, the complete corruption of humanity, and the imperative demands of moral duty. These factors often combined to produce only a perennially guilty conscience in the followers of that religion. Reason was supreme and emotion played little or no role. And the minister's word was law.

But nineteenth-century America was not eighteenth-century New England. New moods were abroad in the land. A heavy wave of Romanticism swept in from Europe and called forth strong emotions among people (see the chapter on Francis Asbury). Reason was no longer sufficient. Religion also had to offer emotion, and no one was more emotional in the nineteenth century than Henry Ward Beecher.

It was also a time for great optimism mingled with great

doubts. The west was opening and there seemed to be no limit to what Americans could accomplish. Most Americans believed that God had given them a manifest destiny to export their style of civilization to all the world. Most Americans still wanted to be religious and to express themselves in religious terms, but they needed a new model for theology and church life. Part of Beecher's strength and appeal as a pastor lay in his ability to provide religious expression and direction to this widespread optimism.

But there were also grave doubts gnawing at America's conviction about its own uprightness and Christian character. Thoughtful people were asking if America could really claim to be God's chosen instrument through which he would offer a blessing to all the nations. In large measure these doubts were caused by the existence of slavery, even as in a later period grave national doubts were caused by the experience of the war in Vietnam. But these problems were also related to the growing gulf between the rich and the poor, to increasing abundance and enjoyment of worldly goods on the part of a few, who themselves had usually been born poor, and to rapidly rising tensions between the western democrats and the eastern aristocrats. To each of these issues and problems, Henry Ward Beecher spoke an authoritative word and the people of the United States loved him for it.

Beecher did not achieve this distinction and importance because he was a man of towering intellect or profound spirituality. Indeed, he was an ordinary man who possessed only two gifts which he used to the fullest. The one gift was that of oratory. He had developed this gift to a remarkably high level in college, and throughout his life he was ranked among the four or five greatest orators that America produced in the nineteenth century. His other gift was the remarkable ability to sense the hopes and fears of the American people and to give powerful expression to them, almost before the people themselves knew what they were thinking. Some critics have argued that Beecher usually said only what people wanted to hear.

But the real foundation of Beecher's success as a pastor rested in his understanding of love: God's love for the sinner, the preacher's love for the people, and the people's love for their preacher and for each other. The people of Plymouth Church eagerly soaked up Beecher's words about God's love, they thrived on the personal love he offered them, and in turn they offered him a love that overcame serious charges of personal corruption levelled against their pastor on at least three separate occasions.

Beecher's understanding of the love of God flowed from what he called his own "conversion" while he was studying theology at Lane Seminary in Cincinnati, Ohio, where his father was president. In an address before the pastors in London, England in 1886, Beecher described how thoroughly religious his home life had been and how these religious experiences left him completely untouched. Then one "blessed morning of May," it pleased God to send to his "wandering soul the idea that it was God's nature to love a man in his sins for the sake of helping him out of them," and that God did this out of nothing but "the fullness of his great heart." In short, said Beecher, he discovered that "he [God] felt toward me as my mother felt toward me . . . who never pressed me so close to her as when I had done wrong." The passage is a perfect demonstration of Beecher's thought on God's love and his gift for highly emotional preaching. For his time, this was radical preaching in contrast with the stern and harsh preaching of his father and other Puritan leaders. It drew the people to Plymouth Church in crowds that regularly overflowed the twenty-six-hundred-seat auditorium.

Lyman Abbott, his successor as pastor of Plymouth Church, recorded something Beecher said about love when the latter celebrated his seventieth birthday. On that occasion, Beecher said, "I love men so much that I like above all other things in the world to be loved. . . . I love love, but I love truth more, and God more yet." To these words of Beecher Abbott adds, "For great as was his love for his fellowmen and his desire for their love, the dominating motives of his life were his love for God, or his love for Christ—and in his experience, the two phrases were synonymous,—and his desire for God's love."

His preaching about God's love struck such a radically differ-ent note from that of his forefathers that it hit many of his hearers with the impact of a new revelation. Abbott described Beecher's impact on his own religious development in terms of profound gratitude, much as Connie does in the Cameo. It appears that most of his parishioners experienced feelings of relief, freedom, and joy at Beecher's preaching. These emotions gave many of them a new lease on religious faith at a time when the old faith and the old convictions were crumbling. In a very real sense, their religious faith and vitality depended directly and fully on Henry Ward Beecher.

One of the basic concerns of this book is to examine the concepts of pastoral authority that various men have developed and applied in their ministries. Beecher is a classic example of the American Protestant preacher who operates with an understand-ing of authority that is largely personalistic in nature: that is, the authority of pastors depends on their personality and the influ-ence that they personally wield in their parish. In this respect, Beecher became the model and prototype for thousands of American ministers down to the present. In a real sense, he himself made the parish go by the sheer force of his determina-tion and enthusiasm. By loving the people, Beecher sought to make them dependent upon him and obedient to his wishes and desires. His personal energy provided the great bulk of the spiritual energy that animated his parish. He ministered to the spiritual needs of his people, not so much by proclaiming the truths of God to them, but instead by freely inviting them to draw on his own apparently limitless reserves of love, sympathetic understanding, and confidence for the future. Although such personalistic pastors may say, "Thus says the Lord!" they may in fact be asking the people to believe the word and accept it be-cause they speak it. Similarly, when they pronounce absolution of sins, the people may hear such pastors speaking in their own name, instead of being able to hear God's voice in the pastors' word.

In many cases, as in Beecher's, such personalitic authority offers great amounts of psychological satisfaction to both pastor and people. Obviously, it places great demands on the psychological strength and resources of the pastor. It can readily lead to a nervous breakdown on the pastor's part. It can also generate factions in the congregation—one group affirming its loyalty to Pastor X, while another group is unable to relate to Pastor X as a person and thus also unable to acknowledge Pastor X's personalistic authority over them.

Another problem often associated with personalistic authority is that the members of the congregation permit themselves to be entertained and even dominated by the pastor. They become passive and take little active part in developing and exercising the five functions of worship, fellowship, witness, service, and nurture.

While Beecher devoted considerable energy to involving the people in parish activities, his efforts largely failed. Several factors combined to frustrate his efforts. One was his own enthusiastic and domineering personality. Another was the huge size of the Plymouth congregation, numbering more than 2600 souls. There was little or no opportunity for fellowship, except for the inner core that attended the Friday night prayer meetings, and those who were involved in the program for fellowship that the Cameo ascribed to Connie. Nor was there much practice of mutual nurture; the preacher provided all the needed nurture in his sermons and Bible lessons. Nor did the members stimulate each other to witness and service. Instead almost everything that happened in Plymouth Church centered in the work of its preacher.

In the American Reformed tradition, this kind of pastoral authority has been and still is quite common. It may also appear in the Episcopalian and Lutheran traditions, although with less frequency because these two denominations have a higher view of sacramental authority and the pastor's sacramental powers. Among Roman Catholics it may occasionally also be found, but it is effectively resisted in both the theology and the practice of that denomination.

By now you are probably beginning to appreciate the crucial importance of the authority question and the great difficulties involved in defining pastoral authority correctly and helpfully.

There is a fundamental difference between the carefully spelled-out authoritarian beliefs of Ambrose and the spontaneous, unsystematic practices of Henry Ward Beecher. Undoubtedly the proper definition of pastoral authority needs something from each of the pastors that have been described in this book.

What are the strengths and weaknesses in Beecher's kind of personalistic authority? Should the pastor's personality play any role in the establishment of pastoral authority in the parish?

Beecher never spoke to the subject of pastoral authority, but had he been asked he would undoubtedly have pointed to Jesus Christ as the highest authority in his parish. Probably he was not at all conscious of the real nature of the pastoral authority he exercised at Plymouth. Certainly his own repeatedly affirmed goal was to present Jesus Christ in such a way that Christian people would follow His example and would base all their decisions on His authority alone.

He developed his understanding of Christ's authority in the parish at some length in a sermon in which he affirmed in clear terms that success in preaching depends on the ability of the preacher to put before people the Lord Jesus Christ as "a living person who gave himself a ransom for sinners and now ever lives to make intercession for them." On the basis of this confession, he went on to argue that "there can be no sound and effective method of preaching ethics . . . which does not derive its authority from the Lord Christ"; that "all reformations of evil in society, all civil and social reformations, should spring from this vital center"; that "all philanthropies are partial and imperfect that do not grow out of this same root"; and that "all public questions of justice, of liberty, of equity, of purity, of intelligence should be vitalized by the power which is in Jesus Christ."

This is a remarkably clear and sweeping description of the centrality and the authority of Jesus Christ. However, despite this classic formulation concerning Jesus Christ, it must be said that Beecher's Christology should be labeled as "moral example Christology," rathe than as "Pauline," in the sense that Paul placed considerable emphasis on Jesus Christ crucified. Beecher affirmed his "moral example Christology" by saying that it was his unswerving purpose to preach the gospel "primarily and mainly for the re-creation of man's moral nature, for the bringing of Christ as a living power upon the living souls of men." In a sermon preached on November 22, 1871, Beecher asserted that the single unswerving goal of the apostle Paul was to preach the gospel to create "a free man; a full manhood; Jesus the model; God's Spirit the inspirer and helper." While this summary does cover many verses in St. Paul's epistles, it can hardly be considered an adequate summary of all that Paul taught about the person and the work of Jesus Christ.

Apparently Beecher never referred to Jesus Christ crucified. Several scholars have reached that conclusion after examining hundreds of his sermons. They quote him as saying that it was impossible for him to preach Christ nailed to the cross; "the subject was too awful and sublime." One suspects that in his reaction against Lyman Beecher's overemphasis upon the ugliness of sin, Henry Ward Beecher tended to deemphasize sin and almost to sweep sin under the rug.

This criticism of Beecher's preaching is fundamental. I surely do not criticize his idea that Jesus Christ is the world's best moral example, but I sharply criticize the fact that he rarely talked about the importance of Christ's suffering and death for the sins of humanity. Because he emphasized Jesus' moral influence so strongly, he erred as fundamentally as the preacher who talks only about the crucifixion and the death of Jesus Christ.

It has been suggested above that Beecher erred in his views of the person and work of Jesus Christ because he misunderstood the power and the nature of sin. It seems that he was too naive about sin's power. While he spoke about it a good deal, at least in the early years of his ministry, he appeared to believe that people can escape from the power of sin by self-improvement. This view of sin, then, supported his unbalanced views of the person and work of Jesus Christ. These views were sounded from many American pulpits in the nineteenth and twentieth centuries, and became the theological undergirding for the Social Gospel.

It is my contention that the church has two basic purposes: the one is to heal and restore lives by dispensing the grace of God's forgiveness through word and sacrament, and the other is to train people so that they live not to be ministered to, but to minister and to give their lives for the advantage of their neighbors. It is only as Christians participate in this twofold action—receiving God's life in Christ and offering their own in imitation of him for the world—that they are truly the body of Christ, the church. In such a community, the word and the sacraments are central as vehicles of grace. Preaching focuses on God's act of deliverance in Jesus Christ. On the basis of that action, Christians support and encourage each other to imitate Christ and to go about their calling of being "little Christs," in a world that is indifferent and often vigorously hostile.

In such a churchly community, the pastor plays a twofold role as administrator of the means of grace in word and sacrament, and as example to and equipper of the saints for their warfare. In such a community pastors discharge their office, not in a personalistic style, but rather in the awareness of the unique sacramental authority that has been bestowed on them to preach the word, to forgive sins, and to administer the sacraments; and the people readily and cheerfully acknowledge that sacramental authority. They are grateful for the sacramental ministry of such a person and they band together to encourage each other to follow the pastor's example of Jesus Christ.

Beecher's naive view of sin and his one-sided thinking about the person and work of Jesus Christ affected his understanding of the nature and purpose of the church. Thus it seems fair to say that the members of Plymouth Church did not regard their community as primarily a sacramental community, gathered around word and sacrament. Instead, they thought of themselves as a group of people who had voluntarily come together to listen to and to be stimulated by Henry Ward Beecher. While they hungered for the love of God that Beecher proclaimed, they had only a limited and vague understanding of the forgiving grace that God offered them in word and sacrament. Instead of a deep appreciation of this kind of sacramental forgiveness, they responded emotionally to Beecher's sermons about God's love. Instead of steeling themselves for sacrificial living, they were encouraged by their pastor to enjoy the new wealth that so many of them were beginning to possess. In the pursuit of this enjoyment, they were not thrown back on the strength and encouragement of other members, but rather most of them seemed to have gone their individualistic ways.

In short, in the descriptive phrases that we have used in this book, Plymouth Church was a non-sacramental, voluntaristic church. The word "voluntaristic" means that the people believed that a Christian church comes into being because a number of people make up their minds to form one. In this book, we have been using "sacramental" as the opposite of "voluntaristic." "Sacramental" describes the belief that congregations are created by God through his Spirit.

It seems that Beecher retained the idea of covenanted church membership, first taught by his New England forebears. Plymouth Church insisted that all members sign the covenant, although the covenant was vague in its religious affirmations. It read: "Do you now avow the Lord Jehovah to be your God, Jesus Christ to be your Savior, the Holy Spirit to be your Sanctifier? Renouncing the dominion of this world over you, do you consecrate your whole soul and body to the service of God? Do you receive his word as the rule of your life, and by his grace assisting you, will you persevere in this connection unto the end?"

How do you respond to and evaluate Beecher's views of the person and work of Jesus Christ? Do you think that the two purposes of the church that are stated a few paragraphs above are Biblical and adequate?

In yet another way the career of Henry Ward Beecher symbolizes a dramatic change in the understanding of pastoral authority, and thus also of the pastoral office. That other way relates to his understanding of Biblical authority. As the Cameo points out, Beecher abandoned the strong beliefs of his ministerial predecessors that every word of the Bible carried God's full authority and was to be interpreted literally and applied in a legalistic fashion to the lives of Christians. Instead he argued that the authority of the Bible meant only that it provided reliable and inerrant moral counsel. He granted that Biblical statements might be proven wrong by new historical and scientific discoveries, but he maintained that the discovery of such errors did not affect the reliability of the Bible's moral influence. The Cameo suggests that Beecher's new point of view enabled him and many of his contemporaries to continue to trust the Bible's moral purpose at a time when Biblical scholars were developing theories and hypotheses that challenged almost all traditional beliefs about the Bible. Although his view of the Bible is inadequate, it did help him rise above the fears that many were experiencing.

At the same time, his views of the Bible contributed to the changing view of pastoral authority. His pastoral forebears had placed their authority almost exclusively upon an inerrant Bible which, when interpreted by the pastor, solved all problems and allowed for no back talk on the part of the people. The Beecher breed of pastors had to redefine their understanding of authority. Many accepted Beecher's personalistic model. However, others have not yet found a model that works for them. One of the most challenging questions that confronts pastors today is the issue of the authority they exercise in the congregation, as this book has repeatedly stressed. Much of the present-day confusion stems from the changes that Henry Ward Beecher and his successors produced in the attitude of Christians toward the Bible.

By insisting that the church had a responsibility toward its culture, Henry Ward Beecher produced yet another radical change in people's understanding about the nature of Christianity. In this emphasis Beecher stands squarely in the train of those pastors who, up to the time of the Reformation and the Enlightenment, insisted that the church was the primary custodian of charity and justice in society. As this book has pointed out in several chapters, this understanding of the church's mission faded out in our modern period. Beecher almost succeeded in placing the church at the center of culture once again. His success is evidenced by the fact that at one time there was serious talk about running Henry Ward Beecher for the presidency of the

United States. The tragedy of Henry Ward Beecher's efforts to involve the church in culture is that his efforts were built on an inadequate understanding of the person and work of Jesus Christ and of the nature of the Christian faith. His optimistic view of human potential continued to shape American Protestant thought down to the Depression of the 1930s. When Protestant theologians finally escaped from the siren song of Henry Ward Beecher, they reacted with an overly pessimistic view about humanity and its potential. The result is that the church today is still struggling to find the proper understanding of the work of Jesus Christ and of human nature in order to build a theological foundation for its own proper role in society.

Much of what Beecher stood for is Christian and correct. He failed because his theological undergirding was inadequate. Had he succeeded in welding concern for culture to a good Biblical theology, the history of Christianity in twentieth-century America would very probably have been quite different. And if Christianity had played a different role in Western history, it is also in order to suggest that the whole trend of life in twentieth-century United States would have followed a different course. Thus Henry Ward Beecher serves to remind Christian congregations of the crucial importance of the theological foundation upon which they build. He also serves to remind congregations that the crux of their theological foundation is the word concerning Jesus Christ, who gave himself for the life of the world, dying and rising again that people might be free.

12.
Harley Theim

CAMEO

It had been a great first day with the people of God at Olivet Church, thought Harley as he and Evelyn came back to the parsonage. There had been no time for even a moment's rest—from the morning service when he was installed, through the dinner, the afternoon program, and an evening service attended by people and pastors from many congregations in that part of Illinois. Some had even come over from St. Louis. Harley and Evelyn felt thoroughly welcome, thoroughly exhausted, and thoroughly happy.

As they walked into the kitchen, they discovered that their people had managed to get into the house during the day and leave an endless number of love gifts of food. Despite their fatigue, they set about putting it away, talking about future plans for themselves and the Olivet congregation.

After that pleasant beginning, things continued to go well at Olivet. Attendance was increasing at both services. People spoke well of his preaching. He managed to visit most of the members in the first year, including some families that had not been to church in years, some of whom began to attend again. He had a gift for working with children and youth, and the parents were delighted to see this. At least some of their responsibility could be shoved onto the young minister.

Although his Bible college professors had urged him to hold the line against drinking, smoking, and card playing, Harley

refused to worry much about these problems at Olivet. As he told
the church council, he had enough to do fighting major sins like
dancing, divorce, broken engagements, failure to witness or to
give ten percent to the work of the church. He felt that in general
the council members supported him, although there were a few
who urged him to hold the line all across the board. "It's like a
domino chain," one of them liked to argue with great finality, "tip
one and they'll all fall."

As usual, Harley encouraged the council to search the Scriptures with him to find guidance and warrant for all they were
doing. He pointed out that there were no passages against card
playing, that Jesus had turned water into wine, and had once
spoken of himself as not being a teetotaler. As far as smoking was
concerned, Harley had to admit that the argument that smoking
killed and was, therefore, against the sixth commandment had
much to commend it. However, he insisted that he would speak
against only those things that the Bible spoke against in clear and
literal fashion. He had such a high view of the final and absolute
authority of every inspired and infallible word in the Bible that
he could not persuade himself to go beyond it in any matter. Nor
would he stop short of any issue on which the Bible spoke clearly.

He spent considerable time with the council and in his sermons, pointing out that the inspired and inerrant Bible was the
sure basis of their faith, the source of all the comfort they needed,
and the infalliable guide to every moral decision. He liked to talk
about Jesus' own statement that not one word of Scripture could
ever be broken and that not even the dot on the letter "i" in the
Bible could be changed. Harley based his own faith on this idea,
and he did everything in his power to lead his people to that same
foundation. Many of them had believed the same thing all their
lives; others were persuaded by Harley's preaching and counseling.

But there were always doubts and nagging questions to
bother him in the wee hours of the morning. For example, he
admitted to himself that on occasion he interpreted the Bible to
gain personal popularity. There was also the growing number of
bad marriages. Carol Hanson's marriage was a classic example of

the problem. Carol was one of the most faithful workers in the congregation, and she had told him with great reluctance the story of the mistreatment that she was receiving from her husband. It was a gruesome account, and Harley knew that she was not exaggerating. But he explained to her that it was God's will that she remain united to her husband for life, unless he broke up the marriage. She had given in, convinced that he truly understood God's will for her. The black eye that she tried to camouflage with extra makeup on the following Sunday caused Harley another pang of self-doubt—and these pangs were growing more frequent and contributing to his sleeplessness.

When a group of his young people attended a square dance at the high school, Harley rebuked them privately, ordered them to stay away from the Lord's Table until they repented, and then brought the matter up before the council. He wanted the council's support. Since about half the council were also parents of the offending children, the discussion became emotional and heated. Finally, the council declined to back Harley on this matter. One father summed up the council's opinion with the observation that times were changing and that the sin of dancing was apt to be more in the mind of the beholder than in that of the young people. It was a major break in the Biblical dam that Harley had carefully constructed to aid his people in leading lives that were pleasing to God.

Jim Wisdom, one of the council members, took him across the street for a cup of coffee after the meeting, to assure him of his personal support and to explore the issue in more depth. "You know, Harley, I like your preaching, I like the way you work with our kids, I like everything you're doing. But I believe the Bible wants you to be more broadminded with respect to some of its teachings. Even the Bible changes its own understanding of its own laws. Moses had said that divorce was permitted, but Jesus said it was not. Why the change? Because the mind-set and the needs of the people change. The Jewish old-timers said that the sixth commandment was about murder, but Jesus said 'No' to that interpretation and pointed out that the sixth commandment was designed to describe a life-style marked by love and concern." After these remarks, Jim paused for a swallow of coffee, and then said, "You know, Harley, I think we can destroy the law by giving it too strict an interpretation." Harley was too tired and too confused to pursue the subject. He thanked Jim for his concern, promised to give it more thought, and went home, suffering from another of his blinding headaches.

In an effort to straighten out his thinking, Harley decided to enroll for two courses at a seminary in St. Louis. Both seemed tailor-made for his needs. One was entitled "The Inspiration and Authority of the Bible" and the other was called "Christian Ethics in a Post-Christian World." For three and a half weeks he worked harder than he ever had in his life. Both professors were tigers and swamped him with reading assignments and papers. But, as Harley had hoped, both courses focused directly on his two personal crises.

In the Bible course, the professor led the students through the history of the idea of inspiration, showing how it originally had meant that in some very real sense the Holy Spirit had been active in the production of Biblical books, but had not dictated each idea and each word to the writers. The professor had the students work through the first three Gospels and certain passages in the Old Testament. Harley had already begun to notice some of these apparent contradictions in the Bible as he prepared for his preaching and Bible class work, but he had pushed these facts into the back of his mind because he had no resources for dealing with them from his own days at the Bible college. There his professors had assured him that the Bible was perfect, without any error or contradiction whatever. It was painful to discover that his professors had been wrong.

For example, Harley noted that in one Gospel account Jesus healed the blind man when he was going into Jericho and in another account he healed him when leaving the city. Now he noticed that the two accounts were so much alike in detail that he could no longer accept his old professor's explanation that the two healings were two separate events. He noted that Pilate's words on the cross were reported in different form in each Gospel. The old theory that this was due to translation no longer

satisfied him. Matthew and Luke reported the events of the temptation in different order. The Old Testament in two separate
accounts reported a significantly different number of soldiers
killed at the battle of Helam. There were other apparent contradictions and discrepancies, so many that Harley was finally forced
to reject that idea which had been the center of his faith: the
inspired, inerrant Bible.

Fortunately for Harley, his professor was a kind and wise
person who spent many hours with Harley as he confronted this
crisis of faith. The professor urged Harley to transfer his faith
from the foundation of the Bible to the more sure foundation of
Jesus Christ himself, but Harley could not make that transfer. He
wallowed in doubt. He was almost immobilized for days at a time
by his headaches. But he continued to do the work and to see one
cherished idea after the other challenged in a way he was unable
to deal with.

Things went no better in the other course. Harley's first reaction to that professor was to label him a "Situation Ethicist" and
thus dismiss the value of anything he had to say. But he soon
realized that the label was unfair. This man was committed to
Scripture as the place where God's will was best revealed, but he
also led his class to understand that there were few instances,
even in Scripture, where God's will was clearly and adequately
understood by human beings. Then he went on to discuss with
his students dozens of cases from real life where two or more
courses of action might have been Christian. In some cases, even
Harley had to conclude that two courses of action, diametrically
opposed to each other, could both be an honest Christian interpretation of God's will.

The professor opened enough church history to the students
to enable them to see that any religious group that chose to
govern and organize itself by law, beginning with Judaism, con-
tinuing with medieval Roman Catholicism, and coming down to
present-day instances, was doomed to wither and die on the vine.
"Law government can be maintained only by the passing of more
laws and the application of more military force," he observed.
Harley winced as he thought of the incident with his young peo-

ple and the dance. He shivered as he realized that the shoe fit him.

But the most exciting part of the course came when the professor began to construct a new understanding of the Christian life, after he had demolished the law understanding. He presented three points which came together and made great sense to Harley. "In the first place," he said, "law is always a limiting, anti-creative principle. It defines strict boundaries around how Christians are to respond to the love of God. In the second place, God has replaced law in the New Covenant with the motive power and example of his own Son. Christians are called to be 'little Christs,' as Luther put it, wherever they are each day. The motive power is God's love for us in Christ, rather than the fear of hell. And in the third place, Jesus Christ takes the Law, which the natural person makes the ceiling of all endeavors, and turns it into the floor, the foundation line from which the Christian moves onward and upward into new realms of hitherto unimagined service and witness." All the students spontaneously applauded the professor at the conclusion of his lecture. Harley clapped as loudly as any. The professor blushed, grinned sheepishly, and observed that applause was more pleasant even than his paycheck, and considerably less frequent.

The summer session solved one of his problems, but as Harley continued to wrestle with the question of the inspiration and authority of the Bible, he discovered that his two problems were so interrelated that one could not be solved until the other had also been settled. His view of the Bible made him an authoritarian legalist, even though his new view of Christian ethics had changed his view of law and legalism.

As Harley wrestled with these problems, his headaches continued to increase. Frequently he would be out of action for two or three days at a time. He assumed that somehow the headaches were psychologically related to his mental struggles, and he tried to calm Evelyn's fears with that argument. In his more honest personal moments he admitted to himself that his faith had lost its foundation in an inerrant Bible and had not yet found another one. There were frightening times when he found no faith in his heart. Preaching became difficult as he tried to preach out of his own unfaith to the people's faith. He wondered whether it would not be more honest to resign. He was sure he could think better if the headaches were not always bothering him.

He finally gave in to Evelyn's urging and that of his optometrist that he see a neurosurgeon. He was shocked almost beyond control when that doctor reported that he had a tumor or cyst on his brain in the region of his eighth nerve. Arrangements were made for immediate surgery. He and Evelyn clung to each other like frightened children. Finally, Harley admitted to Evelyn his faith crisis. Try as he would, he could not address God as his heavenly Father. On the night before the surgery, after the attendants had shaved his head and the resident insisted that Evelyn keep the clippings for the undertaker, he could only pray, "God, if there is a God, have mercy on my soul, if I have a soul."

Harley survived the surgery, even though there were touch-and-go emergency moments. Recovery was a slow process. But after a week of coma, he began to regroup his thoughts, delighted, in the first place, to discover that he was still alive. God had not sent him to hell, as he should have done. An overwhelming emotion of love filled Harley's whole being. At the center of this deep emotion was the crucified Lord Jesus Christ, for whose sake God had forgiven him and spared his life. Harley was participating in a miracle, a strong and personal demonstration of God's love for him. Now he wanted to belong to and serve the God who in love and mercy had spared his life. Now he understood the meaning of faith. Now the power to serve God was located inside himself and it was the power of love. He realized that before the surgery the drive to serve God had been located outside of himself and was in the last analysis some form of fear, which worked on him through the law. He discovered that his faith no longer rested on the Bible, but that instead it rested on God's promise to redeem him in Jesus Christ. Harley experienced emotions of happiness and freedom that he had not known before.

He was ready to return to the pulpit when the doctors finally permitted him to do so. He wanted to share his new understanding of God's love with everyone he could reach. Now he felt that he had the necessary gifts for ministry: faith, hope, and love. Now he realized how dry and poor his leadership of the people had been, how ineffective his own person and example had been. These new gifts became very important to him, for they served to convince him that he was indeed ready for ministry, that he had been called by God and equipped with the necessary gifts. He remembered reading something about necessary gifts for ministry in college, but the primary gift that was required seemed to be the ability to complete four years of Bible college with adequate grades and then to know someone who would find the first congregation for you. He could remember some professors talking about gifts, but as he reflected on their remarks, it seemed to him that the proof of readiness rested in the fact that these young aspirants were offering themselves for lives of poorly paid ministry. Wasn't that proof enough that they were gifted for ministry?

He began to understand the atmosphere of fear and tenseness that he had often noticed at council meetings and in general among the members. It could probably be traced in larger measure to his own style of Christian leadership. He recalled the old proverb "As pastor, so people," and he was convinced that at least in his own case and the people of Olivet it was a true saying. He was determined and anxious to share his new insights, his new personality, his new style of leadership with them for their sakes.

Harley discovered that the new power of love at work in him was leading him to seek new objects for his attention. He became much more concerned about the plight of the poor and the needy in the city and he tried, with limited success, to persuade other members to follow his example. He recalled reading once that Bernard of Clairvaux said that the closer he came to God in worship, the nearer did he find himself standing to his needy fellow people.

However, at Bible college it had been drilled into Harley's mind that the church as church was not to become involved in programs of social reform, but was to limit its activities to saving souls. The belief was that only saved souls through their individual efforts could make lasting improvements in society. Harley was no longer convinced by this argument.

As the months moved on, Harley found the concept of imitating Christ to be at the same time frightening, challenging, and curiously comforting. It challenged almost every one of his Christian values to test them by the model of Jesus' life. Particularly challenging were Jesus' words in Mark 10 about having come not to be served, but to serve and to give his life to ransom or to set people free. As Harley tried to imitate this call, he discovered many things that were imprisoning him, things that he needed to escape from before he could try to set others free, things like fear, the desire for comfort and prestige, the old compelling wish to please and the need to be liked, an intense pressure to conform to social and churchly traditions, especially those he had been taught at college, and so forth. However, as he carried out his ministry, he also saw how poverty, sickness, unfair laws and social structures imprisoned great numbers of people, rich and poor alike. In his sermons, counseling, and daily schedule, Harley began to place more emphasis on the Christian's call to be active in improving society, and even began to suggest ways in which the congregation as congregation could be active in Belleville.

Some members were puzzled by his new approach, others were disturbed and even angry about it. As one old pillar of the congregation put it, "Harley, you know durn well that our religion keeps our daily lives separate from Sunday's preaching. You're starting to get the two mixed up, and it will only make the people angry. We've got a good congregation going here; don't rock the boat."

It soon became clear to Harley that a considerable number of council members were of a similar mind. A confrontation crisis was developing at Olivet. To head it off, one council member suggested a weekend retreat in which Harley would have an opportunity to tell the people where he was going, and they would have an opportunity to express their fears and hopes to him. Out of that retreat, it was hoped, a new sense of direction and a new spirit of love and harmony would emerge at Olivet.

About half the congregation came to the two-and-a-half-day

retreat. The weekend began Friday night with a service and a fellowship hour. Harley led the Bible discussion on St. Paul's words, "Imitate me as I imitate Christ." He assured the congregation that he was not setting himself up as a perfect example or a goody-goody type person, while at the same time he explained to them that he believed that a special responsibility rested upon him as pastor to provide an inspiring example. He spoke to them frankly of his need for their individual prayers and support as he tried to meet this heavy responsibility. Apparently, the idea was so new and radical that the people were not ready for good, animated discussion. Most of the questions showed that either the questioner had misunderstood Harley or else was floundering in water that was frighteningly deep.

In the first Bible hour on Saturday, Harley focused on Matthew 25 and discussed the Christian's call to imitate Christ by visiting the prisoners, clothing the naked, feeding the hungry, and so forth. He argued that both individual Christians and the congregation as congregation had been called by Christ not only to help the poor and the needy but also to change the social, economic, and political conditions that produced poverty and need. He pointed to specific examples of corruption and oppression in Belleville that the church could affect for the better.

This presentation generated a good discussion about the church's mission. Most of those present disagreed with Harley's wider, socially oriented understanding. They recited various Biblical laws which they believed talked only about one person's responsibility toward another person, and never about the church as an institution. They also quoted Jesus' words about his kingdom not being of this world and about seeking first the kingdom of God and his righteousness. The interest was so high and the discussion so promising, that Harley scrapped his third planned presentation and continued with the one on mission.

He offered his own understanding of the crucial passages. He reminded his members, in the first place, that "kingdom" in those passages meant God's activity in this world to bring to people his gifts of forgiveness, love, peace, health, and so forth. He pointed out, in the second place, that he, like Jesus, was not

interested in building a kingdom that was of this world. "Who,"
he asked, "would get excited about a God whose kingdom was
like that of the kings, presidents, or rulers of this world, marked
by greed, ambition, rivalry, power struggles, deception, and ruthless destruction? Or who would seek for a kingdom that offered
only meat and drink? People want a kingdom that brings joy and
peace in the Spirit. Or who, once having discovered God's kingdom, would not want to seek it first, above everything else?"

Harley expected many to disagree with him, but he was not
prepared for the direction the church's discussion took. The first
questioners ignored the subject of mission and kingdom and
concentrated on Harley's new way of explaining the Bible. The
questioners did not conceal their fear that he was twisting the
Bible to suit his own ideas. "Where," they asked, "will all this
end? How long will it be before you conclude that Jesus was not
God, that he did not really die for us?" One of his constant
supporters, in a voice quavering with emotion, asked him, "What
about Jonah? If you can say that 'kingdom' means something else
than the Bible says it means, what about Jonah? Was he swallowed by the whale? What about Adam and Eve? Were they real
persons?"

The murmurs in the audience made it clear that the questioner had touched a raw nerve to which Harley had not really
been sensitive. Harley prayed for the grace of a gentle and wise
answer, but the prayer went unanswered. His own emotional
conviction about faith based on Jesus Christ rather than on an
inspired, inerrant Bible, literally interpreted, his convictions
about the church's mission and the need to reinterpret many
Bible passages in order to stress the mission properly, led him to
speak hastily and thus harmfully. Rashly he said that he didn't
know if Jonah was a historical person or not. What was important
was the mission God gave him and would not let him lay down.
He affirmed that he had learned many good ideas from the use
of historical criticism, and he wasn't sure about Adam and Eve as
real historical persons. Those two comments ended the possibility of any further constructive dialogue with the now clearly
frightened and angry majority. Many of them did not even stay

for the full weekend. Some were sensitive enough to offer lame excuses to Harley, while others simply left.

Some of the wiser men and women in the congregation spoke to Harley to assure him that the remarks were not aimed at him personally, but rather flowed from the irrational fear that his remarks about the Bible and Jonah and Adam and Eve and historical criticism had generated. Jim Wisdom reminded him that he had never before used the phrase "historical criticism" to describe his methods of Bible study, and that it was the term itself that alarmed people. He also reminded Harley that he and many other members had been trained all their lives to put their faith and hope in an inerrant Bible. He admitted that he was not ready to give it up yet, although he expressed his intention to support Harley and to work through these problems with him.

The character of Harley's ministry changed radically after that weekend that had begun with so much promise. Some members began to regard him with suspicion and dislike. A considerable number stopped coming to church or began attending other churches.

However, a minority rallied to Harley with genuine enthusiasm. They supported him in every way and Harley found a new dimension of strength and joy in their support. He remarked to Evelyn that the spirit of the small surviving group reminded him of the descriptions of the small early Christian communities who continued steadfast in the apostles' teaching and in fellowship and in the breaking of bread and in prayer. Despite the large losses, Harley and Evelyn had never known greater happiness or peace of mind.

But the new spirit was not destined to last long. Complaints were brought against Harley before the regional officials of the denomination. Rather than engage in long arguments that had been already answered in the officials' minds and that would only adversely affect the church's image in the community, Harley offered to resign. Regional officials and some friends within the congregation encouraged him to apologize, to affirm that Jonah and Adam and Eve were historical and to promise not to use historical-critical methods any longer. But Harley believed that these statements would so compromise his personal integrity that his imitation of Christ before the eyes of the people would be basically flawed and hypocritical. And so, on the seventh anniversary of his installation, Harley preached his farewell sermon. He was sure that he and Evelyn would find another congregation someplace.

COMMENTARY

The ministry of Harley Theim at Olivet Church can be divided into two phases. In many ways, his change parallels that experienced by many American pastors and congregations in the period following World War II. The tragedy that finally terminated his ministry has likewise been experienced by the members of many congregations.

In its first phase, the center of Harley's ministry was the inerrant Bible and the conviction that faith demanded such a Bible and needed to be based on that kind of book. Probably Harley and his members did not intend to move Jesus Christ to the side and to place the Bible at the center of their faith, but in effect this is what they did. Many studies and surveys indicate that this has happened to many American Christians.

Related to his Bible-centered faith was a conviction that the Christian life was largely shaped by the applications of laws and rules. The Ten Commandments undoubtedly played a major role in Harley's preaching. And related to this emphasis on the commandments was the introduction of fear and the threat of damnation as an important motivation to Christian living. The appeal to law and to fear is not easily documented or proved, but it is safe to say that these are still the twin weapons of many Christian pastors and people. Even the appeal to Jesus Christ is often an appeal to Jesus as a threatening example of what to do and what not to do.

It also seems that in many cases the combination of an inerrant Bible, the appeal to law, and the use of fear as motivation led to a very high and strict view of the pastor's authority. Because pastors knew the Bible best, because they could present the doctrines that were found in the Bible, because they understood God's law and will best, and because they were concerned to save the people from hell by preaching, the people in turn were happy to grant pastors a paternalistic and overpowering authority in their lives. Pastors were not the servants of God in their midst, but often by every test and standard they were God's rulers among his people.

In the case of Harley and many other Christian pastors, there was a further belief that knowledge of pure doctrine was the most important mark of the Christian and the greatest need that the Christian had. Thus sermons were heavily doctrinal in character and a great deal of emphasis was placed on head knowledge. Many members could recite large sections of Scripture and official church books, but this head knowledge frequently did not affect the life-style of these people. The argument almost seemed to be that knowledge of Biblical doctrine automatically produces faith and faith automatically produces good works. In some denominations characterized by this stress on head knowledge, the model seemed to work. At least it worked if the standard of success lay in church contributions and in the building of new buildings.

In many of these denominations, the emphasis upon intellectual knowledge was matched by a narrow understanding of the church's mission that equated mission with "saving souls." Since souls were saved largely through knowledge derived from an inerrant Bible, the mission of the church rested largely in gaining new members and in distributing tracts and in mounting expensive programs of Christian education in Sunday school and vacation Bible schools.

At the same time, this understanding of Biblical knowledge and faith created in many Christians the conviction that they needed to do certain good works in order to gain salvation. The presence of this desire to do good works to save themselves has been documented in recent years by several important sociological surveys. This determination to save oneself appears to be in direct contradiction to many Bible passages that emphasize that salvation is always God's gift in Jesus Christ.

Thus, in summary, the first stage of Harley's ministry was marked by a package of ideas and attitudes that resulted in a narrow understanding of the church's mission and a conviction on the part of his people that they needed to save themselves.

As you look into your own heart, what do you see to be the actual center of your faith? What part does the Bible play in your faith? Do any of the descriptions of the first phase of Harley's ministry ring true with your own religious experiences?

Following his surgery, the character of Harley's ministry changed radically, according to the Cameo. The basic change seems to be that Jesus Christ took up residence in Harley's heart in a dramatically new way.

In this second phase, Harley's understanding of the pastoral office and of pastoral authority also underwent a radical change. Crucial to this new understanding was Harley's discovery of the principle of imitation of Jesus Christ. Harley was especially struck by St. Paul's call to his Christian friends to imitate him as he imitated Jesus Christ.

As he approached his ministry in this new spirit, the people warmed to him in a new way and they began to come to him with a host of problems and troubles that previously they had kept to themselves. They sensed that Harley was now a real brother and a real friend. They sensed in him a warmth and an integrity that drew them to him. In his own mind, Harley understood that his authority centered primarily and basically on his authority to deal with the problem of sin. With every passing day, he discovered new burdens of sins that his people were bearing and under which they were slowly and inevitably being crushed. The burden of sin was never pleasant, and Harley often felt like a stable boy whose lot in life was to perform unpleasant duties. But, in imitation of Jesus Christ, he found great joy and satisfaction in performing those humble duties.

The Bible came to play a new role in Harley's ministry. Although Harley did not spell out this new role to his people, it did affect his approach to them and his methods of dealing with them. He abandoned the old concept that the Bible was a book of laws and rules and that his job was to force people to conform to certain Biblical standards and patterns of behavior. Instead he began to use the Bible as a source book of guidance and counsel and a source book of spiritual strength for troubled people. In a manner of speaking, he came to paraphrase Jesus' words about the sabbath being made for people and not people for the sabbath. Harley began to operate on the principle that the Bible was made for people in the sense that it was there to help each person become more Christlike, rather than being there as a threat and a pattern to which people had to conform or else be damned. This attitude did not mean that Harley was indifferent to the moral teachings of the Bible. He took them as seriously as ever, but he refused to quote a Biblical moral principle as the final and absolute solution to each moral problem that his people encountered. For example, he no longer found it possible to say to people that divorce was always wrong, as he had done to Mrs. Hanson in his earlier history. Instead he tried to help people in need find resources within the Bible that would enable them to make mature and adult decisions that would be God-pleasing.

He had to watch himself quite carefully in this new trust relationship to avoid abuses. Many of the people in the congregation were now quite ready to regard him as their father and to permit him to make all decisions for them. He often found himself tempted to play that fatherly role. At the same time, he gained a firsthand knowledge of how easy it was for the Christian pastor in the history of the church to become such a strong and dominant figure, since both the pastor and many of the people preferred that model. He often asked God for the grace of humility, and discovered the central importance of that particular virtue. At the same time, he sought to avoid a kind of Uriah Heep model of cringing humility. He believed that the pastor could be humble while at the same time a person of strong conviction.

How do the people of your parish define pastoral authority? Are you comfortable with the call to imitate Christ? Is this idea generally understood and accepted by the Christians you know?

As Harley tried to develop the concept of imitating Christ, his understanding of the church and its mission underwent radical changes. These changes showed themselves most evidently in his approach to the mission of the church in this world. Mission was no longer limited to saving souls, but had come to include the whole life of the whole person. Political and social concerns were as much a part of God's mission as the traditional concepts of preparing people for eternal life. As Harley read the Gospels and tried in spirit to imitate Jesus Christ, he found himself spending a great deal of time, alongside of his Master, dealing with hunger and sickness and nakedness. Harley had no trouble convincing himself that if Jesus had been alive in his day, he would have used all forces of politics and economics to heal the ills of people. In this respect, Harley's understanding of church and ministry was directly affected by his understanding of the person and work of Jesus Christ. By now you are aware of the importance of understanding this mutual relationship. In a very real sense, the picture of Jesus Christ that is presented in the Gospels and epistles of the New Testament is the critical factor by which church programs are to be judged. It is also the critial factor by which one's ideas about the nature and purpose of the church are to be judged. Thus a primary responsibility of any congregation is to engage in untiring study of what the New Testament says about Jesus Christ.

The Cameo says little about Harley's understanding of the church as the body of Christ because Harley paid little attention to that Pauline idea. Like many of his pastoral contemporaries, he did not understand the centrality of the church in Paul's thinking, and his ideas about the church were confused and underdeveloped. For example, Harley and many other pastors believed that their denomination, regardless of which one it was, was the only true church and that salvation could be found only in it. Others regarded their congregation as a collection of individuals who had voluntarily agreed to fellowship together for a time and to hire a pastor to do certain things for them. In this book, that understanding has been called "voluntaristic," and I have argued that this view does not do justice to the Biblical definition of

church. It is inadequate because it plays down the work of the
Holy Spirit as the Chief Gatherer. Nor does it give adequate
stress to the close relationships that bind together the members
of the body of Christ. Holy communion as the center of congregational unity is also usually deemphasized.

While Harley changed his definition of the church's mission
with respect to problems of charity and justice in the world, many
of his contemporaries have not done so. They still maintain that
the church's primary task is to save souls. They are concerned lest
religion become too worldly, in the words of Lyman Beecher.
Religion and life, so to speak, are not "confused" in this understanding. Therefore, the major functions are evangelizing and
education. Because many current-day Christians accept only part
of their challenge to be Christlike, they use only a part of the
spiritual resources that the Spirit has placed at their disposal.

In several places in this book, the thesis has been set forth that
one's understanding of Jesus Christ will, inevitably, affect his or
her understanding of the church, its nature and mission. It has
also been argued that the obverse is true: one's understanding of
the church will either reveal his or her subconscious thinking
about Jesus Christ or will actually shape and determine that understanding. This relationship can be traced in Harley's life, and
probably also in the lives of many of his contemporaries. Two
patterns of understanding can be suggested here; there are probably others.

In the first place, Harley did not fully understand the humanity of Jesus Christ. He said repeatedly that Jesus was fully God
and fully man but he also believed that Jesus' humanity was
necessary only so that he might take our place under the law and
die for our sins on the cross. Of course, this is a true and fundamental Christian statement. But it overlooks two other important
reasons why the world's Redeemer had to be human as well as
divine. The first reason was so that he might be tempted just as
we are (Heb. 4:15) and do battle for us with sin, death, and the
devil, overcoming them in his resurrection. Thus his humanity is
like ours and plays a vital, active role in our salvation, rather than
a merely passive role as it did in much of Harley's preaching.

Furthermore, Harley erred in not focusing on Jesus' human nature and human body and the implications that Paul and others
saw in this truth for their understanding of the church. The
church, the group of believers, is also his body, joined by every
ligament and joint so that together the various members can
grow in grace and Christlikeness. In other words, both Harley's
Christology and his ecclesiology were underdeveloped. Which
came first? That question cannot be answered, but both doctrines
supported each other in their abortive development.

Furthermore, Harley had almost no understanding or appreciation of the grandeur and the glory of the holy Christian
church. The attitude of men like John Chyrysostom and Ambrose
of Milan would have made little sense to Harley, if he had become
acquainted with them. Harley had been trained by his professors
to say that the "church is people," and he had not moved beyond
that in his own thinking. That phrase contains a most important
truth and is a necessary corrective for those who identify church
with building or denomination. However, the church is also the
body of Christ, and as such is more than people. Or at least one
can say that the church is people who are joined together as the
body of Christ, and as such are a new entity, always on their way
together to mature personhood, to the measure of the stature of
him whose body they are in the world. This understanding of the
church has implications for one's understanding of preaching, of
the sacraments, and of the church's mission.

*Try once again to articulate your understanding of the person and
the work of Jesus Christ and of the nature and purpose of the church.
How do these two fundamental concepts relate to each other? How
does your view of these two ideas affect your understanding of the
church's mission?*

Following the abortive weekend retreat, Harley made an acci-
dental discovery about the nature of the church that strongly
influenced him at Olivet and that must have played a major role
in his future pastoral assignments. That discovery centered in the
unique strengths of the small group that met together regularly
for the "apostles' teaching and fellowship, . . . the breaking of

bread and the prayers." (Acts 2:42, RSV) Though he did not articulate the dynamics in his own mind at that time, he was experiencing what I have called the five basic functions of healthy Christian community living, and he was discovering that these functions have always developed best in the context of small groups. Surely he was finding a new meaning in the word "fellowship" as he and his people learned to support each other. Furthermore, he was experiencing the importance of "mutual Christian nurture" as he and his remaining handful helped each other to grow in faith and in the prosecution of their Christian mission. They learned to support each other for "witness" and "service" in ways that were far more effective than had been true in the large group. They were surely experiencing new dimensions of "worship," although they undoubtedly missed the worship life that they had shared with a much larger group.

To what degree do you consciously seek to grow in the five functions? To what degree do present congregational structures effectively help Christians to help each other to grow in these graces?

13.
Daniel Daugherty

CAMEO

Father Daniel Joseph Daugherty* lifted his black cassock from its peg in the All Saints' sacristy. He was wearing tennis whites —flannel shorts, polo shirt, tennis shoes, fuzzy white athletic socks. Earlier, he had played three brisk sets with Marvin Klein, managing editor of the *Tribune*, a worthy opponent, whom Daugherty had met in the course of his work with runaway children. Daugherty had been, since age ten, an excellent tennis player. He might well have been Davis Cup or a pro. He kept it up in the seminary and later, on a catch-as-catch-can basis in the Navy. He resumed a regular routine when he reported to All Saints', playing not less than three days a week. The All Saints' pastor, Monsignor Ryan, did not like it. They were shorthanded, like all suburban parishes in Washington, and Ryan resented the time it took. Besides that, Daugherty sensed, Ryan thought his assistant pastor looked undignified in tennis togs, a bit frivolous, a bit too much like the rich playboy. Ryan was strictly old-school.

---

*The pastor in this chapter is a fictitious contemporary Roman Catholic priest who is the leading figure in *The Archbishop,* a novel by Clay Blair, Jr. Material from the novel has been condensed for the purpose of this book by omitting several pages, and by putting between brackets new material that will bridge over the omitted part. The chapter is abridged from pp. 7–15 of *The Archbishop* by Clay Blair, Jr. (World Pub. Co.). Copyright © 1970 by Clay Blair, Jr. Reprinted by permission of Harper & Row, Publishers, Inc.

He had been taught, and believed, that a priest should hold himself aloof from temporal activities, sports, movies, cocktail parties, never be seen out of uniform, nor upset the popular conception of priestly character as popularized by Barry Fitzgerald, Bing Crosby, and Spencer Tracy. The people, the flock, *wanted* the stylized conception, Ryan argued. An aloof and dignified priest was more credible. He helped support their faith, the mystical loyalty and obedience to the Eternal Church. Let them see no chink in the armor. Never let them sense that a priest might have human failings—fear, anxiety, money worries, sex problems. Nor should a priest ever project an image of having *fun*.

To Daugherty, tennis was not precisely *fun*. It was many things. It was a way of keeping in shape physically, which he believed to be important to his general well-being. It was a way of escaping, at least momentarily, the Niagra of trouble that deluged him seven days a week, in the confessional, the rectory, in the hospitals, homes for invalids and aged, the juvenile courts, psychologists' offices, retreat houses, schoolrooms. The steady procession of ill-advised marriages, illnesses, physical and mental, unwanted children, alcoholic parents, wayward teen-agers, unwanted aged, and finally (blessedly!), the funerals and the anguish—some real, some phony. On a good, hard clay court, Dan Daugherty put all that aside, restored his mental equilibrium. Then too (he knew well), tennis was his one way of forcefully expressing his manhood. Facing an opponent like Marvin Klein, Father Daugherty's primitive instincts—aggression and hostility, the territorial imperative—took charge of his being. He played with savage, killing fury. He played to win, usually did, and this gave him intense satisfaction. He would not give it up, no matter how bad it was for his image. Not that he bought a single line of Ryan's argument anyway.

He slipped the cassock over his head. It was fresh from the cleaners yet still smelled faintly of stale perspiration. It was tight in the bodice, with a flaring skirt, like a well-tailored dress. Daugherty did not like the uniform. For one thing, it was feminine, like much of Mother Church. He felt that, in a real sense, it did much to deny the manhood he fought for on the courts.

He snapped on his fresh white collar, walked nimbly from the sacristy to the altar. It was getting dark. The altar was appropriately dark and somber. The red tabernacle light was burning, dramatically signifying the presence of God. Father Daugherty had never understood the need for this showmanship. The first words of the Baltimore Catechism taught that God was everywhere. He did not need a light to call attention to His being.

Father Daugherty genuflected before the altar, hoping his tennis shoes and bare legs would not be noticed. Then he walked down the aisle in the dimness toward the confessional [feeling rising anger toward everything that All Saints' and its new ski-lodge building had come to represent in his mind].

It is not likely that any church, however ingenious, would have pleased Father Daugherty. His views on churches were radical. He was fundamentally opposed to the very concept of a church, that is, a specific structure where people gathered to worship God at a stated time each week in a formalized ceremony, the Mass. All that was obsolete. He believed in what he called a "living religion"; that people should love God, communicate with God all day long, wherever they might be. To Daugherty, churchgoing was a sign of weakness. Weakness on the part of the flock for feeling the need to be congregated specifically to communicate with God; weakness on the part of the Church for fostering that feeling of need, demanding that one attend or face eternal damnation. [He had even suggested that All Saints' not be built; the Catholics and Episcopalians could pool the existing Episcopal church. Naturally, this suggestion was ignored.]

There were now, in the rear pew of the church, a dozen parishioners, kneeling in prayer, preparing their confession. Father Daugherty passed them silently, head bowed, properly aloof, yet longing—feeling an almost uncontrollable compulsion—to reach out and touch them, to prove he was human, sympathetic, compassionate. He wanted to hear noise, to shout, bring the dead building alive, make the big beams overhead reverberate with joy and happiness, wanted *everyone* to rejoice, to celebrate that God had given them life, a being, and then to send them away, to help the less fortunate, to experience the warm glow of giving, to understand, as Christ had said, that there was no greater reward. He wanted to banish them from the ski lodge, so to speak. But if he did, they would surely put him down as a nut. Like Christ, in his time.

He pulled back the heavy green drape and entered the confessional. It was a duty—a chore—he detested. He would remain there on the hard oak seat two hours, sliding open one little door and then the next. He would hear, for the most part, a routine, mechanistic litany of sins from the young, for which he was required, like a judge in court, to dole out routine, mechanistic penance. He would hear of mortal and venial sins—felonies and misdemeanors—and all the while, he would feel monumentally superfluous. After all, no man needed a priest to serve as a go-between to God. God was Man. Man was God. God was everything. Everything was God. One had only to say, sincerely, *mea culpa.* The confessional was obsolete too. Group therapy was an infinitely more effective cathartic.

They came in endless procession. It was not yet a large parish. He recognized them through the screen, knew the shapes of their ears and noses, the smell of their bodies and breaths. The little Burroughs boy. Used the name of the Lord in vain five times. Say five Our Fathers and five Hail Marys and a Perfect Act of Contrition. Pretty Nancy Favrot, leader in the CYO, faltering, twisting her handkerchief, whispering almost inaudibly: she had had evil thoughts seven times. Dear Nancy, he thought, and longed to say, it is the natural human condition. Instead: Did you touch yourself? No, Father—aghast. Say ten Our Fathers and ten Hail Marys and ask God to keep your thoughts pure. Caught in this piddling, false routine, while the greater sin, the dishonesty and hypocrisy of the Church, went unpunished, the crisis went unheeded. He asked the next confessor, the Rogers woman—poor arthritic vegetable—to give him spiritual strength, remember him in her prayers.

He could use a little help. Or perhaps a great deal. For some time now, he did not know precisely how long, he had suffered a crisis of faith. It had begun with his doubts about Church policy on celibacy.

As a young seminarian, it had been easy for Daugherty, approaching the subdiaconate phase of his Major Orders, to sign that solemn Latin document. As a teen-ager, his sex drive had not been strong. He seldom dated, preferring a good book to a silly girl. For him, an erection, a nocturnal emission, had been a rarity. He believed then that celibacy was a gift from God, an extraordinary state of being that lifted him above the common man and brought him into a mystical union with Christ—an "objectively superior state of life," as it had been declared by the Council of Trent. He did not believe in marriage for priests. He accepted the view that Scripture forbade it. He believed that a married priest would inevitably face a crippling conflict of interest—be torn between his obligation to God and his duty to wife and family. Celibacy was, as Pope Paul defined it, a "crowning jewel."

[At this time of crisis, Daugherty became acquainted with an older priest, Andre LeGuiese, who seemed to be on a first-name basis with every liberal theologian and bishop in the Church. LeGuiese had encouraged Daugherty to stay, to tunnel from within. He assured the younger man that great changes were about to happen. He told him that the papal commission had voted 70–14 in favor of authorizing contraception. It was only a matter of time until the Holy Father would make a public announcement in support. "Wait a little bit longer," was always LeGuiese's pastoral advice.]

Father Daugherty was waiting. Like tens of millions of Catholics everywhere.

As he opened the window now on the familiar silhouette of Jean Favrot, Daugherty was conscious of a curious force in the air. As though the mere act of sliding back the little board had somehow released pent-up forces that had long been gathering. The sight of her pretty face through the screen, the smell of her perfume, the recollection of her good work for the parish in spite of the burden of all those children—six tumultuous boys and a baby, plus two girls—and the knowledge of the chaos she endured moved him, profoundly, to pity. In the desperate brown eyes that peered toward him through the screen, he saw, summed up, his own personal crisis. He had an urge to tear away the screen, to see her face to face, without artificial barriers, without ceremonial trappings. Somehow, he sensed that if he could penetrate her spirit, he would find his own strength, that his own problem was inextricably interwoven with hers. It was as though she had appeared as a holy vision, an apparition. A sign?

Jean Favrot had, literally, fallen on her knees in the confessional. The contact with the hard wood hurt. Beyond that, her mind was utter confusion. She had meant to drop the children, rush the groceries home, then return for her own confession. Instead, she had parked and run headlong into the church, leaving the children to straggle inside. She had knelt before a statue of the Blessed Virgin, lit a candle, and waited for the familiar, comforting release. This time, it had not come. Rather, the anxiety, the peculiar feeling that she was separating from herself, floating away helplessly, overpowered her. She did not know how long she had knelt, staring unseeingly at the votive candles. Nor was she aware of Nancy's guiding her to the confessional whispering, "Hurry up. The food's defrosting."

Now she saw, in the dimness of the box (as she always thought of it), the handsome, virile features of Father Daugherty, his dark hair, good clean nose, the jutting chin, the long sideburns sweeping rakishly forward on his cheek, the youthful face turned down and away. She smelled his sweat—athletic sweat. She heard him sigh, too, a deep, tremulous sigh for so young a man. She did not bless herself.

Waiting for her to begin the stylized ritual of the confessional —"Bless me, Father, for I have sinned . . ."—Daugherty turned his head toward her slightly. He saw the tips of her fingers pressing tightly against the outside molding of the window. Then, looking closely, he saw a mask of anguish, a woman desperately reaching to—or beyond—her depth.

"Go on," he said gently.

At last Jean found her voice.

"I've had it," she said through the screen. "Right up to here."

She raised one hand, flat and level, to her eyebrows. Her voice was cool.

Father Daugherty leaned forward, ear close to the screen.

"Go on."

Jean Favrot put her mouth against the screen. Her voice came like the hiss of broken steam pipes: "I've absolutely reached the end of my rope. I can't go on like this. Not a day longer. What kind of God is this anyway? My husband, a damned lush, out playing golf, leaving me with nine children and all their endless errands and the car's broken down half the time and *he* goes on trips and what do I have to show for what I've done? Look at me, worn out, bedraggled, my hair a mess, no clothes, a damned maid, a slave, and believe me, there is plenty in life I *could* do . . ."

She went on, almost incoherently, damning her lot, her family. Father Daugherty sat back, sighed, tapped his right tennis shoe against the carpet. He listened, yet he did not. He heard snatches. All too familiar snatches. Let her blow off steam. The unhappiness of the world knew no boundaries. It was all wrong. Then he heard her voice, sharp, clear, forceful:

"I *hate* God."

The eyes were gone now, buried in her hands. He could see that she was trembling, sobbing. He coughed gently. She looked up, tears streaking down her cheeks.

"I *have* to have peace of mind," she said. "He doesn't give me any."

The clichés and platitudes on the Sacred Sacrament of Holy Matrimony that Father Daugherty had amassed over the years to haul up for such occasions now crowded his mind, lifeless, absurd. We were brought on this earth to suffer, to atone for Christ's suffering, for all the sins since Adam and Eve. Suffering makes us stronger. It leads to the eternal reward, the sight of God, a seat at His feet. Suffering builds character. Suffering reaffirms the Faith. If we do not suffer, then how can we recognize pleasure when it comes? God is punishing you, my dear, in his mysterious way.

"I want to get away," she hissed. "I *hate* my children. My life. I want to take the pill. I want to commit sin. I think about it all the time. The commission . . . they will approve the pill, won't they? Why can't I begin now? I want to live—not just exist. I

. . . I want to *enjoy* sex, but I don't want any more children. Can't you tell me *something?*"

He let her run on, knowing now his premonition had been correct. A strange, indefinable alliance had been joined this day, in this confessional. They were alike in their doubts, yet Jean had faith. That she was here now—however desperate—was proof. He had to help her. In Jean Favrot's spiritual strength perhaps he might find his own. No soul, no family in the parish was in graver danger. She did not need confession. Jean Favrot needed release—urgent release—from the stupid, stifling bonds of the Roman Catholic Church. She must be saved, whatever the price.

"Jean," he said softly, but firmly. "In matters of sex, let your conscience be your guide. Try to make it with Bob, if you can. If your conscience tells you to use the pill, use it. I can't officially condone it. You know that. But if you want my opinion, you've done enough—brought enough life on earth."

He saw in her face a ray of hope, then anger.

"Bob won't buy it. I'd have to do it secretly."

"You can't deceive him. You have to work it out together."

"Why am I in this incredible position? That I have to go groveling to him after I've given him nine children. Answer that."

Father Daugherty sighed again, pausing to gather his thoughts.

"Jean, I can't help you. You know the rules. I can't say, here or elsewhere, use the pill. When I say let your conscience be your guide, you know what I mean. You've been reading the theological arguments. By advising you to follow your conscience, I'm guilty of . . . of heresy, because you know what my meaning implies. I could be fired tonight if this got out. I never told anyone that before . . ."

"I need *help!* This church isn't giving it to me."

"Could . . . could you and Bob come to the rectory later?"

"He'll be stoned. We're going to his boss's for dinner. Anyway, it would be pointless."

What was a religion then, Daugherty thought, that could fail a woman at a time like this? His mind searched feverishly for some answer, a word of hope. Then he thought of Dr. Cantor, the psychologist at the McLean Guidance Center. They had first met at city hall on a juvenile delinquency panel discussion. Cantor was young, brilliant, practical, a non-Freudian who believed strongly in the new theories of group therapy—had in fact developed some techniques of his own. Daugherty had never sent a parishioner from the confessional to the clinic. Yet . . . He turned to the face in the window.

"The best advice I can give you, Jean, from my heart, is go over to the McLean Guidance Center and talk to a psychologist named Dr. Cantor. Join a group therapy session. It may do you a world of good. If I had the time, or the competence, the professional competence, I would gladly give it. But you can get it there, better, I know."

"Bob wouldn't permit it," she said.

"Don't tell him."

"And the pill?"

"I told you. That's for you to decide. Your conscience, and Bob's. That's all I'm going to say."

"But . . ."

"Go in peace," Father Daugherty said, closing the window. And to himself: "Pray for me."

COMMENTARY

Father Daugherty's supervisor, Monsignor Ryan, seems to share rather fully the views of Ambrose of Milan and his concept of the priestly role and function. Daniel Daugherty represents a different model of priestly care. In what follows, the concern is not to defend or criticize either man, but rather to put into sharp focus several questions about the nature of the Christian community and the practice of pastoral care for the mission of the church. The fact that the Cameo is fictitious does not rob it of any of its truth or usefulness. To underscore the applicability of this chapter, the Commentary will pose questions about Fathers Ryan and Daugherty in the light of shorter quotations taken from the Decree on Church and Ministry adopted at the Second Vatican

Council. The Commentary is divided into discussions of priesthood and of the church's nature and mission.

Monsignor Ryan had a very specific view of the priest's nature and role. He was a father-figure, set apart from the people by his ordination to be the incarnate symbol of everything the Church is. Father Daugherty's view was almost the exact opposite. In the light of the conflict between the two men, read the following paragraphs from the decrees of Vatican II on the effect of ordination, priestly nature, and priestly duties. Try to read each paragraph from the viewpoint of Ryan and Daugherty—and from your own perspective.

However, the Lord also appointed certain men as ministers, in order that they might be united in one body in which "all the members have not the same function" (Rom. 12:4). These men were to hold in the community of the faithful the sacred power of Order, that of offering sacrifice and forgiving sins, and were to exercise the priestly office publicly on behalf of men in the name of Christ. Thus Christ sent the apostles as he himself had been sent by the Father, and then through the apostles made their successors, the bishops, sharers in his consecration and mission. The function of the bishops' ministry was handed over in a subordinate degree to priests so that they might be appointed in the order of the priesthood and be co-workers of the episcopal order for the proper fulfilment of the apostolic mission that had been entrusted to it by Christ.

God, who alone is the holy one and sanctifier, has willed to take men as allies and helpers to become humble servants in his work of sanctification. The purpose then for which priests are consecrated by God through the ministry of the bishop is that they should be made sharers in a special way in Christ's priesthood and, by carrying out sacred functions, act as his ministers who through his Spirit continually exercises his priestly function for our benefit in the liturgy. By Baptism priests introduce men into the People of God; by the sacrament of Penance they reconcile sinners with God and the Church; by the Anointing of the Sick they relieve those who are ill; and especially by the celebration of Mass they offer Christ's sacrifice sacramentally. But in the celebration of all the sacraments—as St. Ignatius Martyr already asserted in the early Church—priests are hierarchically united with the bishop in various ways and so make him present in a certain sense in individual assemblies of the faithful.

As to the faithful, they (the priests) should bestow their paternal attention and solicitude on them, whom they have begotten spiritually through baptism and instruction (cf. 1 Cor. 4:15; 1 Pet. 1:23). Gladly constituting themselves models of the flock (cf. 1 Pet. 5:3), they should preside over and serve their local community in such a way that it may deserve to be called by the name which is given to the unique People of God in its entirety, that is to say, the Church of God (cf. 1 Cor. 1:2; 2 Cor. 1:1, and *passim*). They should be mindful that by their daily conduct and solicitude they display the reality of a truly priestly and pastoral ministry both to believers and unbelievers alike, to Catholics and non-Catholics; that they are bound to bear witness before all men of the truth and of the life, and as good shepherds seek after those too (cf. Lk. 15:4–7) who, whilst having been baptised in the Catholic Church, have given up the practice of the sacraments, or even fallen away from the faith.

Priests should, therefore, occupy their position of leadership as men who do not seek the things that are their own but the things that are Jesus Christ's. They should unite their efforts with those of the lay faithful and conduct themselves among them after the example of the Master, who came amongst men "not to be served but to serve, and to give his life as a ransom for many" (Mt. 20:28). Priests are to be sincere in their appreciation and promotion of lay people's dignity and of the special role the laity have to play in the Church's mission.

Even though the priests of the new law by reason of the sacrament of Order fulfill the preeminent and essential function of father and teacher among the People of God and on their behalf, still they are disciples of the Lord along with all the faithful and have been made partakers of his kingdom by God, who has called them by his grace. Priests, in common with all who have been reborn in the font of baptism, are brothers among brothers as members of the same Body of Christ which all are commanded to build up.

The faithful for their part ought to realize that they have obligations to their priests. They should treat them with filial love as being their fathers and pastors. They should also share their priests' anxieties and help them as far as possible by prayer and active work so that they may be better able to overcome difficulties and carry out their duties with greater success.

In carrying out their duties as pastors parish priests should make it their special concern to know their parishioners. Since they are the shepherds of all the individual sheep they should endeavor to stimulate a growth of Christian life in each one of the faithful, in families, in associations, especially those dedicated to the apostolate, and finally, in the parish as a whole. They should, therefore, visit the homes and the schools as their pastoral function requires of them. They should manifest a special interest in adolescents and young people; they should exercise a paternal charity towards the poor and the sick. Finally, they should have a special care for the workers, and should urge the faithful to give their support to apostolic activities.

For the better ordering of the care of souls priests are strongly recommended to live in common, especially those attached to the same parish. This on one hand is helpful to their apostolate work, and on the other gives to the faithful an example of charity and unity. [From Austin P. Flannery, ed., *Documents of Vatican II* (Grand Rapids, Mich.: Eerdmans, 1975), pp. 864–865, 870–871, 386, 880, 881, 582, 581]

The Cameo and Commentary on priestly qualities and roles help to form a set of fundamental questions about the nature of the Christian community and its necessary leadership. The following questions represent only a few of the ideas that need to be studied. You will undoubtedly raise many more as you reflect on the material.

Do you think of ordination to ministry as Monsignor Ryan and the Decree of Vatican II do? What are the strengths and the weaknesses of that "high" view of ordination? How do you think of yourself with respect to your own humanity: like Ryan or Daugherty? Do the paragraphs quoted from Vatican II deal with that fundamental problem?

If small-group community life is essential for priestly work, should it not also be developed among laity, whose Christian calling in some senses is more difficult than that of priests?

The second concern that the Cameo underscores is that of the nature and the mission of the church. In the Cameo, Ryan and Daugherty represent two quite opposite viewpoints. Ryan thinks of the church basically as an institution for salvation and protection. Within the church, priests celebrate the eucharist, hear confession, preach, and generally help people to survive this life until they reach heaven. The building as such is important to Ryan because of his view of the nature and mission of the church. On the other hand, Daugherty thinks of buildings as liabilities. He is more interested in a life of praise that expresses itself in spontaneous worship and self-giving service for the needs of people. As you read the following paragraphs from the Decree on Church and Ministry, try again to read from the perspective of both men, and also from your own.

> The People of God finds its unity first of all through the Word of the living God, which is quite properly sought from the lips of priests. Since no one can be saved who has not first believed, priests, as co-workers with their bishops, have as their primary duty the proclamation of the gospel of God to all. In this way they fulfill the Lord's command: "Go into the whole world and preach the gospel to every creature" (Mk. 16:15). Thus they establish and build up the People of God.

> For through the saving Word the spark of faith is struck in the hearts of unbelievers, and fed in the hearts of the faithful. By this faith the community of the faithful begins and grows. As the Apostle says: "Faith depends on hearing and hearing on the word of Christ" (Rom. 10:17).

According to Vatican II, the highest form that the Word assumes in the congregation is in the eucharist.

> In carrying out their work of sanctification parish priests should ensure that the celebration of the Eucharistic Sacrifice is the center and culmination of the entire life of the Christian community. It should also be their aim to ensure

that the faithful receive spiritual nourishment from a frequent and devout reception of the sacraments and from the attentive and fervent participation in the liturgy. Parish priests must bear it constantly in mind how much the Sacrament of penance contributes to the development of the Christian life and should therefore be readily available for the hearing of the confessions of the faithful. If necessary they should call on other priests who are fluent in different languages to help in this work.

Priests are to be sincere in their appreciation and promotion of lay people's dignity and of the special role the laity have to play in the Church's mission. They should also have an unfailing respect for the just liberty which belongs to everybody in civil society. They should be willing to listen to lay people, give brotherly consideration to their wishes and recognize their experience and competence in the different fields of human activity. In this way they will be able to recognize along with them the signs of the times.

Modern man is in a process of fuller personality development and of a growing discovery and affirmation of his own rights. But the Church is entrusted with the task of opening up to man the mystery of God, who is the last end of man; in doing so it opens up to him the meaning of his own existence, the innermost truth about himself. The Church knows well that God alone, whom it serves, can satisfy the deepest cravings of the human heart, for the world and what it has to offer can never fully content it.

In virtue of the Gospel entrusted to it the Church proclaims the rights of man: she acknowledges and holds in high esteem the dynamic approach of today which is fostering these rights all over the world. But this approach needs to be animated by the spirit of the Gospel and preserved from all traces of false autonomy. For there is a temptation to feel that our personal rights are fully maintained only when we are exempt from every restriction of divine law. But this is the way leading to the extinction of human dignity, not its preservation.

Christ did not bequeath to the Church a mission in the political, economic, or social order: the purpose he assigned to it was a religious one. But this religious mission can be the source of commitment, direction, and vigor to establish and consolidate the community of men according to the law of God. In fact, the Church is able, indeed it is obliged, if times and circumstances require it, to initiate action for the benefit of all men, especially of those in need, like works of mercy and similar undertakings.

One of the gravest errors of our time is the dichotomy between the faith which many profess and the practice of their daily lives. . . . Let there, then, be no such pernicious opposition between professional and social activity on the one hand and religious life on the other. The Christian who shirks his temporal duties shirks his duties towards his neighbor, neglects God himself, and endangers his eternal salvation. Let Christians follow the example of Christ who worked as a craftsman; let them be proud of the opportunity to carry out their earthly activity in such a way as to integrate human, domestic, professional, scientific and technical enterprises with religious values, under whose supreme direction all things are ordered to the glory of God. [*Documents of Vatican II,* pp. 582, 880, 940, 941, 942, 943]

In the church that is described in the Decree of Vatican II, priests play the central role in establishing the church, in preserving it, and in defining its nature and its mission. In this respect, there seems to be a direct line from Ambrose of Milan to the Decree on Church and Ministry. One has to respect an understanding of church and ministry that has evidently served the deepest spiritual needs of millions of people for thousands of years. But at the same time in the long history of the church, another view of church, ministry, and mission has also been present. The questions that are posed in the following paragraph are not intended to criticize the Roman Catholic view, but rather to highlight some of the differences between what can be called the hierarchical and the egalitarian views of church and Christian community.

Do you agree with the statement that is made in the first sentence of the preceding paragraph? If your answer is "Yes," do you approve of that priestly role? In its statements on the mission of the church, Vatican II seems to be more in harmony with Father Daugherty than with Father Ryan. Do you agree with Vatican II? If you do, how successful is your parish in putting that view of mission into practice? What have you personally found most helpful in enabling you to be "about your Father's business"?

14.
Jack W. Marshall

CAMEO

H. Allen Smith once described Jack's town as a good town to be from. More and more, Jack Marshall had come to agree with the humorist. Tonight was the final blow. After three months of patient, weekly instruction of six prospective members, four of them had announced tonight that they were not going to join Jack's Methodist church. Their reasons were vague, but their intent was clear. Jack mentally reviewed the church records of his three years' work. The congregation had numbered approximately seventy-five when he arrived in 1965, and its current membership was sixty-eight. Three wasted years by any standard, Jack reflected bitterly. Whatever he had to offer was of no value or interest to the people in this community. He was a failure and he had to end this chapter of his life and find something else to do.

Hank Early, the arthritic chief deacon who had attended each meeting of the adult group, sensed his preacher's keen disappointment and stayed behind to chat. "You know, preacher, I should have warned you about Colonel and Mrs. Wolff. I knew they had no intention of joining the church, but I decided to keep quiet. I'll tell you why. You see, when you helped the colonel pitch hay in his barn that one morning, you laid an obligation on him. When you invited him to the class, he was trapped; he had no choice but to come. But he and his wife never for a moment thought of leaving their Baptist church and joining a Methodist church." Hank chuckled, and then went on. "The reason I said nothing is that I figured it would do old Sam good to get some good Methodist teaching to go with his Baptist ideas. You did him a real good service. He'll never be quite the same stubborn Baptist again. I don't mean that he's enlightened, but I reckon he's less darkened." Hank chuckled again. But then he became serious, "Preacher, it appears to me that you're down in the dumps about the way things been going here. Well, I guess I can't blame you. But, you know, my wife and I were talking the other night and we calculate that you've brought twenty-four new people into the church to take the place of those who have moved away. That's twice as many people as Jesus got to join his church in three years! I reckon if you was to measure everything by growth in members and in giving, like the Baptists can afford to do in this country where they have a monopoly, then you'd have plenty of reason for giving up. But I figger that Jesus never measured anything the way we do. By any of our measurements, he was a total failure. Twelve members in three years of full-time work and then he ends up on a cross. Maybe we Christians got to learn to spell success f-ə-i-l-u-r-e."

Jack gripped Hank's hand firmly to show his appreciation, forgetting the arthritis until Hank winced against his will. But his mood had not changed by the time he reached the little home on Washington Street that the congregation was renting for a parsonage. Annie had baked a cake to celebrate the new members and had decorated it with six candles, which she lighted as she heard Jack's car pull into the driveway. Jack's first act was to blow them out and to throw himself into his chair. "Only two out of the six, Annie. I can't take this pounding any longer. Let's do something else and go somewhere else." Annie was prepared for Jack's remarks. He had been making them with increasing frequency during the past twelve months.

"Let's not talk tonight, dear. You'll have nothing positive to say. Let it wait until the morning. Now, what would you rather have with your coffee, a piece of candle wax or a piece of cake?"

Jack grinned in spite of himself. That was one of Annie's strengths. She used humor as her most effective means of grace.

Jack was usually powerless against it because it almost always gave him the insight on himself that he needed at that moment. He voted for cake and after an hour's desultory conversation, they went to bed.

By the end of the week, both of them were convinced that their present career should be ended, although their reasons were different. Jack was convinced that he was a failure and therefore should leave. Annie did not believe that Jack had failed, but agreed to leave because Jack was convinced that he had failed.

She recalled the wonderful years in college and seminary, especially after they had married in 1963. Jack was in the middle of most campus activities. Too small to play football or basketball, he became team manager in both sports. He starred at second base on the baseball team, and had been offered an insignificant contract by the Dodgers, calling for him to go to their Chancellorsville farm team at $145.00 a month. He served as president of the student body during his senior year and had always been the leader of the student council during their seminary years. But none of these honors had come easily. Jack had worked, always honorably, to develop friends, to keep himself informed about issues. He had developed a habit of forthright speech that most people appreciated. Both he and Annie had talked about his need to succeed, but had agreed that the need was healthy and constructive, not morbid.

Jack's father had dominated his life and had used sarcasm to goad Jack to new accomplishments. This had left him with deep-seated uncertainty and insecurity that were the chief dynamics in his determination to succeed. He knew that he needed to understand himself better and to learn to control this basic need if he wanted to continue to be helpful to people. Their final decision was to leave and to enroll in a program in Clinical Pastoral Education in St. Louis through Eden Seminary and Barnes Hospital. The year's program would use up their savings, but Jack hoped to receive a scholarship that would take off some of the financial pressure.

Both he and Annie found the year's experience immensely helpful. The frustration and disappointment gradually disappeared. As Jack came to understand himself better, he also learned to work with his deep-seated drives more successfully. Annie was pleased with the recycling job that was being done on her husband. Even three-year-old Kip and one-year-old Kay liked St. Louis. There was the Zoo and there was Daddy around the house more.

As part of his training program, Jack was asked to serve part-time on the staff of the Lakewood United Methodist Church in west St. Louis County. Jack felt at home and welcome. The members were about three-fourths salespeople and middle-management executives and one-fourth farmers, the surviving remnant of the original membership. So well was Jack accepted that he was offered the position of head pastor when the man who had been there for thirty-five years decided to retire. The congregation agreed to wait until Jack's year of training was completed. Then he, Annie, and the two children moved into the lovely three-bedroom ranch that the congregation owned. Jack felt thoroughly at home among these people, but Annie was sometimes tense and uncomfortable. Everything was so different from the Kansas parsonage that she remembered and that she somehow felt was the only proper way for a clergy family to live.

Things went well from the start. Most of the people were relieved by the resignation of the other man, a pastor of the old school, and were charmed by Jack's freshness and openness. He was soon on a first-name basis with most of the people. Even many of the young people called him "Jack," and he welcomed this. Jack's work in the pulpit pleased the people. They appreciated the way in which he brought religion to bear on contemporary problems. They also liked the way in which he tied Biblical texts to daily living. Jack had never tried to be either a Biblical scholar or a theologian, but the people apparently did not want rich food. Jack was content to joke about his sermons with respect to their lack of profound depth. "If illustrations in sermons are windows," he liked to say, "then my sermons are greenhouses." But the people remembered what they had learned in the greenhouse and they grew under Jack's persistent encouragement to apply these truths in their lives.

To his surprise, Jack also discovered that most of the people wanted him to take charge and run things. He supposed that this attitude might be a carry-over from their own careers, where most of them were responsible to someone else who continuously ordered them to accomplish this or that goal. Or perhaps it was that they were so tired from weekday responsibilities that they were anxious not to take on any additional ones after work. Whatever the reason, Jack and his people, especially his men, got along well.

The golf course and the business lunch were the places where Jack carried on much church business. His natural ability soon enabled him to play competitive golf and he began to win some of the community tournaments. The recognition as pastor and golfer combined with the experiences of the Clinical Pastoral Education year to shape a new sense of confidence and leadership in him. He was frequently invited to speak to business and community groups and was elected to the boards of two social service agencies in the St. Louis area. Almost every minute of his day was filled and Jack thrived on this. Annie's gentle admonitions to take time to refill his spiritual tank went unheeded. Or, at best, Jack would occasionally read a book or attend a workshop on pastoral counseling or the application of business techniques to parish management.

Jack was especially good in applying business techniques to parish administration. His interest in this skill began when the congregation engaged a fund-raising organization which asked Jack to attend one of its parish-management seminars as part of the total program. Jack was impressed by the organizational and administrative design of the program and realized how crucial good management was to parish success. He even quipped to Annie that good administration was at least as important as good preaching. Things happened better and more quickly as Jack introduced management skills into more and more areas of parish life. His men appreciated this because they understood this way of parish management and they were comfortable with the language and with the assignments they received. Salesmen were asked to function as salesmen in presenting the congregational program. Accountants were asked to function as accountants, and, most important, executives were asked to behave like executives. They gave orders in the church and they carried out the orders they received.

In the summer of 1971, the congregation urged Jack to attend a Management by Objectives seminar that was being conducted in St. Louis for a one-week period. Jack went and was completely won over by the usefulness of this approach to the mission of the church. Following the seminar, he read all the literature he could find and spent several hours discussing it with a skilled St. Louis practitioner. By late August, he was ready to call an MBO (management by objective) seminar for his congregational leaders. Many of the business people understood the general philosophy of this school of thought, and the rest picked it up quickly. At the end of the three-day retreat, the congregation had committed itself to developing an MBO approach to all their programs.

Each leader was asked to develop a set of goals with respect to a division or department or agency within the congregation. In developing these goals, the leaders were asked to be realistic, realistic about what they were convinced they could achieve and realistic about what they believed their people were ready, willing, and able to do. The men were enthusiastic about the new potentials that all began to see for the parish, and they took seriously their own goal commitment. They agreed to a semiannual review and evaluation of their progress and their goal achievement.

Jack added a new feature that was his own creation, namely the office of Executive Director for Parish Life. In effect, this person was to function as the chief executive officer of the parish and was to be held responsible by the council for the performance of every other officer in the parish. The Executive was to make sure that each person had a clear written description of his or her job and responsibilities, and to maintain continuous supervision so that "things happened," as some of the businessmen put it. The people were impressed with Jack's parish design, although they kidded him about what would be left for him to do. Jack responded in kind and assured them that he would devote more time to his golf game as a major form of community witness.

Again, apparently only Annie noticed that there had been no true spiritual food or life at the retreat. She imagined that what had gone on was what would happen at any well-organized management training seminar. But she resolved to say nothing to Jack. He was far too high on cloud nine to hear anything even remotely critical.

Counseling of individuals and couples was another area of parish service that Jack enjoyed thoroughly and that the people appreciated more and more. It also consumed increasing amounts of his time, but somehow Jack found the energy and the drive to spend these hours also. Although Jack usually kept the identity of the counselees and the content of the discussions to himself, he did share with Annie many of his successes and the good feelings that he enjoyed from them. Occasionally Annie found herself watching the door to Jack's office from the living room corner. It was clear to her that the great majority of Jack's counselees were individual women, although Jack liked to stress his successes with married couples. Annie wished that she had not just read John Updike's *Month of Sundays* and its description of the counseling activities of the preacher.

Annie noted that most of Jack's book purchases were in the area of counseling and that very few of them had religious titles or were published by religious houses. When she asked Jack about this during one of their rare moments together, Jack assured her that there was nothing uniquely religious about what he was doing, except that he was trying to help people because of his own relationship to Christ. This remark surprised Annie. She commented to Jack that she believed that there could and should be unique Christian counseling centering in the forgiveness of sins and reconciliation to God and the neighbor. Jack agreed that those were his goals and tools, but again emphasized that both Christian and non-Christian counselors used the same dynamics and principles. "Do you mention Christ and forgiveness to people?" Annie pressed the point.

"No, I usually don't," Jack replied. "Such religious references only stir up people and make healing a far more difficult process. Oh, have no fear, Annie, I'm first and foremost a Christian pastor."

Annie wondered as she remembered Mrs. Wicksham's comment at their chance meeting at the supermarket, "Jack's at least as good as Dr. Gregory, my former psychiatrist, and he's much cheaper."

Annie found herself spending more time with her mother, a widow who had moved into a retirement home on Highway 40, just a few minutes from the parsonage. They had always been close, largely because in Kansas teamwork had been crucial for survival when both your husband and father were circuit-riding Methodist ministers who believed that Francis Asbury had spoken the last word about clergy finances, mobility, commitment, and love. Annie's mother had shared her husband's vision and the two of them had communicated it to their children.

"Trust," "praise," and "joy" had been the key words in their home. Each was crucially important. They had to learn to trust in God and his promises because they had nothing else in which to trust. Income was limited and precarious. But somehow, Annie's mother remembered, there had always been food. Oh, yes, a lot of bread and oatmeal, but food. She pointed to Annie's present condition as proof and reported that Annie's brother was again twenty pounds overweight. Together they recalled the sense of freedom that had been theirs in those days when they had placed all their trust in God's promises. Both women admitted that they had lost some of that carefree but responsible freedom. Annie spoke to her mother of how trust did not seem to be any longer a part of Jack's vocabulary. Apparently, things were going so well in every part of his life that he did not need to rely on God for anything. Annie confessed that her own greatest fear was that Jack was unaware of what was happening to him. "One day soon," she said to her mother when they were sitting on the expensive lawn furniture on the patio at the parsonage, "Jack is going to reach for his faith, and he isn't going to find anything."

"Praise" had been the second survival word in Kansas. Reverend Francis Cartwright had schooled his wife and children in this until it became a joyful part of their nature. In whatever happened, they found genuine reason for praising God. It had been painfully difficult to praise him when he took away the girl who had followed Annie and preceded her brother, but, spurred on by the genuine joy in Francis Cartwright's heart over his daughter's joy in heaven, Mrs. Cartwright and Annie gave priase to God for the death of the baby. They found time to praise God in whatever they were doing and wherever they went. They praised him in word, song, hymn, prayer, and deed. Praise had become a second basic dynamic in the Cartwright family.

Annie felt personally uneasy when her mother talked about their childhood lives of praise because she herself was not training Kip, Karen, and little Kristine to live this kind of life. She didn't know why. It was easy to blame it on Jack who had abdicated most of his fatherly responsibilities and who had not led them in a hymn of praise since Annie could not remember when. Her mother encouraged her to take this task upon herself, to teach the children to sing the great Methodist hymns, and to train them to run to God and to give him thanks for every happening in their lives.

The combination of "trust" and "praise" created the "joy" that Annie and her mother remembered vividly from the Kansas and Wyoming days. "I guess I never understood how to explain it," her mother said, "but we were always happy, even when Joy died. I believe some people thought we were crazy, but we weren't. And our joy wasn't artificial, something that we made up to impress people. We were a happy family," she paused in embarrassment and corrected herself. "We have always been a happy family, and I believe it's because we trusted God and praised him. Of course, your father also taught us to love each other deeply by being such a loving, giving person himself. Although," she added ruefully, "it seems like we always came out short on the giving end of it. But he always had so much for others that enough spilled over into my life and into your life. I just never would have wanted it any other way." Both women wiped tears from their eyes.

In the course of one of their conversations, Annie gained a

new understanding of the sensitivity and depth of her mother's thought. Unlike Annie, her mother had not graduated from college and had not had college courses in theology. But as Annie listened on this particular day, she realized that her mother had learned much more theology from life than Annie had ever learned from books. They talked about failure. The conversation began when Annie shared with her mother some of the thoughts that had led Jack to resign his first parish. After Annie had finished, her mother began her reply, and it almost seemed that she had moved to another place and another realm as she talked on.

"You know, Annie, I worried a great deal about you and Jack, because your experiences reminded me of what your father and I went through at his first Kansas post. He had seven stations to care for and he really poured his heart into his work. Rain or snow could not keep him home. More than once I feared he was lost in one of those fearsome Kansas blizzards. At the end of two years, three of the stations were closed. People moved away because of drought. One station was transferred to another rider who was twenty miles nearer than Dad had been. A troublemaker persuaded the members of another station to elect him as their preacher, and they told Dad they wouldn't need him any longer. The remaining two stations could not justify a circuit rider any longer. So after two years, Dad had nothing to show for his work. He was transferred to Wyoming, brokenhearted, ready to quit.

"But the first person we met in Wyoming was a woman who turned out to be God's best gift to us. We never stopped praising God for her. She had lost her husband in a blizzard the year before we arrived, and one of her three children had died of smallpox. Another one was mentally handicapped. But this woman, whom some considered terribly unfortunate, had learned life's greatest lesson, and she taught it to us. The lesson is very simple: There need not be such a thing as failure in anyone's experience and what the world calls 'failure' is very important to Christian growth.

"She pointed to the good things her husband had done for the town. He had helped bring through the railroad; he had developed cattle pens. He had fought for and supported the elementary school and had the town thinking hard about a college when he died. As a matter of fact, not too many years later, after we returned to Kansas, she wrote us that the town had a college and that it was named in her husband's honor!

"Then she talked to us about her two children and how she and her husband did not consider either of them a failure or a loss. Rebecca, she said, did more good for people in her ten years by being herself than most people do in a lifetime. Jeremy almost singlehandedly taught that town how to be gentle and considerate. Nobody laughed at him. The whole town loved him. She told me about one day when a stranger rode into town with a chip on his shoulder, looking for trouble. He ran into Jeremy at the stable, and Jeremy must have somehow converted the man on the spot. At any rate, he rode on the next day and nobody was hurt while he was here. She always maintained that they had had no failures to worry about or to feel sad about.

"That was her first lesson. We applied it to ourselves when Joy died, and it works. But her second lesson was much more important. I still remember that we were standing in Gardiner's dry goods store when she explained this one to me. She was talking about all the 'failures' that people encountered in life. She, of course, did not recognize them as failures, but she understood that most people saw them that way. So many failures forced her to do a lot of thinking, and as usual she turned to the Bible and to prayer for her answers. It came to her one day in a flash, she told me. Her answer was that failures are more important than successes if life is to go on and to get better. Success, she said, rarely made a person better and rarely helped a community for long."

Mrs. Cartwright paused for a moment, then went on, "You know, I had never thought about that before, but I have thought about it many times since, and she is absolutely right on that point. That's why I'm so worried about what success is doing to Jack." She stopped abruptly and a deep blush spread over her face. "Annie, I'm so sorry; I didn't mean to; please, forgive me."

Annie reached out and took hold of her mother's hand.

"Mother, it's good that you finally mentioned it. I've been afraid to burden you with it, hoping that you hadn't noticed it. I've talked to no one, and I'm so glad you brought it out. But let's get back to your Wyoming friend. I think she has something to teach me too."

Mrs. Cartwright continued. "Well, let me see if I can recall her words." She was obviously confused by her slip. "Like I was saying, she decided that failures were more important, more necessary, more helpful than success. And finally she found her idea in the Bible where Jesus said that unless a person dies like a grain of wheat that you throw into the ground, that person cannot grow. She pointed out that failure is like dying. You die to your dreams; you die to your self-confidence; you die to your own plans—and then you're finally ready to start growing.

"Francis and I applied it to our own situation, and we discovered how right she was. There had been no real failures in Kansas, only a lot of helpful experiences for many people. The people who had moved away carried Francis's understanding of Jesus and the church's mission with them to other parts of the States. We learned later that the other station soon turned the troublemaker out and became one of the Methodist strongholds in western Kansas—which isn't saying much," she added ruefully. "And who knows how much more the new man may have been able to do than your father could, for all kinds of reasons.

"Now personally, I think—and Francis and I talked a great deal about this—that we learned the importance of t, p, and j—remember? That's what we always called it—after the Kansas experience. We became so much stronger, so much closer to each other, such better parents. We learned to praise God for it and to trust him more fully for the future. We learned then that though maybe somebody intended it to hurt us, God turned that 'failure' into a blessing. I hope Jack can learn that lesson before it's too late."

Both Annie and her mother knew that time was running out for Jack, if they were right in their theologizing, and that Jack was in no mood to listen to any talk about the glory of failures and the evil of success. Annie tried, but with no apparent success.

Finally she said to him one night, "Jack, this success machine you're building here is a tiger and you're holding it by the tail. Either you'll have to hold on and swing it to death or if you let it go it'll turn on you. And I don't want that to happen to you." Jack was so amazed by Annie's inability to see what God was doing through him that he stormed out of the house and to the bar on Clayton Road, sure that he would find there some of his members who would reassure him about the wisdom of his pastoral leadership.

Two events in the following week supported Annie's observations, but neither did much to crack Jack's armor of success. The first one involved his friend Father Joe Sant'Ambrogio, priest at the Roman Catholic church on Ballas Road. He and Joe liked each other, and they spent much time together. But while Jack's parish was growing by leaps and bounds, Joe's was at best holding its own. As they were having a beer in the clubhouse after nine holes, Joe brought up a problem that had been bothering him for several days. It involved two of his families who had transferred to Jack's parish without Joe's blessing, but who now wished to be readmitted as communing members of Joe's parish. "I asked them to talk to you," Joe observed, "but both said they would much rather not. So I agreed to do it in their place."

Joe tried to summarize their reasons in an impersonal way, but it was evident to Jack that Joe was voicing his own convictions through these two families. In essence, it boiled down to the fact that the families were sorely disappointed in what had been happening to their spiritual lives since they joined Lakewood United. They had originally transferred because they were drawn by the strong social activism of Lakewood, which was in marked contrast to the inaction of their own parish. Jack and Joe had discussed this difference many times, but neither would budge an inch.

"These are ordinary people, Jack. They are not eucharistic nuts. They're not high on prayer and piety. But they're not getting God's word from you; they're not getting the nourishment from you that they used to get from the sacraments at Sacred Heart. Now, old buddy, I don't want to make a federal case of this, but I think they've put their fingers on something that's important to you."

Jack finished his beer, glanced at his watch, and urged Joe to take both families back: "That's no problem to me. Tell them they have my permission. And then you can put them back to sleep." He pushed back his chair and started for the door, unperturbed by Joe's comments. But Joe grabbed his sleeve.

"Hold it, Jack, for God's sake. This is too important and you mean too much to me to drop it. I've been trying to get up enough courage for eighteen months to talk to you." Jack paused, but did not sit down. "Jack, you're running a super corporation. My God, are you successful! I'm surprised you're not president of the church by now. But there is nothing Christian about what you're doing, except maybe taking the offering." Joe tried a lop-sided grin, but got no response from Jack. "Man, when was the last time you got down on your knees to God? When was the last time you preached a sermon about sin and forgiveness? That's what people need to hear. Then you can add all these other things to it. When was the last time that you allowed one of your hot-shot executive directors to fail, either in the congregation or in his business or in his family? When was the last time you failed?"

Jack's anger was becoming obvious. Joe knew that he had scored a point, and he did not want the conversation to end. But Jack did. He turned and left.

When he reached home several hours later for a bite to eat before addressing a Rotary meeting, Annie informed him that the Breckenridges had stopped by a few minutes earlier to tell him that they had decided to move their membership to the small church at Pond. George Breckenridge had been Executive Director of the congregation for two separate one-year periods and was one of the strongest financial supporters. Their loss would be serious. Jack's mind immediately computerized the membership profiles in his office to see who could take George's place. Annie told Jack that they would make an appointment with him to talk about it, but that their minds were firmly made up.

When Jack, George, and Fran met for lunch at Stouffer's

Tower on Tuesday, George repeated their decision. Then, in words that were almost identical with Joe Sant'Ambrogio's, George and Fran stated their reasons.

"You've got to understand how much you mean to me, Jack," said George. "No minister has ever helped me to get interested in church work the way you did. I enjoyed my two years as Executive Director, but now that I look back over the last five or six years, I realize that Fran has been right all along. She's been talking about her shrinking faith at the same time that I thought mine was growing. But for the last three or four months, things have not been going well for us. Our kids are messing up their lives, sales are way off, and I'm beginning to discover that I have nothing left inside myself to meet these problems. Jack, I'm sorry, and we shouldn't have been this abrupt, but we've got to do something in a hurry to keep ourselves together. And frankly, Jack, I'm afraid that you've got a tiger by the tail in that congregation you built."

Four or five other families also decided to leave the church during the next few months. Most of them were like the Breckenridges, good members and good supporters. Two of them tried to explain their reasons to Jack, but they lacked the Breckenridges' clarity and openness. Jack told Annie that they were leaving because they wanted to belong to smaller congregations. "I think," said Jack, "that they need a great deal of affirmation and they're not getting it here at Lakewood. But I've been giving that whole area some thought and I have a few ideas to suggest to the council at our next meeting. I believe I've put together a super program to help people know each other better and care for each more effectively."

Annie did not ask Jack for details and Jack was not bothered by her silence. Annie was sure that Jack had put together another high-powered program and that the program would help people to experience deeper relationships with each other. Annie was equally sure that the program would not be distinctively Christian but would probably adapt the principles of *I'm OK—You're OK,* the book everyone was reading. Annie was also sure that Jack's new program would draw more people to Lakewood and thus the departure of the Breckenridges and others would soon be forgotten. Annie regretted this because she shared the Breckenridges' feeling to a degree that she had decided never to admit to Jack. Annie had been trained to refuse to even consider divorce and Jack was finding so much stimulation and so much success in so many different ventures that he apparently was failing to notice what was happening to their marriage.

COMMENTARY

The Marshall Cameo is fictitious but it poses several questions that concern pastors and people today. How important is success in the parish and what kinds of "success" should Christians expect? Are the strategies and techniques of the business world compatible with the nature and goals of Christian congregations? How do pastors' individual personalities affect their theology and style of pastoral care? Is Christian counseling different from secular counseling? How important is the pastor's personal devotional life?

The Cameo is fictitious, but at the same time is so true to the history and experiences of thousands of pastors and lay people that almost all readers will recognize at least part of their own pilgrimage in it. Certainly the Marshall Cameo does not apply only to pastors of wealthy suburban churches. The same questions and pressures exist in every congregation.

Pastors and lay people are under great pressure to succeed. No one likes a failure, and the failure does not hang around for long. Many Christians define success in terms of more members, increased giving, and larger buildings. Of course, no pastor or lay member will admit that the foregoing sentence is true for him or her. Most books on building successful parishes begin with a statement that the author is not interested in numbers and is not playing the numbers game. The rest of the book is then devoted to discussions of how to increase numbers in the three categories mentioned above.

Of course, no Christian is opposed to success with reference to members, giving, and buildings. And, of course, each Christian adds that he or she is interested in numbers only as an index of what is happening to the souls of people or as a sign that the congregation can undertake more ambitious Christian programs. But despite all these disclaimers, there is an influential school of thought that identifies growth in numbers, giving, and buildings, with God's blessing. Decrease or failure in one or more of these areas is taken to be evidence that either the pastor has not yet caught the vision of church leadership or is indeed a failure. Success is the name of the game.

Success is also the name of the game in another way potentially even more troublesome. Along the highways of the United States today one sees signs exhorting people to place their trust in God with the guarantee that they will prosper, their barns will be filled, and their ventures will be blessed. Of course this is a natural hope for Christians, and many Christians have experienced such blessings in rich measure. The problem arises when faith is understood to be the vehicle that secures such blessings for the Christian. From this it follows that the Christian who is not richly blessed in material things has an inadequate faith or no faith at all. This is especially troublesome when physical or mental health is the sought-after blessing.

By almost anyone's standards, Jack Marshall was a successful pastor. The Cameo indicates that success was especially important to Marshall because of some childhood experiences. Annie, the Breckenridges, and a few others did not share Jack's commitment. Annie's mother is used as the agent in the Cameo to set forth another understanding of the role of success and failure in Christian life and in Christian congregations. The point of the Wyoming woman's story is that Jesus turns human definitions of success on their heads and offers his own instead.

Jesus' definition of "success" is set forth in clear and radical terms in Mark 10:41–45, especially verse 45. James and John were evidently convinced of the dignity of Jesus' person and the importance of his message. They wanted to develop structures that would guarantee success for the spread of what Jesus sometimes called his "kingdom." As James and John cast about for models of successful organizations, one came immediately to their minds, the Herodian kingdom. Herod the Great had been a success by almost every standard, despite his miserable final months. He had been the second most powerful and the second wealthiest individual in the Roman Empire. He had been the greatest builder of his day. He had exercised almost unlimited power over his subjects. He had been a true success! And so the brothers propose to Jesus that they adopt and adapt the kingdom organization. In that way they could assure success for his wonderful message.

Jesus' answer must have surprised them, "Can you drink my cup and be baptized with my baptism?" he asked. The brothers assured him that they could, although they did not understand that the cup and baptism referred to suffering. In an effort to make clear to the disciples the difference between success by Herod's standards (which they apparently shared) and success as measured by God's criteria, Jesus said to them:

" 'You know that those who are supposed to rule over the Gentiles lord it over them, and their great men exercise authority over them. But it shall not be so among you; but whoever would be great among you must be your servant, and whoever would be first among you must be slave of all.' " Then came the clincher in Jesus' understanding of success and failure. " 'For the Son of man also came not to be served but to serve, and to give his life as a ransom for many.' " (Mark 10:42–45, RSV)

With these words, Jesus offered a new definition of "success" in terms of self-giving service rendered to others in the name and in the place of God. This is the only definition of "success" that Jesus ever offered to his followers. The people of God have no other goal to pursue nor any other criteria of faithfulness to their calling and to their Lord. If more members, increased giving, and bigger buildings are essential to more self-giving service in the name of God, then "numbers" of that sort are important. However, growth can become an end in itself and the Cameo suggests that this had happened in the life of Marshall and in the thinking of most of his members.

Furthermore, I have suggested at several places in this book that smallness is an essential ingredient for "success" in the Christian mission. Historical research reveals clearly that small groups have always been a major source of vitality and renewal in the history of the church. That does not mean that bigness is in itself bad. It does mean that bigness presents special problems to the mission as Christ defined it in Mark 10, while at the same time it can offer unique combinations of spiritual, financial, and physical resources that can significantly contribute to the achievement of mission goals. The problems run out of control when congregations forget Jesus' definition of "mission" and "success."

The purpose of this Commentary is not to exalt smallness and failures. Far from it. The purpose is to focus on mission and then on the important role that failure has in the lives of God's people individually and collectively. The pattern of understanding is again furnished by Jesus himself both in words and deeds. At several points in his ministry, he stressed that death is the necessary prelude to all Christian growth. Death is one aspect of failure. Illness and disappointment are other aspects of it. Joe Sant'Ambrogio grasped this central truth and tried to communicate it to Marshall. But Marshall was unable to hear or even to think about the fundamental point his friend was trying to make.

The Wyoming woman had had several experiences in her own life that taught her Jesus' lesson that failure is the necessary prelude to "success." From those experiences, she had also learned that failure is an essential part of life; no one is exempt from that experience. If in no other way, all people will experience the final failure, death itself. She had also learned that failure (or death) is not the real enemy. As a matter of fact, she had probably learned that failure and death are part of God's way of achieving his mission goals. She may even have begun to think that God himself participated somehow in her tragedies, her failures; that he was not an aloof God seated on a golden throne, wrapped in a heavy protective plastic sheet.

In the daily disappointments of life she had learned the importance of what Martin Luther and many other religious leaders call the "theology of the cross." The point of this theology is fundamental to creative living and simple once you have washed the stardust of success out of your eyes. The theology of the cross affirms that God himself was a failure, that God revealed his intimate nature to us most clearly when in the person of his son he hung on the cross for all people. As Luther dramatically expressed it, "If you would find God, then go look under Christ's cross for he is hidden beneath it."

Out of Calvary's defeat came new life and new power, power to transform millions of people and to inspire them with a vision of self-giving service that changed the course of the world. Admittedly Christians have not always understood the theology of the cross, and even when they have understood it, they have not always been faithful to that understanding.

It is the grasp of that theology and the baptismal determination to live it out in the world that forces Christians to depend on each other for strength, forgiveness, reassurance, and training.

The opposite understanding of God's nature and purpose is usually called the "theology of glory." The theologians of glory like to minimize the brutality and the significance of God's suffering in Christ. They prefer to stress Christ's victory and emphasize that his followers are already triumphant over failure, disappointment, and death. Theologians of glory like to exalt humanity and its potential at the expense of Christ's atoning work. They offer considerable comfort to Christians who are not personally experiencing real failure, disappointment, or death. But they offer no lasting comfort in the face of reality. Nor do they call Christians to serve in imitation of Christ. They prefer to challenge Christians to great deeds of commitment that do not expose them to the threat of death after the pattern of Jesus Christ.

In the light of what has been said here about failure and the theology of the cross, you may be better prepared to monitor the direction of your own congregational programs. And I hope you have been sensitized to the "theology of glory" pitfalls that can so easily be associated with successful congregational programs.

Evaluate your congregation's goals and programs in the light of what the Commentary has said about the theology of the cross. Do you agree that "failure" is often more beneficial to Christians than success? Which do you find more helpful, a large congregation or a small fellowship group?

Related to the first focus on success and failure in the parish is the second focus on the nature of the Christian congregation in relation to worldly structures and techniques. Recall that in the Cameo Jack Marshall built Lakewood United Methodist by using management techniques borrowed lock, stock, and barrel from the world of business. The point was made that his members willingly adopted these management strategies because they understood them from their own careers in business. In introducing these techniques, the business people at Lakewood United were not asked first to wrestle with theological or Biblical concepts or to use religious language that they may not have fully understood. Instead, they heard their pastor using the same language they used and suggesting techniques that they understood as least as well as he did to achieve the same goals that their management groups at work were pursuing: growth in sales, in income, and in physical plant.

These remarks are not designed to debunk business techniques in the congregation. Many of them are made to order for many congregational programs. Rather, my purpose is to raise a more subtle question, the answer to which will affect the entire future of any congregation. In what ways is the congregation like a business organization? If there are basic points of similarity, what is unique about each? Several answers have been suggested in this Commentary and at other points in this book.

First, the basic character of the congregation is established by the fact that it is the body of Christ and that members consciously understand themselves to be his body. That means several things. It means that the congregation is not a corporate structure with a president who gives orders and sees to it that they are carried out. It means, further, that the congregation exists to help the members grow in the grace of imitating Jesus the Christ. That is, they come together and they hang on to each other so that they might better understand and practice the fundamental principle that they exist, not to be served, but to serve and to stand ready to give their all to set people free from whatever it is that oppresses them. This is a radically different goal from that which any well-organized, self-respecting business pursues. In a manner of speaking, the people of the congregation are in the business of dying for others, while the people of the business world are in the business of living for tomorrow and hopefully a better profit report. Of course, a good business wants to achieve profit by providing a fine service that helps people somehow to be more fully human, more free from worry, better clothed and fed, and so forth. There are superficial similarities between the goals of a good business organization and the goals of a good congregation.

However, congregations and businesses seek such radically different goals and derive their strength and power from such radically different sources, that each needs to be very leery about borrowing techniques and strategies from the other. It's probably true that a business that adopted Jesus' motto as its operational principle would not survive for long. Is the reverse also true, namely, that a congregation that adopts the methods and techniques of business in a wholehearted manner will also not be around for long—as a Christian congregation? The point is so fundamental that members of congregations need to devote much thought to it.

Can you write a paper on what it means to you to say that your congregation is the body of Christ? What management techniques has your parish adopted? Do you believe that they are all productive in terms of the Christian mission?

The third focus in the Marshall Cameo is on the relationship between his personality and personal needs and his theology and style of pastoral care. Perhaps to stress this as I have already done at several places in this book is like shipping steel to Pittsburgh, but there are several reasons for this emphasis. One reason is to stress the basic point that every Christian's theology is an odd mixture of Biblical study, church tradition, and his or her own personality. In a very real sense, every Christian is his or her own theologian. This fact is often denied by denominations with strong theological traditions or with strong hierarchical control patterns. Leaders in such denominations are apt to stress "pure" doctrine or church law as something that everyone understands in the same way and accepts completely. The consequence of this approach to theology and church custom is often that the troubled, seeking individual sees no relationship between theology and life's problems. Such individuals are told repeatedly that all questions have been answered and that it is only necessary for them to accept and obey the church's "position." Any deviation is considered sinful, and the person in pilgrimage is almost forced to keep thoughts and questions locked up in his or her heart.

One reason why Christians entertain such views of theology is that they have confused the opinions of leading theologians in the past and in the present with the beliefs of the rank-and-file membership. In all probability, there are scarcely any pastors, even theologically well-trained pastors, who agree on their understanding of key words and concepts.

In a healthy congregation, this fact of Christian life is recognized and affirmed. Steps are taken so that God's people can theologize together in an atmosphere of openness and trust and shape theological positions that deal directly with the realities of their daily lives. Of course, the members of each denomination want to reach theological opinions that are reasonably compatible with the chief teachings of their church body.

There is a second reason for this emphasis on the relationship between the pastor's personality and his or her theology, and that is to stress the living, dynamic character of theological thought. Doing theology is never a completed task where the last word can be said, the ink dried with a blotter, and all of life's questions finally answered. Therefore, pastor and people should learn to share together in this pilgrimage. Often this mutual search is frustrated by guilty consciences or by inadequate training on the part of both pastors and people. There are remedies for these problems. These remedies should be pursued so that this vital and refreshing search can go on in a responsible way. The Christian's understanding of an involvement in mission is directly affected by his or her theological beliefs.

Static and stubborn views concerning theological answers will usually lead to static, imperialistic approaches to the church's mission. Furthermore, such static views usually result in mission work being identified with the proclamation of "pure doctrine."

Is your personal theology complete and genuinely helpful to you? Does your parish recognize the importance of ongoing theologizing? How does your present theology control your understanding of mission?

The fourth focus of the Cameo is on the question of whether Christian counseling is unique. So many leaders of the church have devoted so much time to this question that this chapter cannot even pretend to offer a final solution. However, I can offer several observations on the basis of the historical research that has been presented in other chapters of this book.

The first observation is that individual counseling has always been one of the primary tasks of the Christian pastor, although the counseling situation has taken different forms. In the first few centuries, counseling of individuals was often done by the entire congregation. Today we may debate the effectiveness of this approach, but it should be remembered that this kind of group counseling of the individual was very effective at several crucial periods in the church's history.

Our understanding of this group process will be more accurate if we remember that often these counseling groups consisted of only a handful of Christians, perhaps numbering somewhere between ten and fifty. Because of the small size, the members of these groups knew each other well and came to love and depend on each other as they sought to be faithful to their understanding of God's mission. Thus when a person was counseled by this group with respect to his or her sinful ways, and was then separated from the fellowship, this counseling by friends made a strong impact upon the sinner. It was not unusual for the disciplined person to spend three, four, five, and even as many as ten years under discipline until the group was ready to receive him or her back into its fellowship. This counseling and discipline emphasized obedience to the Christian mission, high moral standards, and the eucharistic fellowship of the group. It was, in other words, different from contemporary secular counseling in every important way.

In the medieval church for almost a thousand years, from A.D. 500 to A.D. 1500, counseling was done largely on a one-to-one basis in the rite of private confession and absolution. The emphasis was placed on human sinfulness as a barrier to the presence of God. The confessor offered the precious gift of forgiveness for Christ's sake, and then urged the repentant offender to amend his or her sinful ways by imposing a specific duty upon the person. Priests stressed that they were both servants and representatives of Jesus Christ and that they offered forgiveness for Christ's sake alone. As the centuries passed, many who went to confession believed that their own good deeds earned forgiveness, but there were countless others who went to confession in order to hear Jesus speaking through the mouths of priests and forgiving them fully and freely.

Thus at least until the time of the Reformation, counseling was at the center of the church's life, it was strongly ecclesiastical in character, the work of Jesus Christ was the central focus, and confession, absolution, and satisfaction were designed to help people to become better representatives of Christ in their daily lives.

This churchly pattern of confession seems to have disappeared rather soon from the Protestant branch of the Christian church, although it survived in strong and weak forms in the Catholic branches of the church. Only in recent years has it begun to lose its centrality in the Roman Catholic Church.

Beginning with the work of Sigmund Freud, private psychiatric counseling began to be practiced by medically trained doctors and to be appreciated by growing numbers of troubled persons. Probably the rise of this kind of individual counseling can be linked with the disappearance of counseling in any kind of creative or helpful form from most Protestant congregations. Shortly after World War I, the clergy became interested in this new approach to people, and psychiatric counseling began to be offered by many of them. Some of these people were adequately trained for this highly skillful work while others were not. To increase clergy skills, programs like Clinical Pastoral Education were introduced at almost all seminaries in the United States. In many cases, it was impossible to recognize any specifically Christian principles in the clergy training programs. Pastors were often the first to recognize this, and tried to find a Christian approach to individual counseling. Other pastors, like Jack Marshall, denied that there were any specifically Christian elements in counseling and deliberately rejected the patterns that the church had used for almost two millennia. That is, in their counseling they usually made no references to sin, forgiveness, God's justice, the work of Jesus Christ, their commitment to the church's mission, and so forth.

Many other pastors regrettably denied that there was any value in the skills of the psychiatrist. They continued to stress God's anger against sin and the sole sufficiency of the work of Jesus Christ. They were in effect repeating the crude and often brutal counseling "skills" of the revivalists of the nineteenth century in the United States.

This book presented a churchly type of counseling in the chapter devoted to the work of Wilhelm Loehe of Neuendettelsau in Germany in the mid-nineteenth century. Loehe insisted that confession and absolution was a churchly rite and must always be conducted in the congregational setting. By that he did not mean a return to the practices of the first centuries, but rather that the pastor should keep the parishioner acutely aware of the fact that counseling was first and foremost a transaction betwen God and the repentant sinner. Furthermore, Loehe stressed that confession and absolution must always be done in the center of congregational life. Again, he did not mean that this should go on in the church service, but rather that both the repentant person and the entire congregation should always be mindful of the unique gift of God's forgiveness that was being offered in the ritual of confession. Loehe also stressed, perhaps too strongly, the almost Christlike authority and power of the pastor. He did this in the hope that each sinner would truly hear Christ speaking in the pastor's voice and would therefore be assured of Christ's personal forgiveness for him or her. Loehe stressed human sin and God's grace and the special role of the sacraments in the life of the Christian.

Thus there were fundamental differences between counseling as practiced by Jack Marshall and that carried on in the long history of the church. Like many of his contemporaries, Jack did not refer to sin or to grace as a normal part of counseling. Instead he stressed various Freudian understandings of human problems and tried to help people to "get in touch with themselves" by understanding the source of their troubles. Jack also assumed that his counseling sessions were strictly a matter between himself and the other person. It was in his opinion no concern of the congregation. Their prayers were not solicited, nor were the troubled individuals encouraged to draw strength from the sacraments. Instead, he believed that his primary responsibility was to make the troubled person understand that at least he, Jack Marshall, accepted the individual, even though he was aware of the actions that the person had committed. People told him repeatedly that his acceptance helped them to begin to travel the road to recovery and mental health. Jack never used the counseling situation to challenge people to better performance in God's mission. His only concern was that they find a higher level of wholeness as a result of their sessions with him. It had not occurred to him that they should in turn use their new wholeness for those who were less whole than themselves.

If you had a problem, would you prefer secular or Christian counseling, as these two are briefly characterized in the Commentary? How do you see your congregation participating in the pastor's counseling work?

The fifth focus of the Cameo was on Jack's personal spiritual life. This emphasis was noticeable in a few of Annie's thoughts and in the conversation that Jack had with Father Sant'Ambrogio. Jack's schedule allowed him no time for private prayer and meditation, but Jack's psyche apparently did not require that kind of close relationship with God. Research into the history of pastoral leadership suggests that this may have been his most serious failing, as we have indicated in one or two other Cameos. How private prayer and meditation increase the effectiveness of the pastor is difficult to determine. However, research confirms that it does. Those who have left real marks on Christian communities have almost always been persons who found it necessary to spend time alone with God and who therefore made time for this, despite demanding schedules.

Does your schedule allow any time for personal devotion? Have you experimented with disciplined patterns of devotion versus free-form, spontaneous acts?

In many ways Jack Marshall is a typical American pastor, and in many ways he has abandoned the attitudes and practices that have marked the great pastors in the church's history. But the blame should not be placed on Jack Marshall alone. It must be shared by the seminaries of the church and it must be shared by his people who played such a major role in supporting the style of pastoral care that he developed.

Marshall's passionate quest for success, his uncritical adoption of business techniques, and his style of strong executive leadership resulted, in my judgment, in a bad pattern of community organization for mission in his congregation. But to offer that judgment is not to offer a helpful corrective. What *could* happen at Lakewood United Methodist to establish a congregation more in conformity with the Biblical understanding of community, "success," and service?

It is conceivable that Jack might change his style as a result of additional experience and study. Perhaps Annie could play a constructive role in helping Jack to recognize a non-Biblical elements in his present leadership and to work to change them. Perhaps the people of Lakewood United Methodist might insist on orienting their program toward service rather than toward numerical and financial success. Perhaps some of the congregational leaders might begin to make critical judgments about Jack's uncritical use of the techniques of the business world.

Perhaps more members might vote against him with their feet and their pocketbooks. However it happens, the pastor and the people of Lakewood Church need to reassess their goals, resources, needs, and strategies if they are to become a church which like its Master does not seek to be served but to serve and to do its best to set people free from whatever oppresses them.

15.
Toward Reform and Renewal

In this chapter I propose to offer some comments on the themes that were listed in the introduction and on some of the questions that appeared in the Commentaries. Every reader, especially those who serve in the pastoral office, will have worked out some answers to most of these pivotal questions during years of actual service in parishes. But perhaps the answers here will further sharpen your own ideas and may even challenge you to look at some of them again.

Each Cameo and Commentary has tried to underline the principle that God's presence and work in this world involve three centers of reality and action in the congregation: (1) the person, work, and presence of his son; (2) the person, work, and presence of the pastor; and (3) the persons, work, and presence of the members of the Christian communities.

Christians build communities on the foundation of their conviction that Jesus Christ is in their midst as the word about him is preached, signed in the sacraments, and shared in the conversation of believers. Christian communities come into existence for the sole purpose of enabling members to become more like Jesus Christ in their daily lives. Therefore, it is crucial (the word comes from "cross") that communities work very hard at finding and developing ways that urge members to focus their thinking, praying, and daily doing upon the Leader who is always present in their midst.

Research reveals that there are two ways in which Christian communities over the centuries have forced Jesus Christ out of his central position. One way is by stressing his deity at the expense of his humanity; the other way is the reverse—stressing his humanity so strongly that his true diety is deemphasized or even lost altogether. In either case, the result is the same: the community loses its basic Christian character and ceases to perform a Christian service to the world.

The ramifications of this principle are manifold. A few examples must suffice. Churches that tend to be quietistic and inactive in matters of justice frequently have a Christology that stresses his deity at the expense of his humanity. Pastors who put great stock in their unique pastoral authority and who tend to posture in front of their people probably also stress Christ's deity at the expense of his humanity. On the other hand, many leaders of the Social Gospel movement stressed his humanity at the expense of his deity, with eventual unfortunate consequences. The same thing can be said in general about many current-day pastors.

Furthermore, the history of Christian doctrine shows that many major theological controversies centered in the question of how Jesus could be divine and human and how these two facets of his person related to each other. It is, therefore, not surprising that many pastors and many Christian communities have problems finding and maintaining a good constructive balance. But to maintain it is the primary intellectual assignment that each Christian group has.

The crucial necessity for understanding Jesus Christ correctly is further emphasized by the principle that one's Christology determines one's ecclesiology. Or to put it in other words: what one thinks about the person and the work of Jesus Christ determines what one thinks about the nature and the mission of the church. The Jonathan Edwards Cameo and Commentary stressed this principle in great detail, but it was present, at least by implication, in each chapter.

The reverse principle is also valid, namely, what one thinks about the nature and mission of the church will also determine what one believes about the person and the work of Jesus Christ.

It is probably correct to suggest that Roman Catholic and Eastern Orthodox pastors tend to approach Jesus Christ from the perspective of their understanding of and love for the church. Thus their ecclesiology shapes their belief about Jesus Christ. Protestant pastors, at least in the past, tended to take the opposite tack. What they believed or thought they believed about the person and the work of Jesus Christ usually shaped what they believed about ecclesiology.

Both groups erred. The Catholic groups lost the corrective balance that comes from stressing the person and the work of Jesus Christ. Protestant pastors regularly failed to appreciate the church as Christ's body. As a result, both they and their people were frequently cavalier in their thinking about the church and its liturgy, hymnody, and history. Protestant church life was seriously impoverished. In this ecumenical age, both parties are correcting improper emphases as they engage in dialog. Finally all dialog has as its real end the improved practice of pastoral care.

The proper focus on the person and the work of Jesus Christ also leads to a proper stress on the kingdom of God, and this concept needs to be emphasized if pastoral care is to be true to its original Scriptural objectives. As several Commentaries pointed out, the church at its best is always committed to the proclamation and establishment of God's kingdom. That is its only reason for existing. The church has regularly failed to be true to this mission because it has frequently misunderstood the nature of God's kingdom. It is his rule, already here in this world and leading on to its climax in the afterworld. To proclaim the kingdom of God means, then, that one devotes time, effort, and prayer to creating godly conditions in this world and to spreading the good news that the king is coming. Too many churches have instead spiritualized the kingdom and thought of it as the place where the souls of the departed will be forever with the Lord. The Commentary on Francis Asbury placed particular emphasis on the importance of a balanced understanding of God's kingdom, as did the Commentaries on Ambrose and Jonathan Edwards.

The second focus of Christian life in community is the person, work, and presence of the community's pastoral leader. Historical research makes it clear that for two thousand years the pastor has been the hinge, the key figure in Christian community life. In my research, I set out to prove that the pastor is *not* the hinge. I thought that if the pastor's position and authority could be limited, then the congregation would automatically be stronger and more energetic in mission. But almost all my research forced me away from the conclusion I set out to reach. Instead, I had to conclude that for almost two thousand years the pastor has been the hinge and that we ought not try to destroy or radically alter that historical lesson. The Latin proverb is correct: *qualis rex, talis grex.* "The people will be like their leader." Modern-day group studies show that this is by no means a uniquely Christian idea. Every group will eventually take on the characteristics of its leaders. It can do this positively by affirming the leader's style and values, or it can do it negatively, by rejecting these. The net result is the same: the leader contributes heavily to shaping and molding the group's personality and identity.

The pastor is the hinge between Jesus Christ and the people. In a sense, the people turn or swing on that hinge. The pastor has been equipped by God with special gifts and abilities to be a Christlike person, and is obligated to inspire the people by word and example to grow to the measure of the stature of the fullness of Christ. Because a direct appeal to Jesus' own example will frighen and discourage most people, God's Spirit has created this intermediary example. It is also true, as will be pointed out later in this chapter, that a pastor cannot serve effectively as hinge without the parallel example and inspiration of the people served. This is one of the many paradoxes that need to be kept in mind if Christian communities are to mature in self-understanding and in service to their neighbors.

But many will say that the requirement to imitate Jesus Christ and to call on others to follow his example is too heavy a burden to place on anyone. Who would be so foolish as to claim the necessary spiritual gifts? If that is one of the chief responsibilities of the pastor, who would dare accept that office? Before we despair, let us review several theological and historical facts that bear on this principle of imitation.

1. For sixteen centuries and more, pastors assumed that responsibility. Look again at the Cameo of John Chrysostom. He accepted this awesome responsibility for himself, and so did many others.

2. In our day this concept of imitating Christ is not popular with many Christians, although the Daniel Daugherty Commentary shows that some Roman Catholics try to take it seriously even today. In some cases it has disappeared from the Christian understanding of the meaning of discipleship. In other cases, the idea has been misunderstood and has led to disastrous results.

What happened after 1700 to all but banish the idea from the minds of Christians? In a nutshell, Christianity underwent another radical change, just as it had done earlier in the period from Justin to Ambrose. After 1700 Christianity was driven out of public life in Europe and shortly thereafter (say after the American Civil War) also in the United States. The learned of the Enlightenment period ridiculed what they called the outrageous claims of Christianity to possess all truth. They also rejected the church's claim that it had the divine right order even kings to do its will. Their attacks and criticisms broke the public power of the church and reduced Christian faith to a matter of private, interior dispositions and actions. As a result, Christ's example had little or nothing to offer to these private Christians, since his example could be effective and important only as it influenced and controlled all of life and inspired Christians to do their best for their neighbors. A partial Christ could not inspire people to live the full Christian life, and so imitation language disappeared from the vocabulary of many Christians to this day.

3. The ability to imitate Jesus Christ is a gift from the Spirit, given to certain individuals for the benefit of the entire community. Thus no one can boast if he or she possesses it. The possessor must also be helped to realize that this gift is a gift of service; it equips one person to equip others. Thus this individual learns to give thanks to God for this special opportunity to be useful to fellow believers.

4. Even St. Paul realized that he had a long way to go to become the perfect imitator. But this did not keep him from

urging others to follow his example, even as he tried to follow the example of Jesus. Paul probably came to know Jesus' example by talking to those who had known him during his days on earth and perhaps also by direct revelation. Today we acquaint ourselves with Jesus' example chiefly through the pages of Scripture, particularly the Gospels.

5. The gift and ability to imitate Jesus can flourish only in a strong and supportive Christian community. This principle is basic for two reasons. In the first place, the gifted pastor needs the support and prayers of other Christians. The pastor depends on them and they give support and encouragement in many different ways. In effect, the people "pastor" the pastor so that the pastor can "pastor" them! This idea of mutual "pastoring" applies to almost all other pastoral duties as well, but it is particularly important in this crucial area of imitating Jesus Christ. In the second place, there must be a strong and close community so that the people can be directly impressed by the pastor's example. In many large congregations, the pastor's example of personal dedication and service is neither known nor experienced by most members. Usually the pastor's only impact is made through the sermon. Many of the pastors in this book provided an effective example because the group was small (compare Justin and Tertullian), or they provided an example that inspired other priests who in turn inspired the people to whom they ministered in smaller and more personal groups.

6. No pastor in the history of the church has provided a perfect example to follow. But that point needs to be modified by the principle that in most Christian groups, in the variety of gifts that the Spirit gives to individual members, one can find a "corporate" portrait that resembles the ideal portrait quite closely. When the community is of such a size and structure that the gifts of the Spirit can work freely within the community, the entire group will develop a personality like that of the ideal pastor! Again the group's personality will not be a perfect, Christlike personality, but the whole group, functioning together in the Spirit, will be more Christlike than any individual member. The theological way of expressing this principle is to say that the local

group becomes the body, that is, the presence of Christ, in its place! As the group grows toward the full height of Christ, it will pull individual members in that same direction, and non-Christian people in that community will sense the presence of Christ in their neighborhood.

It is in order, therefore, to look next at the qualities of the person who serves the community as its pastoral leader. If a composite sketch is prepared of the pastors who appear in this book, a portrait of an ideal pastor will emerge. And that is what I now propose to do. Of course, no person in the long life of the church has looked like this composite sketch, not even St. Paul.

The *ideal* pastor is marked by deep love for God and for people, beginning with the people the pastor is called to serve. Usually the pastor has had a life-changing and profound experience of the goodness and the power of God. This experience has taken so many different forms in the lives of Christian pastors and people that it is wrong to say that it must happen in one way only, and it is impossible to describe a typical way. But it happens in a way that the pastor feels and can usually describe to others.

The pastor is compassionate and translates that compassion into the ongoing pursuit of charity and justice for everyone, and into the consistent determination to bring the good news of Jesus Christ to all the people who can be effectively reached. A humble person, the pastor does not seek glory or profit, or expect to be served, but is always serving and offering to help set others free. But this humility does not cause the pastor to be wishy-washy or spineless. The pastor knows what must be done and said to be true to the calling, and possesses the courage to do those things. Where there is a course of action that is recognizably right, the pastor prays for the courage to follow that course.

The pastor is deeply involved with the Bible, drawing power from it and devoting much time to explaining and proclaiming its truths to others. The pastor maintains a rich devotional life, both in public and in private. The pastor is aware of dependence on the grace of God, and seeks out this grace in worship and meditation. Each day the pastor feels a strong inner compulsion to give thanks and praise to the God who created, redeemed, and now empowers with the divine Spirit.

The ideal pastor practices the art of spiritual self-discipline or asceticism. This latter word unfortunately conjures up distasteful images in the minds of many Christians. The spirit of Christian asceticism is spelled out by St. Paul in Philippians 3. Like Paul, the Christian pastor counts everything as loss in order to know and experience the love of Christ. The pastor manages all aspects of personal life so as to grow daily in love for Christ, and thus develops a personal life-style to witness to others about what Jesus Christ means. Through this ascetic discipline the pastor finds a noticeable measure of spiritual power, and it seems that people sense this, even though this self-discipline is practiced quietly and, as it were, in a closet.

The pastor possesses the gifts of faith, hope, and charity in special measure. Because personal hope and confidence are placed in God, the pastor cultivates moderation and calmness. The pastor trusts God's promises for daily life and is able to instill this trust and confidence in others. What the pastor says and does are always of a piece; they demonstrate integrity. The pastor possesses special ability to lead and influence others. And, interestingly enough, the pastor loves nature and seeks to commune with God in the wilds.

It is important to note the resemblances between this portrait of the *ideal* pastor and the portrait of Jesus Christ that is presented in the church's gospel. Although our intention was not to paint a portrait of Jesus, the result is not surprising, for Christian pastors are persons who have been equipped by the Spirit with special gifts to be like Jesus in thought, word, and deed so that they, in turn, can urge others to follow their example. It is to be expected that Christians see Christ in their pastor and are thereby inspired to new levels of Christlike living.

However, the portrait does not represent a perfectly kind and idealized person, a holy Joe. For in imitating Jesus, the pastor also shares in Jesus' doubts and disappointments, his anger, his moments of rebellion against his Father. That is why, once again, it is so important to keep the humanity and the deity of Jesus in delicate balance. At the same time, the pastor's example consists primarily in demonstrating constant, personal dependence upon Jesus for forgiveness, strength, and guidance. The ideal pastor is human as Jesus was human. In this humanity, the pastor needs the support and inspiration of the people. The pastor needs to be able to depend on them as fully as on Jesus Christ. The pastor's own sins and weaknesses become ways of drawing the people closer to their mutual Lord and Savior.

At another level, the portrait of the ideal pastor is also a portrait of each Christian. Like St. Paul, the Christian wants to make progress toward the goal of maturity in Jesus Christ. The Christian wants to resemble Christ more completely from day to day. Pastor and people, then, are like looking-glasses. Each sees a growing Christlikeness mirrored in the life of the other. Thus one can reverse the old Latin proverb so that it reads *qualis grex, talis rex:* "The pastor is like the people."

Almost every Cameo and Commentary reveals that the problem or question of pastoral authority is always a fundamental one that needs to be resolved if the relationship between pastor and people is to be mutually constructive and supportive. St. Paul's Cameo presented him as a person who understood pastoral authority and in general used it wisely to help Christians mature. Two things were underscored about his understanding.

1. Paul's authority was in large part derived from the fact that his conduct led the people to love him and to trust him. They almost always recognized that Paul was not working for his own benefit, but, rather, that he had given up everything in order to bring the gospel to them. Some passages in his letters show that not everyone regarded him in that way. Chapters 10 to 13 of 2 Corinthians especially describe some who accused Paul of selfish motives. But such people were in the minority. Authority flowed from Paul's personality and from the fact he had truly come to serve and, if necessary, to give his life for the sake of Jesus Christ. This can be called "personal authority" in the good sense. (Henry Ward Beecher also operated with a highly "personalistic" authority, but the Commentary on him pointed out that this is not a good and solid kind of authority.) In the Gospels, Jesus Christ

also demonstrated this kind of good personal authority. People who came into contact with him sensed his unusual love for them and often followed him willingly without a moment's hesitation.

2. But Paul not only *received* cheerful obedience because people liked what he was doing; at times he insisted on obedience because he held the office of an apostle. This insistence appeared especially in his letter to the Galatians and in his correspondence with the Corinthians. The moment Christ's followers began to organize themselves (institutionalize themselves, if you will), there had to be some kind of institutional or official authority. Paul always tried to make it clear that he was not insisting on obedience to himself, even though he was an apostle, but that he was demanding obedience through him to the apostolic word from and about Jesus. This is a neat, but sophisticated distinction, and many persons in the church, including thousands of pastors, have not been able to understand it or to make it function.

The result of this confusion is that many pastors have insisted on personal respect and obedience because of the office they held. Sometimes they insisted on this completely apart from the question of the services they were performing or the spirit in which they were working.

In the case of St. Paul, his claim to authority was closely linked to the word that he proclaimed. The thrust of this apostolic word is most clearly set forth in passages like Romans 1:16–17 and 2 Corinthians 5:18–19. The center of the apostolic word is always the word of God's gracious forgiveness for the repentant sinner. Jesus summarized that word in John 20 when he said to the disciples after his resurrection: "Receive the Holy Spirit. If you forgive the sins of any, they are forgiven; if you retain the sins of any, they are retained." (RSV) From this it follows that the pastor's basic authority is the authority to proclaim forgiveness of sins in the name of Jesus Christ. This authority is clearly that of a servant and not a ruler. In all his letters, Paul was concerned to build Christian communities around the experience of God's forgiveness, for he knew that only this center would make these communities different from others in his world.

However, almost from the beginning, this servant model of authority to forgive was mixed with other models of pastoral authority. For example, many Christian pastors modeled their pastoral roles on the Old Testament priests, rather than on the forgiving-servant pattern of Paul. After the example of Old Testament priests, they often behaved more like rulers with dreadful powers to perform Christian sacrifices than like servants. From at least the time of Cyprian, the model of pastoral authority began also to resemble the authority that Roman public officials claimed for themselves in their offices as mayors, senators, and so forth. Ambrose is an example of how the Roman model contributed to confusing and changing the Pauline model.

As several Commentaries suggested, there was conflict from the beginning between the egalitarian (or democratic, community-oriented, forgiving-servant)model, and the hierarchical (or aristo-cratic, pastor-oriented, ruling-shepherd) model. A number of historical developments contributed to the eventual "triumph" of the hierarchical model in most parts of the Western church. An obvious historical factor was the growing size of congregations, as some of the Commentaries pointed out. Another one involved changing ideas concerning the eucharist, the mystery of the real presence of the body and blood of Jesus Christ, and the dreadful powers possessed by the priest who could change bread into Christ's body. This was emphasized especially in the chapter on Ambrose and Marcus. Yet another factor related to changing views on the church's place in the world.

From what has been said about the person and work of Jesus Christ and the person and work of the pastor, it follows that the Christian community, the third focus of this book, must define itself as a seedbed, a *seminarium*, in which weak and struggling plants can help each other to achieve Christlike strength and maturity.

In several chapters, a five-point program was used to monitor the spiritual health and vitality of various Christian communities. This five-point program, shaped like a star, called for balanced and continual growth in five Christian actions or graces: worship, fellowship, witness, service, and nurture. I argued that people assemble in Christian communities to help each other grow in these graces. I believe that this is the only proper goal of Christian congregations. It is also crucial for Christians to remember that they help each other to grow for the sake of the world and those people who need to experience the presence and the love of Jesus Christ.

I argued in some Commentaries that the absence or malfunctioning of any one of these five graces will soon cause the other four to become weakened, nonproductive, harmful, or die. Historical research confirms the basic importance of this principle. For example, a community that is not service-oriented will soon find that its worship becomes self-centered, as do all other aspects of its program. Or a parish that is not worship-oriented soon discovers that somehow the uniquely Christological flavor and motivation have disappeared from their lives. A community that neglects nurture is apt to experience the same deadly result.

The five functions must not only be present, they must be balanced and they must be growing. Research and present-day experience show that many Christian communities resist involvement in witness and service. One soon notes that every other part of their program becomes eccentric and nonproductive. Similarly, when members of the community do not push and encourage each other to maintain balanced growth in all five functions, the community tends to become despiritualized and dry.

So that this balanced growth will occur, several things need to happen. The congregation must be so structured that it is clear to every member what membership in that community entails. More will be said about congregational structures below. Furthermore, all Christian resources must be clearly focused on this single five-part objective. The chief resource, of course, is Jesus Christ present in his Spirit and in the word in its many forms. The power of the word comes in the sermon, in the sacraments of baptism and holy communion, in confession and absolution, and in the conversation, encouragement, and admonition of the members for each other. The pastor is a unique resource, but so is every member of a healthy parish.

Again historical research suggests that this fivefold growth happens best, and perhaps only, in closely knit communities where the members feel some sort of compulsion to help each other and to lean on each other. In the history of the church, especially, but not only, in the first five centuries, a pattern repeats itself with regularity, and many Christians have experienced this in their own communities. As the congregation grows, fellowship decreases, and when this happens, the total vitality of the congregation decreases. The percentage of people involved in worship falls off. The practice of service declines as individuals begin to distance themselves from other members. The wealthier people find it possible to ignore the poorer ones. They begin to change their earlier habits of commitment to charity and justice through personal action and substitute for that gifts of money or property. As fellowship declines, nurture changes its appearance completely. In smaller congregations, people were concerned about nurturing each other, as the Commentary on Tertullian and Justin reveals. As congregations grew larger, nurture became the exclusive responsibility of the preacher, who discharged this responsibility almost exclusively through preaching. Members stopped caring for each other.

The gradual breakdown of the balanced operation of these five functions in the first five centuries (and at many other times in the church's history) was accompanied by a radical change in the Christian understanding of the nature and purpose of the church. Ideally, Christians view themselves as yeast and leaven, a force for good turned loose in the world, bothered with only a minimal structure and organization. Pastors and people are in mission together, and they help each other to avoid counting the cost, and instead do what the moment demands—in imitation of their Master. They see themselves called by the gospel to love and embrace the world and to infiltrate it with the power of the gospel. But as the world continues to reject the church, or as the world overcomes the church through gold or other more subtle pressures, Christians build walls between themselves and the world. This wall is primarily designed for self-protection and its construction is motivated by fear and guilty consciences. Important bricks in this wall are church law and church officers. Eventually, the clergy seize exclusive control to protect the church from the world. This cycle marks church history from the beginning, and probably will to the end of time.

The chart on the facing page puts these developments of the first five centuries into graphic form, although the reader should be aware of the difficulty of reducing great movements of the human spirit to graph form. But despite serious limitations, the chart may help to illustrate the complex developments that effected basic changes in the people's understanding of the nature and mission of the church, the person and work of the pastor, and thus also—and much more seriously—the person and the work of Jesus Christ.

From what has been said, it follows that the church must find ways of structuring itself in groups so that mutual spiritual nurturing and growth, centering in word and sacrament and inspired by the example of the pastor, can happen. Most of today's churchly structures almost guarantee that the "imitation principle" and the "group-support principle" cannot function. If the church will find ways of developing such small group structures, it also follows that the church will need a great many more pastors than there are now. For example, a congregation of six hundred people is usually served by one pastor. But if this congregation were to develop small groups of fifteen to twenty-five members each, that congregation would need about thirty pastoral leaders. My experience suggests that there are in each congregation enough pastorally gifted people to lead the number of groups that the congregation needs. The Spirit always provides the necessary gifts to those groups that are open to its leadership. Most of these additional pastors will not be full-time pastors nor will they be products of four to eight years of highly specialized theological study. They can in most cases continue in their present jobs, and in most cases the present head pastor will be able to provide the religious and pastoral training that they need.

It is encouraging to note the number of seminaries and church renewal agencies that have begun to emphasize the crucial importance of small groups for the mission of the church. For the past several years, I have served as Executive Director of

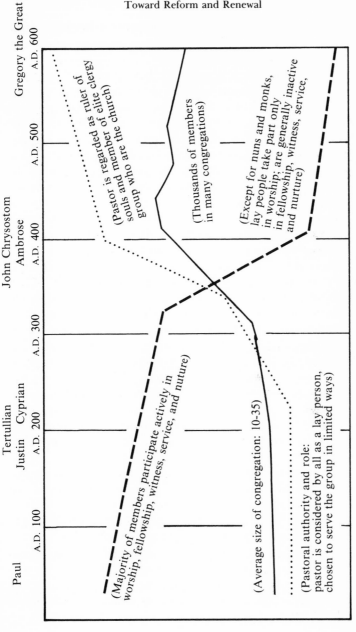

Paul

Tertullian
Justin   Cyprian
A.D. 100   A.D. 200   A.D. 300

John Chrysostom
Ambrose
A.D. 400   A.D. 500

Gregory the Great
A.D. 600

(Pastor is regarded as ruler of
elite clergy
(Pastor is regarded as ruler of
souls and member of the church)
group who are the church)

(Thousands of members
in many congregations)

(Except for nuns and monks,
lay people take part only
in worship; are generally inactive
in fellowship, witness, service,
and nurture)

(Majority of members participate actively in
worship, fellowship, witness, service, and nurture)

(Average size of congregation: 10-35)

(Pastoral authority and role:
pastor is considered by all as a lay person,
chosen to serve the group in limited ways)

A chart showing the general relationship between individual participation in the life of the church,
congregational size, and growing pastoral importance from A.D. 30 to 600

Congregations Organizing for Mission Endeavor, Inc. (C.O.M.E.), a St. Louis-based organization that stresses the small group as the best environment in which effective mutual growth in the five functions can happen. This program was launched with help from the Lilly Endowment and the Aid Association for Lutherans, and is being accepted in a growing number of congregations around the world.

These small groups have been helpful to many participants, but one pattern has recurred in almost every congregation, and that is the resistance to effective witness and service on the part of Christians. The seriousness of the problem and the potential solution were well expressed by a group leader in one of the C.O.M.E. congregations who commented at an evaluation session: "We're doing good with worship; we're having fun with fellowship; we're enjoying nurture. And please be patient with us, we're learning that we're supposed to witness and serve."

The recapture of this five-pointed objective is crucial to the renewal of the church. The implementation of this vision will happen best as the church's structures again make it possible for Christians to teach and to inspire each other. This mutual inspiration will happen most fully as congregations offer to their members the best of two worlds, the glorious experiences of the traditional large congregation, and the equally glorious experiences of the small group.

This is the proper point to end our review of what Christians have thought about the person and the work of Jesus Christ; about the pastoral office, duties, and authority; and about the life and organization of Christian congregations. Wherever we have turned in our investigation, we have been confronted by our Lord Jesus Christ, and we have heard the call to imitate him. Some readers may say that the vision in this book is too demanding, too idealistic, and will be taken seriously only by a few "messianic oddballs." I think better of most Christians. As I have come to know them, they want to take their baptismal vocation seriously. They are willing to live it out, although many of them need more help than they are now receiving. They are ready to pay the price of discipleship, although they are often frightened as they count it. This book is intended to be a resource book of historical facts and ideas that they can use for the reform and renewal of the church. It can help all God's people, whether they are called clergy or laity, in this task—for the sake of the world.